A Guide Book of
MINERALS, ROCKS,
AND GEMSTONES

■ ■ ■

THE OFFICIAL RED BOOK®

A Guide Book of
MINERALS, ROCKS, AND GEMSTONES

INCLUDING A SECTION ON METEORITES

Whitman
Publishing, LLC
PUBLISHING SINCE 1934
© 2008 Whitman Publishing, LLC
www.whitmanbooks.com

A Guide Book of
MINERALS, ROCKS, AND GEMSTONES

■ ■ ■

INCLUDING A SECTION ON METEORITES

© 2008 Whitman Publishing, LLC
www.whitman**books**.com

© 2008 Whitman Publishing, LLC
3101 Clairmont Road · Suite C · Atlanta GA 30329

Correspondence concerning this book may be directed to the publisher, at the address above.

ISBN: 0794825559
Printed in China

Disclaimer: This book is presented as a collecting guide only. Expert opinion should be sought in any significant mineralogical purchase. Auction prices realized and other sale-price data is presented for informational purposes, and they apply only to the specific specimens pictured or mentioned. Minerals, rocks, and gemstones are not commodities that can be traded sight-unseen; their values vary widely from specimen to specimen, depending on multiple qualities and characteristics. Such factors as changing demand, popularity, quality interpretations, strength of the overall market, and economic conditions will influence the market, which can fall or rise.

For a complete catalog of antiques/collectibles reference books, supplies, and storage products, visit Whitman Publishing online at
www.whitmanbooks.com

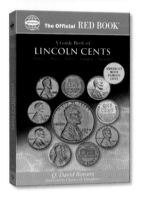
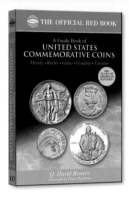

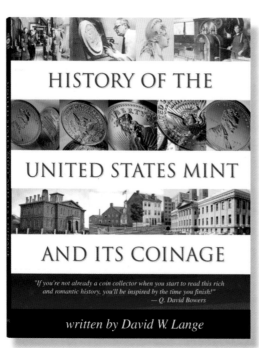

TABLE OF CONTENTS

PREFACE

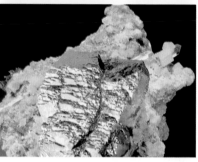

No matter where you live in the United States, you're not far from someone who collects minerals, rocks, or gemstones. Dozens of local, regional, and national clubs are devoted to "rock hounding." Every day of the week you can find Americans with shovels, hammers, and homemade egg-carton specimen boxes exploring the countryside to add to their collections. This hobby—this passion—is shared by hundreds of thousands of people here and around the world.

Undoubtedly humans have always been fascinated by the shiny, attractive treasures yielded by the earth. Since Europe's Renaissance, as early as the 1500s, collectors have studiously gathered rare, valuable, and interesting mineral specimens. For centuries mineral collecting was the domain of kings, princes, and other wealthy and educated people who could afford the leisure and had the resources to gather beautiful and expensive specimens. (Today many formerly royal collections occupy the status of national treasures in state museums.) In the 1600s John Tradescant, horticulturalist to various English nobles and later to King Charles I, was a famous naturalist and collector whose cabinets included minerals and gems. Archduke John of Austria, who wasn't much of a general fighting against the French in 1800, proved to be a much better businessman, naturalist, and mineral collector. In 1820 Czar Alexander I had a special collection of Russian minerals assembled (68 salts, 354 stones, 411 metals, 13 combustibles, and 175 rocks, according to an inventory), to be presented as a gift to his childhood tutor.

Eventually this "hobby of kings" expanded to scientists, doctors, merchants, industrialists, and others who could afford books (and read them) and had the time to devote to intellectual pursuits. The earliest collection to be brought to America from the Old World may have been that of Dr. William Douglass, a Scottish physician and writer who, after traveling in the West Indies, settled in Boston in 1718. John Pierpont Morgan was one of the United States' most important collectors at the turn of the 19th century; in 1911 morganite was named after him, at the suggestion of George Frederick Kunz of Tiffany & Co. (who just happened to be Morgan's main supplier of gemstones).

Today, mineral collecting is a popular hobby that nearly anyone can jump into. Public museums hold millions of fascinating specimens, preserved for study by specialists and newcomers alike. Dealers nationwide have large stocks of minerals, rocks, and gemstones for every budget. Clubs and societies gather people together from all walks of life to share in the fun and the intellectual rewards of collecting. And today's collector has access to more books, journals, Web sites, and other resources than ever before. Whitman Publishing is proud to contribute to those resources with the *Guide Book of Minerals, Rocks, and Gemstones.*

AUCTION PRICING

Throughout Whitman Publishing's long history of serving the numismatic and philatelic communities, valuation charts and auction records have been standard procedure. With the *Guide Book of Minerals, Rocks, and Gemstones,* our task has been to balance what we do best with the needs of a new audience—mineral collectors.

Unlike coins, minerals, rocks, and gemstones are formed naturally. They have no standard shapes and sizes with which to categorize them, nor is there quality control of the end product. Each mineral is unique. Minerals are not commodities, and cannot be bought and sold sight-unseen with specific pricing in mind.

So why do we include some auction prices in the text? If they can't be used as an indicator of future performance (and they can't), why report on auction prices at all? Because auction prices are a part, however small, of the hobby community.

Many collectors are born from childhood days spent exploring rock formations and forest floors for fossils and arrowheads. In time (if not immediately), they are struck by the different materials that make up their treasures, and curiosity drives

them to research rocks and minerals. Other collectors develop an interest in crystals and their properties through an awareness of New Age practices. Still others are interested in minerals because of their technological or economic value. Countless paths bring people to the hobby, beginning an often lifelong pursuit that combines intellect and knowledge with visual and tactile pleasure.

The hobby of mineral collecting encompasses a wide range of people—from professional mineralogists to amateur collectors. It doesn't have to be your vocation or consume all of your leisure time. One of the beauties of collecting minerals is that, regardless of where you live, minerals are in nature around you. An hour's drive should get you to deposits of various rocks or minerals, perhaps even gemstones. There are countless types of collections to build. Don't have much space? Work on a thumbnail collection. Short of direct sunlight? Collect minerals that must be kept in the shadows because of sensitivity to light. Have a den or basement or other large space to house your treasures? Create a large, eclectic collection of rocks and minerals that fascinates you.

Whatever type of collection you choose, you are likely to obtain a large percentage of it through your own exploration. This may include classroom field trips or field trips taken with local clubs. Eventually a collector may start purchasing specimens to round out a collection or to build one that is impossible to find in nature locally. Even so, there is no consistent or progressive value for minerals, and current sales do not determine future prices.

The true value of minerals is not monetary. Their value lies in their benefit to mankind. In the millennia since man first picked up a rock to use as a tool, our lives have been enriched by—sometimes even saved by—the treasure trove the earth yields. Minerals are major components in medicines, food and dietary supplements, matches, building materials, cosmetics, dishes and utensils, personal grooming products, coinage, paving materials, aircraft, fireworks, and electronics, among other items.

And for as long as minerals have been used, they have also been gathered and studied. Collections have even been found in ancient tombs. This text will give you an overview of the world's minerals, rocks, and gemstones. We hope it motivates you to take another look at the crystal you found years ago or the stone you picked up on your walk last month, and determine what it is. Once you've done that, go on a hike and find more offerings from Mother Nature. Build a collection that excites you, enjoying each unique piece you find. We hope you'll become a "rock hound" for the fun of it!

Which brings us back to our original question: why *do* we include auction prices in this book? We do it because the information is of interest. Many of these auctioned pieces have some significant historical value or are of such unusual forms that they are sought by high-end collectors. Most of all, we do it because auction prices give insight into another level of the hobby. But never forget that these natural works of art are best studied for their scientific value and collected for their curiosity value.

Happy hunting!

The staff at Whitman Publishing

CREDITS AND ACKNOWLEDGMENTS

Whitman Publishing extends thanks to everyone who assisted in the creation of the *Guide Book of Minerals, Rocks, and Gemstones*. **James Bassett** assisted with preparation of the text manuscript. Most of the book's full-color mineral photographs are from the archives of **Dakota Matrix Minerals** of Rapid City, South Dakota; **Heritage Auction Galleries** (Department of Natural History) of Dallas, Texas; and **Stack's of New York.** Special thanks to **Tom Loomis,** photographer for Dakota Matrix; **James Elliott,** photographer for Heritage; and **Douglas Plasencia,** photographer for Stack's. Other photographs were obtained from the **U.S. Geological Survey, Department of the Interior.** Images of mineral- and mining-related ephemera, and photographs of meteorites in the appendix, are from the Stack's auction catalog of The Tucson Sale (2008).

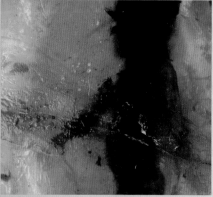

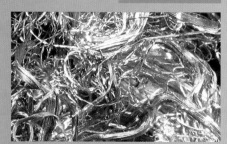

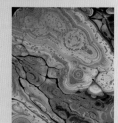

Minerals,
Rocks,
Gemstones

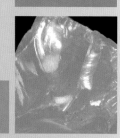

MINERALS, ROCKS, GEMSTONES: WHAT ARE THEY?

BASIC DEFINITIONS

Many people use the words *rock* and *mineral* interchangeably (and therefore incorrectly), but anyone interested in collecting will want to know the proper definitions of the terms and use them appropriately.

In the most general terms, a mineral is a single substance, a rock is made of several minerals, and a gemstone is simply an ornamental mineral.

Minerals

A dictionary definition of a mineral might be "a solid homogeneous inorganic substance occurring in nature and having a definite chemical composition." The key word here is *homogeneous*—a mineral is a single chemical compound, with a specific composition. A mineral can be composed of just one element, such as gold, or it can be a combination of elements, such as pyrite (also known as fool's gold), which is a chemical compound called iron disulfide (FeS_2).

All this really means for the collector is that a mineral is a single uniform substance, so all specimens of a mineral will have a uniform appearance and will exhibit uniform properties. Some might be larger or prettier than others, but in general they all will be more or less the same inherently. This makes identifying most minerals relatively easy, as we shall see in the section on mineral properties.

Currently there are more than 4,000 officially recognized minerals, of which only about 150 are considered common. More than half of all known minerals are so rare that they have been identified from only a few samples—sometimes from only a single grain!

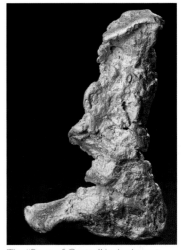

The "Boot of Cortez" is the largest surviving natural gold nugget ever found in the Western Hemisphere. In the Mexican state of Sonora, a local man bought a metal detector and taught himself to use it by combing an area where placer nuggets had been found. He found the "Boot of Cortez," measuring 10-3/4" in height and 7-1/4" in width, and weighing 389 troy ounces. In early 2008, this nugget was sold at auction for $1,553,500.

Rocks

A rock is an aggregate of minerals. Some rocks are composed almost entirely of just a single mineral; limestone, for example, is a sedimentary rock composed predominantly (and sometimes entirely) of the mineral calcite. Other rocks contain many minerals, and the specific minerals in a rock can vary widely. Granite varies widely in composition, usually containing feldspars, muscovite, biotite, and hornblende, but often also including smaller amounts of apatite, garnet, hematite, ilmenite, magnetite, pyrite, rutile, titanite, zircon, and other minerals.

Gemstones

Gemstones are minerals with qualities that make them highly attractive and valuable: beauty, durability, and rarity. Among the characteristics that create beauty are transparency, clarity, luster, color, "fire," chatoyancy, iridescence, and adularescence. The hardness of gemstones makes them durable enough for use in jewelry.

Gemstones are not always true minerals, however. Amber, coral, ivory, and pearl are organic substances; lapis lazuli is technically a rock.

Gemstones are classified into groups, species, and varieties, often based on appearance. For instance, rubies and sapphires are both transparent varieties of corundum (Al_2O_3); rubies are a red variety (the color caused mainly by chromium impurities), while all other colors are called sapphires.

Although often used interchangeably, *gemstone* usually refers to the uncut specimen, and *gem* is reserved for the cut and polished stone.

A Note on the Organization of Specimens

The specimens included in this book are organized according to the classification found in *Dana's New Mineralogy*, eighth edition. First developed by James Dwight Dana in 1837, his system of mineralogy is the standard classificatory system used in English-speaking countries. (A slightly different system, the Strunz Classification, is used in Germany.)

This rare specimen of amber contains the fossilized remains of a 3-1/2 inch lizard and various small insects. Found in the Dominican Republic, it brought $143,400 at auction in early 2008.

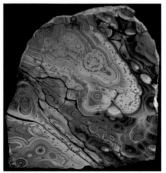 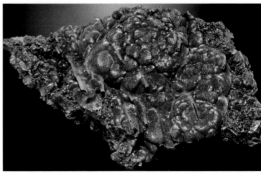

This cut and polished multicolored slab of malachite (left) is a gem reminiscent of those found in fine mineralogical museums. Before it was cut, it could have resembled this green gemstone (right). Both found in Cochise County, Arizona. At auction in February 2008, the cut piece brought $920 and the natural stone brought $690.

■ HOW TO START COLLECTING ■

Humans have been collecting rocks and minerals for thousands of years—graves containing ceremonial or decorative artifacts made of gold, gems, and ivory have been found dating from the beginning of the Upper Paleolithic period (40,000 B.C.). Evidence of mining activity dates back more than 6,000 years, proving that humans have been seeking out these minerals (and not simply finding them by chance) for at least that long.

Rocks and minerals have always held a fascination because of their particular nature. They are literally pieces of our world, hard and enduring, symbolic of eternity. Many specimens are very beautiful—and the more beautiful they are, the rarer they also seem to be, so they became symbols of wealth and status as well.

Today, mineral collecting is more popular than ever before, and absolutely anyone can enjoy the hobby. New varieties and new sources are constantly being discovered and made available on the world market. It is now easy to find affordable specimens from anywhere in the world at just about any local mineral store, rock show, and especially online.

A mineral collection is also one of the easiest to begin casually; much like sea shells, you can start a collection simply by picking up interesting specimens you find in the course of your daily activities and display them on your desk, on a shelf, or even just in a box. Eventually, though, you will probably want to become more organized in your collecting.

A complete collection of all known minerals is an unachievable goal. Aside from the cost and special storage needs of many species, the scarcity of most minerals (some are known to exist from only one or two samples) makes them impossible for amateurs to collect. Also, there are more than 4,000 known varieties of minerals, and more are being discovered every year. Nowhere in the world is there a "complete" collection of minerals—not even in any government or university museum or archive.

Instead, as you become more interested in and more knowledgeable about rocks and minerals, you will inevitably discover a personal focus for your collection. Unless you already have such a focus, it is best to start with a general collection of the most common and easily obtainable specimens. This can help to familiarize you with the characteristics of minerals and increase your knowledge of geology and mineralogy; then, as your

The South African diamond rush of the late 1800s produced a multitude of claims around the DeBeers farm where the first concentration of diamonds was found. Cecil Rhodes and Charles Rudd finally consolidated those claims under the name "DeBeers Consolidated Mines, Ltd." by 1887. The DeBeers brothers had long since tired of the horde of miners descending on their farm and sold out; only their name remained, as it does today. This 18.70 carat octahedron was mined in those early days before consolidation. While it has too many inclusions to be faceted, its size, sharpness, and luster make it a valuable gemstone. After being placed in the national collection at the Smithsonian Institution, the stone was eventually deaccessioned and sold into private collections.

collection and your knowledge grow, you can begin to specialize. Your personal interest might lead you to build a collection of specimens from your own local area, or samples of all known varieties of quartz, or even as many different green (or red, or blue . . .) minerals as possible. Because collecting is always a matter of personal taste, there is no "right" or "wrong" collection. All that matters is that your collection appeals to you.

Books such as this one are an important resource, but there is no substitute for getting to know other collectors. Until you reach the point where you are doing your own field collecting, you will buy most of your specimens from mineral shops or at collectors' shows. Other collectors are usually happy to share their knowledge and to display their collections, and sellers will welcome the opportunity to cultivate new customers. Like any community of people with a common interest, rock and mineral collectors will always be eager to share their knowledge and welcome new members into the fold.

Organizing and Displaying a Collection

It is perfectly acceptable to keep your collection in boxes or egg cartons at first; in fact, this is often the easiest and most efficient method for storing the bulk of your collection. But once your interest grows beyond a few random samples, you will probably want to organize your collection and display it.

To organize your collection, use a cataloging system (such as the Dana system used in this book), or simply keep a chronological record of your

A collection may revolve around unique mineral growths, as seen in this example of native silver. The combination of thick and delicate wire silver looks very much like a tree. Mined in Saxony, Germany, this specimen sold for $18,400 at auction in early 2008.

Another unusual piece is this manganese nodule formed around a fish tooth (species unidentified). While manganese nodules occur throughout the oceans of Earth, they are not widely mined. Nodules remain in the domain of marine biologists, with most mined specimens in research collections. A three-quarter inch segment of the fish tooth is visible.

specimens with data including where and when you acquired each. For larger specimens, paint a small white rectangle on the back or in some other inconspicuous area, and write the catalog number on this with ink; for smaller specimens in thumbnail or micromount collections, affix a label to the box instead. Specimens that are prone to tarnish in the air can be given a thin coat of spray lacquer or polyurethane to protect them without harming them or affecting their appearance too much.

There are several general methods for displaying a collection; choose whichever one is most appropriate for the nature of your collection, or whichever one you feel most comfortable with.

Display Collection

A "display" collection is exactly what it sounds like: a collection arranged and presented for display. Shallow drawers or shelves, covered in glass for protection, are excellent ways to show off your collection. At first you will want to display every specimen, but as your collection grows you may want to display only the best examples. Replace lesser specimens as you acquire new, better samples.

Thumbnail Collection

"Thumbnail" specimens are small, generally no more than 1" (2.54 cm) across. They are more affordable than larger, showier pieces, and usually are of better quality—it is often difficult to find larger crystals without flaws or inclusions of some kind.

Thumbnail specimens are glued into individual clear plastic boxes with hinged tops. The box protects smaller samples while you are handling them, and the hinge allows easy access for close examination under a magnifying glass or microscope.

These beautiful boxes, all handcrafted in Italy, reveal some of the decorative work possible with gemstones and other materials. The green malachite humidor has bull's-eye inlays with no visible seams, attesting to the skilled craftsmanship at work. The variegated tiger's-eye box exhibits mirror image pieces of stone, achieved by butterflying a block of fine tiger's eye and resulting in a strong chatoyancy. The final box, made of fossil stromatolite, shows concentric rings of varying sizes that have been matched from the top to the sides. The stones for these boxes were found in the Democratic Republic of the Congo, South Africa, and Bolivia, respectively.

Top: Rhodochrosite thumbnail collection. These seven matched specimens of brilliant red rhodochrosite from Northern Cape Province, South Africa, illustrate the range of different crystal habits from a single locality. Center: Choice thumbnail collection. This collection houses native silver from Norway, tanzanite from Tanzania, pink fluorite from France, wulfenite from Arizona, anatase from Norway, rutile from Brazil, bixbyite from Utah, and heliodor from Ukraine. The collection brought $1,092 at auction in early 2008. Bottom: Gold thumbnails. Three well-crystalized samples of native gold from Michigan Bluff, Placerville, and Volcano, California. This California collection sold for $690 in February 2008.

The small size of a thumbnail collection makes it very convenient for those with limited storage and display space. A desk drawer or a single, small display case can hold dozens or even hundreds of specimens.

A variation of the thumbnail collection is the "micromount" collection. Micromount specimens are 1/16" (1.5 mm) or smaller. Other than the small size, a micromount collection is treated in the same way as a thumbnail collection.

Systematic Collection

A systematic collection is arranged according to some scientific or mineralogical system, such as Dana's System of Mineralogy. Generally, systematic collections are more appropriate for scientific study or for the very serious collector with a large collection.

Field Collecting

Mineral shops and rock shows are an excellent source of specimens for any collection. Many fine and reputable dealers have online catalogs, and Internet auction sites provide another good place to obtain specimens. Many people have assembled beautiful collections from these sources alone. Additionally, auction galleries such as Bonhams, Christie's, Heritage, Sotheby's, and Stack's sometimes offer collections of minerals, rocks, and gemstones.

Eventually, though, you may want to seek out your own specimens in the field. While it is always nice to add a new or a better specimen to your collection no matter where you find it, nothing can match the thrill of discovering a piece yourself.

Certainly, it is difficult for many people these days to do their own collecting. But field collecting need not involve weeks of trekking through uninhabitable wilderness. A day trip out of town to a public park or private land is often more than sufficient, and even urban landscapes present opportunities. Depending on the geology of your region, road and railroad embankments, riverbeds, and even city parks can yield a surprising range of specimens.

This unassuming milky quartz specimen comes with a surprising historic connection. Tied to the quartz with a fine piece of string is a very old label. It sits in what appears to be the original box. The label reads "Crystallized quartz from the grave of Jefferson Monticello Vir." This piece appears to be a portion of a quartz lens saved from the digging operation for Thomas Jefferson's grave in July 1826. After spending time at the Franklin Institute in Philadelphia, this specimen brought $5,750 at auction in February 2008.

Rules for collecting on public land vary, so it is always wise to check specific regulations before setting out on your trip. Most of the public land managed by the U.S. Bureau of Land Management (BLM) is open to collecting. Some sites require a permit from local governments or the BLM, or are open only to noncommercial (hobby) collecting. It is

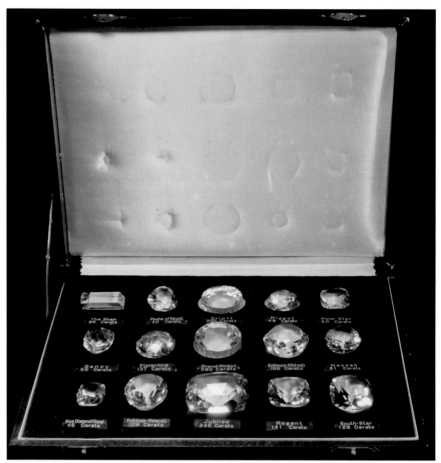

This beautiful and well made collection replicates, in quartz, 15 of the world's most famous diamonds. Probably made 75 years ago, the set sold at auction in early 2008 for $1,840.

against the law to collect at National or State Parks or Monuments; however, private land just beyond the official boundaries of these areas often holds similar species.

Many parts of the country have privately owned quarries where you pay an entrance fee and take your chances. Any time you are collecting on private property, be sure to ask the owner's permission and to use common sense and observe proper etiquette. Pack out all of your trash, stay out of areas posted "No Trespassing," and don't cause unnecessary damage to the environment. Don't destroy or damage specimens you are unable to collect; leave them for other collectors or for yourself on a later collecting trip. It can take only one bad experience to make a landowner decide that his property is henceforth off limits to other collectors.

Clubs

Enthusiasts have formed local clubs throughout the United States and participate in various activities, including trips to mineral-rich areas. The American Federation of Mineralogical Societies is an educational, nonprofit federation of seven regional gem, mineral,

This rare 1890 certificate from the Elizabeth Mining Co. in Montana includes vignettes of the obverse and reverse of the U.S. Morgan silver dollar. The certificate measures 10" x 7-3/4", and brought $575 at auction in February 2008.

and lapidary societies. Links to the regional organizations, hundreds of local clubs, and other sites of interest can be found on the AFMS Web site at www.amfed.org.

Equipment

A toolkit for field collecting can be as simple as a rock hammer and a pair of goggles. It is imperative that you buy a good rock hammer, also called a prospector's pick—or at the very least, a mason's or bricklayer's hammer—as any hammer not made specifically for stone may be too brittle and could chip or shatter. Because stone fragments are liable to fly off in any direction no matter how careful you are, you should always wear eye protection.

Beyond these basics, the size of your toolkit will depend on many factors: the nature of your collecting trip; how serious you are about collecting; even the types of specimens you are looking for. A sledge hammer and cold chisels or a wrecking bar can be very useful, as can a folding shovel of the type commonly available at Army surplus stores. A sieve or piece of metal screen can be used to sift through loose rock or gravel. Keep in mind the weight of your tools and the distance you will have to carry them—and don't forget to factor in the weight of the samples you will carry back!

Take a knapsack or backpack, along with newspaper to wrap and protect your specimens. Egg cartons, film canisters, or small plastic cases are invaluable for storing and protecting especially fragile specimens or those small enough that they might otherwise get lost in your bag. A magnifying glass is very helpful for examining small specimens.

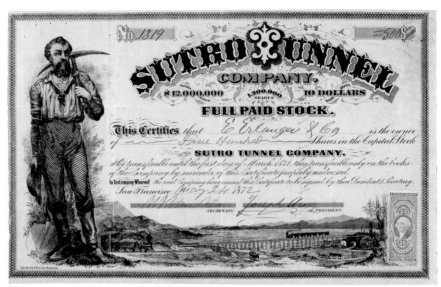

An 1872 certificate from the famous Sutro Tunnel Company, which dug a 20,000-foot (nearly four-mile) tunnel into the flooded Comstock Lode. Work started in 1869 and after the tunnel was completed in 1878, Adolph Sutro sold his interest in his brainchild and invested in San Franciso real estate, later serving as the city's mayor. He left a considerable estate on his death. The certificate is lithographed by Britton and Rey of San Francisco and has a 25¢ U.S. Internal Revenue stamp affixed to it. It measures 12-1/4" × 7-1/2". This specimen sold for $5,290 at auction in February 2008.

Masking tape and a pen or marker, along with a notebook, will let you label specimens or keep track of data about where and when they were collected, and a camera can help to further document your discoveries.

Field Safety

In addition to tools and supplies specific to collecting, be sure you are dressed appropriately for the weather and the terrain. Hiking boots, a hardhat, gloves, bandages for small nicks and cuts or even a complete first-aid kit, and insect repellent may be necessary. A compass and/or GPS unit are handy for navigation in more remote areas, and a cell phone is always a good idea for emergency communication. Always be sure to have food and plenty of water with you, even if you are only out for a few hours.

If you are unfamiliar with the area or with wilderness activities in general, it can be helpful to join a group of collectors with more experience. This is also a good idea if you are unfamiliar with field work, as more experienced collectors can show you the "tricks of the trade." In any case, always check the weather forecast before you go out, and let someone know where you will be, just in case.

Methodology

Until you are used to the hammer, you may want to "practice" on plain rock before you work around any specimens. Only experience can teach you the best way to wield your hammer—too light a blow will be ineffective, but if you strike too hard you risk shattering the specimen you are trying to collect.

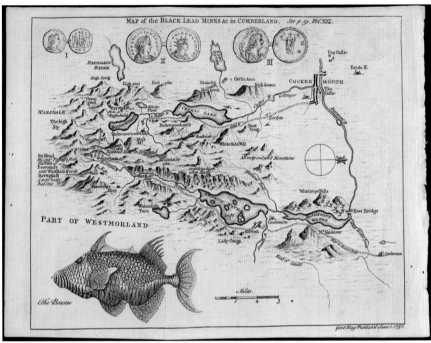

From 1791, this early map shows the black lead (galena) mines of Cumberland, England. It sold for $218.50 at auction in early 2008.

As long as the weight is not an issue, you may want to carry a variety of hammers and chisels with you. A sledgehammer and wrecking bar or crowbar can break through or dislodge large masses of rock to reveal specimens hidden within. It may be safer to extract small, fragile minerals—especially crystals—with cold chisels or a smaller, lighter hammer to minimize vibrations that risk fracturing the specimens.

The size of the specimens you collect depends on the nature of the minerals and on your collection. In general, though, specimens do not need to be any larger than the size of your fist. Crystals in particular are often more important to a collector when they retain some of their native matrix (the material in which they formed), and they may be more valuable this way, too. Once you have extracted a specimen, a few careful, light blows from your hammer can trim it to a more manageable size, or remove sharp projections that might damage other specimens while being carried home in your bag. However, you should resist the temptation to do too much trimming in the field. Trim only as much as necessary for transporting the specimen; delicate work such as removing small portions of the matrix or shaping a specimen to make it more attractive for display is best done at home, with light, careful taps of the pick end of your hammer or more delicate instruments such as dental picks and jeweler's tools.

You don't need to identify specimens in the field, but it is a good idea to label them with the place and date, and to make a note of any other information that might help with identification once you return home. Small specimens should be kept in a small plastic box or film canister so you don't lose them, and fragile specimens should be wrapped to prevent damage. However, it is generally a good idea to wait until the end of

This large 10.6" × 10.6" advertising card produced by the T.C. Williams Co. of Virginia depicts a miner holding a large gold nugget. The card sold for $276 at auction in early 2008.

the day to wrap most of your specimens—if you find multiple examples of one mineral, they might not all be worth keeping, and there is no point in carrying more than you want. Cotton or similar materials can snag small, delicate crystals, so newspaper is actually preferable for wrapping.

Once you have returned home and trimmed your specimens, you will want to wash them. In most cases, scrubbing with water and a stiff brush will suffice to remove loose dirt and debris—although delicate crystals or very soft minerals should of course never be scrubbed. An acid bath or ultrasonic cleaner may be necessary in some cases, but beginners should always consult a more experienced collector before trying this.

IDENTIFYING MINERALS

Mineral Properties

Advanced chemical tests, electron microscopy, and x-ray crystallography are the only absolutely foolproof methods of mineral identification. In fact, most of the newer species of minerals have been discovered not in the field, but in the lab—it is only through such

Sutter's Mill — where gold was discovered in 1848.

First Day Cover. California Gold Centennial stamps are featured here on a first day cover. (First day covers are U.S. postage stamps canceled on the first day of issue, on special envelopes bearing a "cachet" or illustration pertaining to the stamp's theme.) These attractive stamps, issued in 1948, marked the 100th anniversary of the discovery of gold at Sutter's Mill and the start of the California Gold Rush. Interestingly enough those who flocked to the state in search of gold are referred to on the stamp as "Argonauts." This was a reference to Jason and the Argonauts who (in ancient mythology) searched for the "Golden Fleece."

high-tech tests that these minerals have been found to be distinct from very similar specimens.

Obviously, such testing methods are beyond the means and expertise of the hobbyist collector. Minerals traditionally have been identified from several easily observed physical properties, and most of the minerals listed in this guide book—and almost all common specimens that you will encounter in the field—can be identified from these properties and by a few simple tests.

Cleavage

Minerals break through fracture (see page 15) or cleavage. Cleavage is a smooth break producing a flat plane. The tendency for minerals to cleave in specific directions is very characteristic, and so is one of the most important mineral identifiers.

Cleavage is reproducible, meaning that a crystal can be broken along the same parallel plane over and over again. Cleavage occurs in minerals that have specific planes of weakness; these planes of weakness are inherent in the structure of the mineral, and are related to its crystal symmetry. (See "Crystal Classification.") All of a mineral's cleavage planes must match that mineral's symmetry and must parallel a possible crystal face.

Cleavage is often described by what are known as Miller indices, and written as a series of three 0's or 1's contained in square brackets (hexagonal crystals have four axes of symmetry, so they will have four numbers in their Miller indices). It is not necessary that you

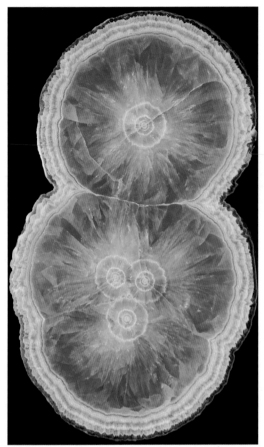

Rhodochrosite. 15 x 9.0 x 1.0 cm. Originally cut from a stalactite, this spectacular slice of two banded, adjoined sections of rhodochrosite shows beautiful color—slightly transparent pink with a few white highlights. Capillitas, Argentina.

understand the mathematics behind Miller indices, only that you understand the notation. The first number refers to the front-back symmetric axis, the second number to the left-right axis, and the third number to the up-down axis; a 1 means the mineral exhibits cleavage along that axis. So a mineral with good cleavage in the [010] direction means that it cleaves along the left-right axis; a mineral with [111] cleavage exhibits cleavage along all three axes.

Cleavage is said to be *basal* when it occurs perpendicular to the major axis of the mineral and *prismatic* when it occurs parallel to the major axis. Multiple cleavages that produce geometric polygons are referred to using the name of the geometric polygon, such as the octahedral cleavage of fluorite.

Color

Color is generally the first thing we notice about a mineral. It is the most striking property of most minerals, one that gives them their beauty and that attracts most people to collecting in the first place. However, color is a notoriously unreliable property for identifying minerals. While a specific color is a fundamental property of some species, such as the blue of azurite or the green of malachite (both caused by copper), many minerals can have a range of colors. Quartz can be colorless (in which case it is called rock crystal); it can also be purple (amethyst), pink (rose quartz), yellow (citrine), or a variety of other colors.

Color is caused by the absorption of various wavelengths of light by the chemical elements that compose the mineral. While most elements typically produce a specific color or range of colors—such as the green and blue from copper, or the red from iron—trace amounts of some elements can often "contaminate" a specimen, altering its color.

Diaphaneity

Diaphaneity is simply a measure of the transparency of a mineral. Diaphaneity ranges from transparent to opaque.

Fracture

Fracture is a type of breaking distinct from cleavage. While cleavage is a smooth break producing a flat surface, fracture is less regular. All solid minerals fracture, whether or not they exhibit cleavage. Fracture is not as important a means of identifying minerals as is cleavage, but it can still be useful.

A related property is *tenacity*, the resistance of a mineral to bending, cutting, or breaking. In this guide book, however, tenacity is combined with fracture in the property descriptions.

Fracture is described in the following terms:

brittle. Easily broken

brittle – conchoidal. A brittle fracture with small, conchoidal (smooth, shell-like) fragments

brittle – irregular. A brittle fracture with irregular fragments

brittle – subconchoidal. A brittle fracture with subconchoidal (semi-curving) fragments

brittle – splintery. A brittle fracture leaving splintery fragments

brittle – sectile. A brittle fracture with slightly sectile (curved) shavings possible

brittle – uneven. A brittle fracture with uneven fragments

conchoidal. A smoothly curved fracture, such as that seen in broken glass

conchoidal – irregular. An irregular fracture with small, conchoidal (smooth, shell-like) fragments

conchoidal – uneven. Uneven fracture with small, conchoidal (smooth, shell-like) fragments

elastic. Springs back after bending

fibrous. Exhibits long, thin, fractures producing strands like hair or cotton

flexible. Characterized by flexible fragments

friable. Crumbly

granular. Fractures into separate grains

hackly. Characterized by jagged, torn surfaces, usually a metal

irregular. Flat surfaces (not cleavage) fractured in an irregular pattern

micaceous. Sheet-like flexible fragments

malleable. Deforms rather than breaking apart

plastic. Deforms, like soft plastic

plastic – splintery. Characterized by long, thin, soft, flexible fractures

regular. Characterized by flat surfaces (not cleavage) fractured in a regular pattern

subconchoidal. Similar to conchoidal; not as curved, but still smooth

sectile. Characterized by curved shavings or scrapings

splintery. Characterized by long thin, splinters

sugary. Characterized by fine-grained fracture

tough. Difficult to break apart

uneven. Flat surfaces (not cleavage) fractured in an uneven pattern

Hardness

Hardness measures a mineral's resistance to being scratched. Mineralogists generally measure hardness on the Mohs Scale, developed by German mineralogist Friederich Mohs in 1822. Mohs selected ten well known, readily available minerals and arranged them in order of their "scratch hardness"—if a specimen can be scratched by a known mineral from the list, it is softer than that mineral; if it can scratch another known

Agate Geode. 10 x 6.0 x 9.0 cm. This unusual polished geode shows an odd checker pattern quartz interior. Chihuahua, Mexico.

mineral, it is harder than that mineral. The higher a mineral's Mohs number, the harder it is. The Mohs scale is relative, however, rather than absolute; it measures only what can scratch what. While corundum (hardness 9) is about twice as hard as topaz (hardness 8), diamond (hardness 10) is almost four times as hard as corundum.

There are many scientific tests to determine the absolute hardness of minerals, but the Mohs test is sufficient for the collector. Standard hardness test kits are available for purchase, but approximations can be made. For instance, if a specimen can be scratched by a penny but not by your fingernail, you know it is approximately hardness 3.

When testing hardness, it is important to test across a fresh surface; brittle or fibrous minerals may crumble easily despite their inherent hardness. Also, some minerals have different hardnesses depending on the direction in which you test—kyanite has a hardness of 5.5 across one axis and of 7.0 across a perpendicular axis.

Values for hardness in this book are given to two decimal places, but remember that these numbers are somewhat arbitrary, based only on a specimen's hardness relative to other minerals.

Mohs Hardness	Mohs Description
0	Liquid
1	Talc
1.5	Between Talc and Gypsum
2	Gypsum
2.5	Fingernail
3	Calcite
3.5	Copper Penny
4	Fluorite
4.5	Between Fluorite and Apatite
5	Apatite
5.5	Knife Blade
6	Orthoclase
6.5	Pyrite
7	Quartz
7.5	Garnet
8	Topaz
8.5	Chrysoberyl
9	Corundum
9.5	Silicon Carbide
10	Diamond

Luster

Luster describes how a mineral's surface reflects light. Like color, it is a subjective property. Luster is described in the following terms:

adamantine. Having a high index of refraction

adamantine – greasy. Between adamantine and greasy

adamantine – metallic. Between adamantine and metallic

adamantine – pearly. Between pearly and adamantine

adamantine – resinous. Between resinous and adamantine

adamantine – silky. Between silky and adamantine

chatoyant. Featuring numerous hair-like inclusions aligned to produce "cat's-eye" figure

earthy (dull). Completely dull

greasy (oily). Having a greasy or oily surface

metallic. Characterized by specular reflection

metallic – dull. Having a dull metallic luster

pearly. Formed by numerous partly developed cleavages

resinous. Having the luster of resin

resinous – greasy. Having a high index of refraction with surface alteration

resinous – metallic. Having a high index of refraction, in nearly opaque minerals

schiller. Having a bronzelike luster, sometimes with iridescence

silky. Characterized by a noticeable shiny direction

silky – pearly. Featuring silky and pearly lusters

submetallic. Having almost metallic reflection

subadamantine. Not quite adamantine

vitreous (glassy). Having the luster of broken glass

vitreous – adamantine. Having aspects of both vitreous and adamantine lusters

vitreous – dull. Having aspects of both vitreous and dull lusters

vitreous – greasy. Having aspects of both vitreous and greasy lusters

vitreous – metallic. Having aspects of both vitreous and metallic lusters

vitreous – pearly. Having aspects of both vitreous and pearly lusters

vitreous – resinous. Having aspects of both vitreous and resinous lusters

vitreous – silky. Having aspects of both vitreous and silky lusters

vitreous – waxy. Having aspects of both vitreous and waxy lusters

waxy. Characterized by fairly dull luster

Streak

Streak is the color of a mineral when it is ground into powder. This is usually tested by scratching the specimen across an unglazed white porcelain tile, although minerals with hardness above 7 (the hardness of the tile) cannot be tested this way because they will scratch the tile rather than pulverize on its surface.

Streak color often differs from specimen color, and so is very useful in identification. Streak color is also less variable than specimen color—for instance, all forms of quartz show a white streak, no matter the color of the specimen.

Streak is most useful for identifying dark-colored minerals such as oxides and sulfides.

Other Properties

There are a few other properties that, while important to the identification of a few species, occur relatively rarely, so they are only listed in this guide for those minerals in which they do occur.

magnetism. A few iron-bearing minerals such as magnetite exhibit varying degrees of magnetism.

radioactivity. Minerals containing the elements uranium and thorium are radioactive and can be identified with a Geiger counter. However, these minerals can be identified well enough through other properties, so it is not necessary for the hobbyist collector to invest in a Geiger counter.

luminescence. Many minerals will fluoresce, or glow under exposure to ultraviolet light. Fluorescence is caused by impurities in the minerals, and these impurities can cause a spectacular array of fluorescent colors. Fluorescence can help to confirm identification of a specimen, but by itself is not enough to identify a mineral.

A property related to luminescence is phosphorescence, in which the specimen will continue to glow for a time even after the ultraviolet light source is turned off.

A much rarer but striking luminescent phenomenon is triboluminescence, in which a specimen will emit flashes of light when struck or crushed. Rock crystal quartz and corundum may sometimes exhibit triboluminescence.

Diamond Mining Stereo Views. Pictured are two very fine Keystone View Company stereo views depicting diamond mining in South Africa. The individual cards are titled " The Premier Diamond Mine Transvaal, Union of South Africa" (2) and "Taking Out the 'Diamondiferous Blue Earth' at Wesselton Diamond Mines, Kimberley, Africa" (581).

Mineral Testing

In addition to the properties listed above, some minerals can be identified through simple lab procedures such as flame tests and acid tests that can be performed at home.

Until these procedures are mastered, they can be quite dangerous, so they are not covered in this guide book. If you are interested in learning these procedures, consult more technical mineralogy texts.

If you need help identifying field samples, seek the advice of more knowledgeable collectors at your local mineral shop or club. You may also find someone who is willing to teach you the testing methods, if you are interested in learning them.

CRYSTAL CLASSIFICATION

All minerals have characteristic crystal structures or geometric arrangement of the specific atoms that compose them. Crystal structure has a strong effect on a mineral's physical properties, and minerals with similar crystal structures will have similar properties.

A mineral is defined by both its chemistry and its crystal structure. Many minerals have identical chemical compositions, but are classified as different minerals with different properties because they have different crystal structures. Diamond and graphite are both composed of pure carbon, but the flat, tabular crystals of graphite make it soft and slippery, while diamond's atoms interlock in strong cubic crystals, making it one of the hardest substances known. Similarly, some minerals have the same atomic arrangement but different chemistry.

A crystal is simply a regular geometric shape bounded by flat planes. A cube is a crystal form, as are a pyramid and a prism. When a mineral grows without constraint, it will always form a perfect crystal; however, environmental factors will often affect the mineral's development—it might form in a space where it cannot grow as it normally would, or interactions with other substances might alter the crystal expression. This can make it difficult to identify a mineral based solely on its crystal shape, but it also leads to the wide range of shapes in which specimens are found, adding to the beauty and allure of minerals for collectors.

Crystal System

Crystals form symmetric shapes, and their symmetry is used for classification. There are six crystal systems, based on the lengths of their axes and the angles at which these axes intersect. As mentioned above, environmental conditions may affect the appearance of individual crystals, but it is important to note that in all crystals of the same mineral the angle between the same two faces will always be the same.

If a crystal is symmetric when rotated 180°, it is said to have twofold (or binary) symmetry. A crystal that is symmetric when rotated 120° has threefold (trigonal) symmetry. A crystal that is symmetric after 90° of rotation has fourfold (tetragonal) symmetry. And a crystal that is symmetric when rotated 60° has sixfold (hexagonal) symmetry.

The six crystal systems are isometric (or cubic), tetragonal, hexagonal, orthorhombic, monoclinic, and triclinic.

isometric. Isometric crystals have three axes of equal length at right angles to each other. Isometric crystals are generally shaped like a rough cube or ball.

tetragonal. Tetragonal crystals have three axes at right angles to each other, but only two of these axes are of equal length. Tetragonal crystals are usually long and slender.

hexagonal. Unlike the other five crystal systems, hexagonal crystals have four axes of symmetry: three axes of equal length, lying in a plane and intersecting at 120°, and a fourth at a right angle to the plane formed by the first three. This fourth axis can be of any length. Hexagonal crystals generally form three or six-sided prisms.

orthorhombic. Orthorhombic crystals have three axes at right angles to each other, like the isometric and tetragonal systems, but all three axes are of different lengths.

monoclinic. Monoclinic crystals have two axes at right angles to one another, and a third axis that is inclined to the plane formed by the first two. All three axes are of different lengths.

triclinic. Triclinic crystals have three unequal axes that intersect at three different oblique angles.

Krantz Crystal Models (various sizes). Rene Hauy introduced wooden crystal models at the end of the 18th century. During the 19th century, such models were used increasingly by both scholars for teaching purposes and by important mineral collectors. At the beginning of the 20th century, Fredrich Krantz offered collections of these in different sizes. Because of the difficulty, time, and expense in making precise wooden models, they are no longer being created. Antique models such as these are highly prized.

Crystal Forms

Within each crystal system there are various classes of symmetry. These are subdivisions of the system based on symmetry. A mineral belongs to (has the symmetry of) a crystal class. The symmetry is observed by studying the crystal forms. For example, the cube is a crystal form. It is made up of six square faces that are related by 120-degree rotations about the axes that run between opposite corners (i.e., [iii]).

As with the Miller indices used to denote cleavage, it is not necessary to understand the technical aspects of crystal form—it is merely a physical description that can help you to identify minerals. Most minerals occur in the highest-symmetry class within a crystal system. Low-symmetry classes within any crystal system have few, if any, mineral examples.

Isometric

Tetartoidal	3 axes of twofold symmetry
	4 axes of threefold symmetry
Diploidal	3 axes of twofold symmetry
	4 axes of threefold symmetry
	3 planes of symmetry
	center of symmetry

Hextetrahedral	3 axes of twofold symmetry
	4 axes of threefold symmetry
	6 planes of symmetry
Gyroidal	6 axes of twofold symmetry
	4 axes of threefold symmetry
	3 axes of fourfold symmetry
Hexoctahedral	6 axes of twofold symmetry
	4 axes of threefold symmetry
	3 axes of fourfold symmetry
	9 planes of symmetry
	center of symmetry

Tetragonal

Disphenoidal	I axis of twofold symmetry
Pyramidal	I axis of fourfold symmetry
Dipyramidal	I axis of fourfold symmetry
	I plane of symmetry
	center of symmetry
Scalenohedral	3 axes of twofold symmetry
	2 planes of symmetry
Ditetragonal pyramidal	4 planes of symmetry
Trapezohedral	4 axes of twofold symmetry
	I axis of fourfold symmetry
Ditetragonal-Dipyramidal	4 axes of twofold symmetry
	I axes of fourfold symmetry
	5 planes of symmetry
	center of symmetry

Orthorhombic

Pyramidal	I axis of twofold symmetry
	2 planes of symmetry
Disphenoidal	3 axes of twofold symmetry
Dipyramidal	3 axes of twofold symmetry
	3 planes of symmetry
	center of symmetry

Hexagonal

Trigonal Dipyramidal	I axis of threefold symmetry
	I plane of symmetry
Pyramidal	I axis of sixfold symmetry
Dipyramidal	I axis of sixfold symmetry
	I plane of symmetry
	center of symmetry

Ditrigonal Dipyramidal	3 axes of twofold symmetry
	1 axis of threefold symmetry
	4 planes of symmetry
Dihexagonal Pyramidal	1 axis of sixfold symmetry
	6 planes of symmetry
Trapezohedral	6 axes of twofold symmetry
	1 axis of sixfold symmetry
Dihexagonal Dipyramidal	6 axes of twofold symmetry
	1 axis of sixfold symmetry
	7 planes of symmetry
	center of symmetry

Trigonal

Pyramidal	1 axis of threefold symmetry
Rhombohedral	1 axis of threefold symmetry
	center of symmetry
Ditrigonal Pyramidal	1 axis of threefold symmetry
	3 planes of symmetry
Trapezohedral	3 axes of twofold symmetry
	1 axes of threefold symmetry
Hexagonal Scalenohedral	3 axes of twofold symmetry
	1 axis of threefold symmetry
	3 planes of symmetry
	center of symmetry

Monoclinic

Domatic	1 plane of symmetry
Sphenoidal	1 axis of twofold symmetry
Prismatic	1 axis of twofold symmetry
	1 plane of symmetry
	center of symmetry

Triclinic

| Pedial | no symmetry |
| Pinacoidal | center of symmetry |

Crystal Habit

Crystal habit refers to the shapes and aggregates that a mineral is likely to form. Often this is the most important characteristic for mineral identification. Although most minerals have a number of different habits, the shapes they create are sometimes very distinct and characteristic of only one or two minerals.

acicular. Having needle-like crystals
aggregate. Made of numerous individual crystals or clusters
amorphous. Having no definite crystalline form

anhedral grains. Characteristic of granular minerals without out crystal shapes

arborescent. Having tree-like growths

bladed. Featuring aggregates of thin blade-like crystals

blocky – rhombohedral. Having rhombohedral crystals (six faces, each a rhombus)

blocky. Characterized by crystal shape that tends to be equant (having axes all the same length)

Their cubic crystals play a large part in making diamonds one of the hardest substances on earth. Pictured here are two natural diamond crystals in their most common forms, cube and octahedron. In 2008, these gems sold at auction for $862.

botryoidal. Characterized by rounded grape-like forms

capillary. Very slender and long; threadlike

cog-wheel. Characterized by twinned crystals forming cogwheel shapes, usually six-sided

colloform. A gel or colloidal mass

columnar. Characterized by a tendency to form columns

compact. Characterized by a dense, firmly packed mass

concretionary. Consisting of rounded massive fine-grained materials

cruciform. Taking the form of twinned crystals with a cross-like outline

cryptocrystalline. Characterized by crystals too small to distinguish with the naked eye

crystalline – poor. Occuring primarily as crudely formed crystals

crystalline – fine. Occuring as well-formed fine-sized crystals

crystalline – coarse. Occuring as well-formed coarse-sized crystals

cubic. Occuring as box-shaped crystals

cylindrical. Shaped like a cylinder

dendritic. Exhibiting branching tree-like growths

disseminated. Characterized by small, distinct particles dispersed in matrix

divergent. With crystals radiating from a center without producing stellar forms

druse. Characterized by crystal growth in a cavity, resulting in numerous crystal-tipped surfaces

earthy. Having a dull, clay-like texture with no visible crystalline nature

efflorescent. Having a powdery deposit on the surface, formed as mineral-rich water evaporates

encrustations. Characterized by crust-like aggregates on matrix

euhedral. Having well-formed crystals with good external form

fibrous. Having crystals made up of fibers

flakes. Exhibiting thin, flat crystals or aggregates

foliated. Characterized by two-dimensional platy forms

friable. Crumbly

globular. Having rounded forms

granular. Occuring as anhedral to subhedral crystals in matrix

hexagonal. Featuring six-sided crystals

inclusions. Occuring as inclusions in other minerals

indistinct. Having unremarkable or poorly formed crystals

intergrown crystals. Occuring as crystals grown together or even through one another

irregular grains. Occuring as splotchy, anhedral crystals forming inclusions in other minerals or rocks

lamellar. Characterized by thin laminae producing a lamellar structure

liquid. Liquid at room temperatures

massive – fibrous. Distinctly fibrous and fine-grained in form

massive – granular. Having large grains, as observed in granite

massive – lamellar. Having distinctly foliated fine-grained crystals

massive. Having uniformly indistinguishable crystals forming large masses

micaceous. Characterized by platy texture with flexible plates

nodular. Taking tuberose forms having irregular protuberances over the surface

nuggets. Irregular lumps produced by stream transport of malleable metals

octahedral crystals. Taking the form of eight-sided crystals

oolitic. Having small (< 3mm) spherical grains

pistolitic. Having spherical grains larger than oolitic (> 3mm)

platy. Characterized by sheet forms (e.g., micas)

plumose. Mica-like minerals forming aggregates of plume-like forms

porcelainous. Fine-grained, translucent, and massive, like broken china

prismatic. Having crystals shaped like prisms

pseudo cubic. Having crystals showing a cubic outline

pseudo hexagonal. Having crystals showing a hexagonal outline

pseudo octohedral. Having crystals showing an octohedral outline

pseudo rhombohedral. Having crystals showing a rhombohedral outline

pseudo tetragonal. Having crystals showing a tetragonal shape

pseudo orthorhombic. Having crystals showing an orthorhombic shape

pseudomorphous. Occuring in the form of another mineral

pyramidal. Having crystals shaped like pyramids

radial. Having crystals radiating from a center without producing stellar forms

reniform. Kidney shaped

reticulate. Characterized by net-like crystalline growths

rhombohedral. Characterized by rhombohedral crystals

scaly. Occuring like fish scales

skeletal. Having crystals forming crude outlines with missing faces

spherical. Characterized by spherical crystals

square. Occuring as square crystals in shape or outline

stalactitic. Occuring in columns, as stalactites or stalagmites

stellate. Occuring as spherical, radial aggregates radiating from a star-like point

striated. Featuring parallel lines on crystal surface or cleavage face

tabular. Thin in one direction

thin. Characterized by flat crystals

triangular. Occuring as triangular crystals

twinning common. Characterized by crystals usually twinned

wheat sheaf. Characterized by bundled crystals resembling sheaves of wheat

Quartz Gwindel. 5.0 x 4.0 x 1.5 cm. This beautiful pale smoky quartz crystal is slightly twisted. Zinggenstock, Guttanen, Canton Berne, Switzerland.

Twinning

Crystal twinning occurs through an error during crystallization when two crystals intergrow, either in contact or penetrating one another. *Contact twins* share a single "composition plane" forming a boundary between the two crystals; the twinned crystals often appear as mirror images across this boundary of contact. *Penetration twins* actually pass through one other symmetrically. Penetration twins often form crosses, stars, or other regular shapes that make them much prized among collectors.

Twinning is fairly common in minerals, although perfectly formed twins are rare, adding to their allure. Staurolite often forms right-angle penetration twins known as "fairy crosses." Fluorite, pyrite, arsenopyrite, and monazite are other minerals that exhibit classic penetration twinning. Quartz, gypsum, feldspars, and the spinel group often exhibit striking contact twinning.

■ IDENTIFYING ROCKS ■

Rocks are made of minerals, and the Earth is made of rocks. (Indeed, so is the Moon, and the other so-called terrestrial planets: Mercury, Venus, and Mars.) Rocks form mountains, of course, but sand is rock that has been ground down by time and weather, and soil is rock that has been ground finer still, and mixed with organic materials and other substances.

Technically, a rock is simply a solid composed of one or more minerals. (Note, however, that sand and soil are not rocks—they are derived from rocks but lack coherence.) Rocks are described variously by composition, grain size, texture, structure, color, and method of formation.

Of these, method of formation is the most general and therefore the most convenient way to classify rocks. *Igneous* rocks are formed by the cooling and solidification of molten material: lava or magma. *Sedimentary* rocks are formed by the slow accumulation and layering of granular material. *Metamorphic* rocks are produced through the alteration by several means of igneous, sedimentary, or even of previously altered metamorphic rock.

Rocks are constantly (though very slowly) undergoing a process of change. All three kinds of rock are ground down by wind, weather, and water, becoming sediment of some sort—sand, silt, or clay. This sediment will eventually compress into sedimentary rock.

Garnet variety Spessartine and Muscovite. 9.0 x 7.0 x 5.0 cm. Several spessartine garnets and a small schorl crystal grow on a remarkable cluster of "star" muscovite crystals. Shengus, Gilgit District, Pakistan.

Sedimentary or igneous rock may be altered by heat or pressure, eventually becoming a metamorphic rock. Deep within the Earth, or in the presence of rising magma or lava, igneous or metamorphic rock can be melted into magma, from which it will eventually re-solidify into igneous rock again. This never-ending process of formation, alteration, and reformation is known as the *rock cycle*.

Igneous Rocks

Beneath the Earth's crust is a thick layer called the mantle, where heat and pressure liquefy the rock there. This liquid rock—called *magma*—migrates upward into the crust, where it cools and forms solid rock. If magma rises all the way through the crust and flows out onto the Earth's surface before solidifying, it is called lava. Any rock formed from cooling magma or lava is an igneous rock (from the Latin *ignis,* meaning fire).

Igneous rock is differentiated into subcategories based on where it formed: *plutonic* (or intrusive) igneous rock is that which forms underground, from magma; *volcanic* (or extrusive) igneous rock is that which forms on the surface, from lava. But no matter where it forms, all igneous rocks share many characteristic properties. Igneous rock is typically very hard (5-1/2 or greater hardness) and dense, and generally lacks any distinctive structures such as layering.

The classification and identification of igneous rocks is based primarily on their particular mineral content, but the boundaries between rock names are arbitrary, and no sharp distinction between species exists, as it does for minerals. Fortunately, while magma is a complex stew of melted silicates, you need only to be able to identify a few minerals to identify a rock—as long as the grains are large enough to see without a microscope, it is easy to determine the presence and relative amounts of these minerals, and from that you can identify the rock. A *classification diagram* provides a general key to identifying the minerals by color and grain size.

In technical terms, these minerals are referred to as felsic and mafic. *Felsic* is short for feldspar/silica; felsic rocks contain a great degree of silica, sodium, and calcium, and therefore form quartz and feldspar minerals. Felsic rocks are generally very light colored. Mafic rocks have a great degree of magnesium and iron—*mafic* is short for magnesium/ferrous—and are much darker than felsic rock.

Igneous rocks are further described by their texture, which ranges from glassy (amorphous, lacking any crystalline mineral grains) to aphantic (fine-grained) to phaneritic (coarse-grained). In general, the more slowly igneous rock cools, the larger its constituent grains will be.

While color and texture can provide clues to identifying an igneous rock, only its specific mineral content determines its actual species.

For instance, granite is a generally light-colored phaneritic felsic rock, containing (according to one definition) between 20 percent and 60 percent quartz and both alkali and plagioclase feldspars, with not more than 65 percent of the feldspar content being plagioclase feldspar. But again, there is no absolute definition—a rock that is 50 percent quartz, 25 percent alkali feldspar, and 25 percent plagioclase feldspar is definitely granite, while a rock with 50 percent quartz, 17 percent alkali feldspar, and 33 percent plagioclase feldspar might be classified as granite by one person and as granodiorite by another!

Igneous Rock Texture

glassy. Amorphous and lacking any crystalline mineral grains. Formed of volcanic flow or ejecta that cooled too rapidly for crystals to form.

aphanitic. With mineral crystals too fine-grained to be seen with the naked eye. Generally formed from lava that cooled before large crystals could form (but not as quickly as glassy rock).

porphyritic. Aphanitic rock with some larger crystals (phenocrysts) embedded in its matrix. Porphyritic rock can be formed when different minerals within cooling magma crystallize faster than others, or when cooling magma begins to form large crystals but is then erupted by a volcano, and the rest of the rock cools quickly.

phaneritic. Even-grained rock with all crystals large enough to be visible to the naked eye. Phaneritic rock forms when magma cools slowly, giving the minerals inside time to grow and form large, sometimes complex arrangements.

pegmatitic. Very coarse-grained rock, with uneven texture. Occurs when some minerals in cooling magma grow massively large.

pyroclastic. Also called *fragmental.* Lava violently ejected from a volcano may include fragments of solid rock broken in the eruption. Pyroclastic rock is formed by lava that solidifies around these fragments.

Sedimentary Rocks

Sedimentary rock is formed from the accumulation and compression of mineral sediment in a process called lithification. As wind, water, and glaciation erode rock surfaces, the particles worn off are carried away to other locations, where they settle in layers. As these sediments build up, the weight of the upper layers compresses the lower layers, and this compaction transforms the sediments into solid rock. Materials dissolved in water may also act to cement the sediments together into solid rock. Often, both compaction and cementing act together to form sedimentary rock. Sedimentary rock covers more than 75 percent of the Earth's surface, but only in a thin layer—it accounts for just 5 percent of all solid rock on Earth.

Sedimentary rocks contain important information about the history of Earth. The sediments themselves provide clues about the original rock that created them. The layers, or *strata,* provide a timeline of their formation, and hence of the age of materials found within them. Differences between successive layers provide evidence of environmental changes. And most spectacularly, sedimentary rocks contain fossils—the calcified remains of ancient plants and animals. (The processes that form igneous and metamorphic rocks destroy such remains, but sedimentation actually acts to preserve them.)

Sedimentary rock is differentiated into three types by the source of the sediments from which it forms.

Clastic sedimentary rock forms from the sediments produced by mechanical weathering and erosion of other rock. Also called detrital rock because it forms from the detritus of other rock, clastic rock is very loosely graded according to particle size—from shale (individual particles less than 0.004 mm in diameter) to conglomerate and breccia, which can include rock fragments as large as boulders.

Chemical sedimentary rock is nonclastic rock whose constituent particles precipitated out of salt water or freshwater. Just as you can only dissolve so much sugar in a glass of water before the excess begins to settle to the bottom, beyond a certain concentration, minerals will no longer dissolve in water but will instead settle, or precipitate, eventually cementing together into solid rock. If the water environment becomes "super-saturated" with minerals as a result of evaporation, the resulting chemical rock is referred to as an evaporite. Travertine and flint are chemical sedimentary rocks; gypsum rock and rock salt are evaporites.

Biochemical sedimentary rock forms from the remains of living organisms. Corals, seashells, and skeletons will form limestone; coal is a biochemical rock derived from the remains of plant material. It should be noted that carbonate rocks—those composed primarily of calcium carbonate ($CaCO_3$), such as limestone, chalk, and dolostone—tend to form by both chemical and biochemical processes, even within the same individual specimen, and plant-based biochemical rocks always form in the presence of clastic rocks. In fact, biochemical rock is differentiated from clastic and chemical rock only because it forms from organic remains—its content is biological in origin, but in reality it still forms through mechanical and chemical processes.

Sedimentary rock texture is simply described as being fine-, medium-, or coarse-grained, or crystalline if it consists entirely of crystals or fragments of crystals. Sedimentary rocks are not easily differentiated by texture alone; the boundaries of grain size are set rather arbitrarily, and even within categories particles are further divided by size. Clay and silt are both fine-grained particles, with clay being finer than silt, but the determination between siltstone and mudstone (which is made of clay) can really only be made under a microscope.

A much more important property for determining a sedimentary rock is its structure. *Structure* refers to large-scale features deriving from the environment and condition in which the sediments formed. Structures are particularly obvious in the field, and so are the best means by which to recognize and identify sedimentary rocks when collecting "in the wild."

Sedimentary Rock Structure

strata. Strata (singular *stratum*) are simply the layers in which sedimentary rock forms as the sediments are deposited in successive layers. Strata can be distinguished by variations in color, texture, hardness, and composition. Strata thicker than 1 cm are called beds; thinner strata are called laminations.

cross-stratification. Caused by the action of wind or water on sand, cross-stratification results in straight or scalloped rock strata forming at angles to successive layers.

graded bedding. Graded bedding refers to rock strata where the size of the grains increases from top to bottom. It is caused by a current gradually slowing down, so that larger and therefore heavier particles settle out first.

ripples. Ripples are parallel, undulating ridges caused by wind or water on sand. They can be seen on a beach or a sand dune.

Metamorphic Rocks

Metamorphic rock is exactly what the name suggests: rock that has been transformed. Any existing rock can be changed into metamorphic rock—igneous, sedimentary, even other metamorphic rock.

Metamorphic rock forms under intense heat and pressure. This can happen deep within the Earth, where such heat and pressure are the normal environment; tectonic forces such as continental drift can also create metamorphic rock. Such widespread metamorphism (which is responsible for creating massive structures over a great area such as mountain ranges) is called *regional metamorphism.* Or the heat of rising magma can alter the rock it moves through; this is known as *contact metamorphism.* However, if rock is heated enough that it melts into magma, it will then form igneous rock when it cools and re-solidifies, not metamorphic rock. Metamorphism only refers to changes that take place before actual melting occurs.

Because of the wide range of temperatures and pressures under which they may have formed and the variety of rocks from which they may have formed, metamorphic rocks vary widely in their characteristics. Metamorphic rocks can contain unaltered fragments and even entire structures of their parent rocks. Particles may recrystallize, forming new structures without otherwise changing composition. As limestone metamorphoses into marble, for instance, the small calcite crystals become larger, giving marble the characteristic texture and appearance that make it so highly prized for sculpture and construction.

Native Gold. 1.7 x 1.6 x 0.5 cm. 10.8 grams. This native gold formed in hoppered, octahedral crystals. Zapata Field, Bolivar State, Venezuela.

Above about 200°C, the individual crystals of many minerals begin to break down and will form new chemical compounds and new crystals. Different minerals form at different temperatures. Certain minerals that form only at the high temperatures and pressures associated with metamorphism are called *index minerals* because they can therefore be used to determine the degree of alteration a rock has undergone. Some of these index minerals are biotite, chlorite, garnet, kyanite, muscovite, sillimanite, and staurolite.

When stress (such as pressure) is applied to a recrystallizing rock in one direction, minerals such as micas and chlorite will grow with their long axes perpendicular to the direction of the force. These parallel mineral flakes produce a planar or banded texture called *foliated rock*. Foliated rock is described by its particular texture. *Slaty* rock is fine-grained with a prominent cleavage along which it splits into thin sheets. *Schistose* rock is coarse-grained, but still has a high mica content and distinct layers, and so splits easily. *Gneissose* rock is coarse-grained, composed mainly of quartz and feldspar; the layers are thicker and often less regular than in other foliated rock.

Among non-foliated rock, textures include *hornfelsic,* which is dense and even-textured, and fine-grained without any evident crystalline structure; and *granuloblastic,* which has larger mineral grains of the same general size.

Metamorphic rock may also be *porphyroblastic* or *poikiloblastic.* A porphyroblast is a large, well-shaped mineral crystal that has grown within the fine-grained matrix rock. A poikiloblast is a porphyroblast that contains inclusions of the original parent rock.

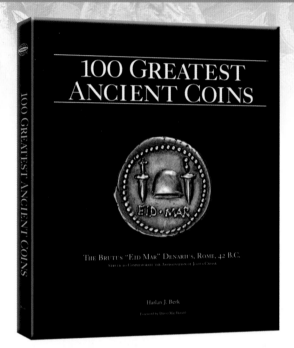

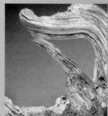

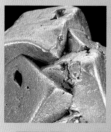

MINERALS

CATALOG OF MINERALS
NATIVE ELEMENTS

Gold

Chemical Formula	Au
Environment	Quartz veins and alluvial deposits
Locality	Many places worldwide, including California, South Dakota, Alaska; Siberia; South Africa; Canada
Etymology	Uncertain Anglo-Saxon origin

Physical Properties of Gold

Cleavage	None
Color	Yellow, pale yellow, orange, yellow white, reddish white
Diaphaneity	Opaque
Fracture	Hackly
Habit	Massive, granular, dendritic
Hardness	2.5–3
Luster	Metallic
Specific Gravity	16–19.3, Average = 17.64
Streak	Yellow
Indicators	Color, density, hardness, sectility, malleability, ductility

Gold. This sharply crystalized native gold is sprinkled with minor amounts of quartz. Placer County, California. Brought $6,325 at auction in February 2008.

In the United States, gold is found in all of the western states as well as in Georgia, Maryland, Michigan, North Carolina, Pennsylvania, South Carolina, South Dakota, Tennessee, Texas, and Virginia. Although California and Alaska are famous for their respective gold rushes, more than three-quarters of all gold mined in the United States now comes from Nevada.

The world's largest gold nugget on public display can be seen in the lobby of the Gold Nugget Casino in Las Vegas, Nevada. The "Hand of Faith" nugget weighs almost 62 pounds and was discovered by an Australian man using a metal detector near Kingower, Victoria.

Silver

Chemical Formula	Ag
Environment	Sulfide ore veins
Locality	Many places worldwide, including United States, Canada, Mexico, Norway, Germany
Etymology	Unknown Anglo-Saxon origin

Physical Properties of Silver

Cleavage	None
Color	Silver white, gray white, gray
Diaphaneity	Opaque
Fracture	Hackly
Habit	Arborescent, dendritic, massive

Hardness	2.5–3
Luster	Metallic
Specific Gravity	10–11, Average = 10.5
Streak	Silver white
Indicators	Color, tarnish, ductility, crystal habit

According to the British Geological Survey, in 2005 Peru was the world's top producer of silver (producing almost one-seventh of the world supply), followed closely by Mexico. In the United States, silver has been mined extensively in Alaska (recently the nation's leading silver-producing state), Arizona, California, Colorado (a major producer in the 1800s), Idaho (home of the Couer d'Alene silver district, the nation's top producer of all time), Missouri, Montana, Nevada (where the discovery of the Comstock Lode in 1858 launched large-scale silver mining in the United States), New Hampshire, New Mexico, Oregon, Pennsylvania, Texas, Utah, and Washington. In many states silver production is a by-product of copper mining.

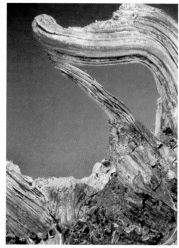

Silver. The thick wire silver growing out of a silver matrix shown here produces a sculpture-like quality. British Columbia, Canada. Brought $1,265 at auction in February 2008.

Copper

Chemical Formula	Cu
Environment	Cap rock of copper-sulfide veins; some types of volcanic rocks
Locality	Michigan and Arizona; Cyprus; Greece; Germany; Australia
Etymology	Greek, *Kyprios*, "Cyprus"

Physical Properties of Copper

Cleavage	None
Color	Copper red; when oxidized may be brown, black
Diaphaneity	Opaque
Fracture	Hackly
Habit	Arborescent, botyroidal
Hardness	2.5–3
Luster	Metallic
Specific Gravity	8.94–8.95, Average = 8.94
Streak	Rose
Indicators	Color, ductility, crystal habit

Copper. Ray Mine, Pinal County, Arizona.

Copper is abundant in the United States, being found in Alabama, Alaska, Arizona, California, Connecticut, Maine, Maryland, Michigan, Missouri, Montana, Nevada, New Jersey, New Mexico, New York, North Carolina, Oklahoma, Oregon, Pennsylvania,

Tennessee, Texas, Utah, Vermont, Virginia, Wisconsin, and Wyoming. Many of the commercial sources are now mined out, however, and only Arizona, Utah, New Mexico, and Montana still produce significant amounts.

Lead

Chemical Formula	Pb
Environment	Hydrothermal origin
Locality	United States; Mexico; Langban, Sweden; Russia
Etymology	Anglo-Saxon, *lead*; Latin, *plumbum*

Physical Properties of Lead

Cleavage	None
Color	Lead gray, gray white
Diaphaneity	Opaque
Fracture	Malleable
Habit	Blocky
Hardness	2–2.5
Luster	Metallic
Specific Gravity	11.37
Streak	Lead gray
Indicators	Color, density, hardness, luster, ductility

Lead slag.

The United States is the world's largest producer of lead. Primary localities are Alaska, Idaho, Montana, Illinois, Missouri, and New York.

Mercury

Chemical Formula	Hg
Environment	Secondary mineral from oxidation of cinnabar deposits. Solid below −38.9°C
Locality	California, Oregon, Arkansas, Texas; Almaden, Spain; Idria, Slovenia; Italy
Etymology	Arabic

Physical Properties of Mercury

Cleavage	None
Color	Tin white, gray white
Diaphaneity	Opaque
Fracture	None
Habit	Liquid
Hardness	0
Luster	Metallic
Specific Gravity	13.6
Streak	none
Indicators	Liquid at room temperature (the only liquid mineral)

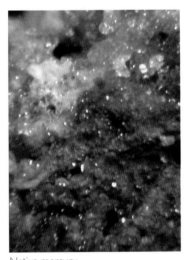

Native mercury.

Mercury has not been mined in the United States since 1992, but mercury ores can still be found in Alaska, California, Nevada, Texas, and Arkansas. Mercury is very rare in its native form; it occurs most commonly in the ore cinnabar. Because its soluble forms are extremely toxic, mercury should always be handled with great care.

Iron

Chemical Formula	Fe
Environment	In meteorites and, rarely, basalt intrusions of carbon-rich sediments
Locality	Germany, Russia, Greenland, New Zealand, meteor fragments worldwide
Etymology	Anglo-Saxon

Physical Properties of Iron

Cleavage	[001] Perfect, [010] Perfect, [100] Perfect
Color	Iron black, dark gray, steel gray
Diaphaneity	Opaque
Fracture	Hackly
Habit	Disseminated, granular, massive
Hardness	4–5
Luster	Metallic
Magnetism	Naturally strong
Specific Gravity	7.3–7.9, Average = 7.6
Streak	Gray
Indicators	Color, malleability, magnetism

Iron (terrestrial).

Iron is the 10th most abundant element in the universe, and the fourth most abundant element in the Earth's crust, composing as much as 35 percent of the total mass of our planet. Primary industrial sources in the United States are located in Minnesaota, Wisconsin, and Michigan, although iron in its various compounds can be found practically anywhere.

Platinum

Chemical Formula	Pt
Environment	Grains and nuggets in alluvial deposits
Locality	United States; Ural Mountains, Russia; South Africa
Etymology	Spanish, *platina*, "silver"

Physical Properties of Platinum

Cleavage	None
Color	Whitish steel gray; steel gray; dark gray

Diaphaneity	Opaque
Fracture	Hackly
Habit	Granular; nuggets
Hardness	4–4.5
Luster	Metallic
Magnetism	Naturally weak
Specific Gravity	14–22, Average = 18
Streak	grayish white
Indicators	Color, density, weak magnetism, hardness, associations, ductility

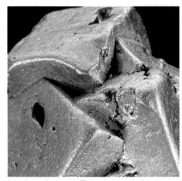

Native platinum. This sharp platinum group, composed of cubic crystals, has a metallic luster and steel-gray appearance. 23.33 carats (4.67 grams); Eastern-Siberian Region, Russia.

Platinum is extremely rare, and because of this is more valuable than gold. Its only sources in North America are in Montana and Ontario.

Arsenic

Chemical Formula	As
Environment	Ore veins in crystalline rocks
Locality	United States, Germany, Great Britain, Japan, France, Norway, Italy
Etymology	Greek, *arsenikon*, originally used for orpiment

Physical Properties of Arsenic

Cleavage	[0001] Perfect
Color	Lead gray, gray, white
Diaphaneity	Opaque
Fracture	Uneven
Habit	Lamellar, nodular, reniform
Hardness	3.5
Luster	Metallic
Specific Gravity	5.7
Streak	Black
Indicators	Tarnish, density, softness, crystal habits, color, garlic smell, associations

Native arsenic.

Arsenic is toxic and very dangerous environmentally; arsenic poisoning in drinking water is a problem in many parts of the world. In the United States, arsenic is found in Arizona, California, Colorado, Connecticut, Idaho, Louisiana, Nevada, New Hampshire, New Jersey, New Mexico, South Dakota, Utah, Virginia, and Washington, with the most widespread occurrences being in Neavda and Idaho.

Antimony

Chemical Formula	Sb
Environment	Hydrothermal veins

Locality	United States, Canada, Mexico, Sweden
Etymology	Arabic, *al-uthmud,* and Latin, *antimonium*

Physical Properties of Antimony

Cleavage	[0001] Perfect
Color	Light gray, tin white
Diaphaneity	Opaque
Fracture	Brittle
Habit	Massive – lamellar, massive, reticulate
Hardness	3–3.5
Luster	Metallic
Specific Gravity	6.61–6.72, Average = 6.66
Streak	Lead gray
Indicators	Density, softness, color, crystal habits, lack of smell, associations

Native antimony.

Antimony occurs in more than 100 compounds, but is not often seen in its native state. Like arsenic, which it resembles, it is toxic, and care should be exercised when handling antimony or any of its compounds. It is found in Arizona, Arkansas, California, Colorado, Connecticut, Idaho, Michigan, Nevada, New Jersey, North Carloina, Oregon, Texas, Virginia, and Washington.

Tellurium

Chemical Formula	Te
Environment	Hydrothermal vein mineral
Locality	United States, Romania, Australia
Etymology	Latin, *tellus,* "earth"

Physical Properties of Tellurium

Cleavage	[100] Good
Color	White, grayish white
Diaphaneity	Opaque
Fracture	Brittle
Habit	Columnar, massive
Hardness	2–2.5
Luster	Metallic
Specific Gravity	6.2
Streak	Grayish white
Indicators	Tarnish, density, color, cleavage

Tellurium. A trace of tellurium runs through the central band of pyrite, while the outer portion of the vein contains a considerable amount of tellurium.

Tellurium is one of the rarest elements on Earth and is almost never found in its native form. It can be found in Arizona, California, Colorado, Connecticut, Michigan, Nevada, New Mexico, North Carolina, Utah, and Virginia.

Bismuth

Chemical Formula	Bi
Environment	Hydrothermal ores of copper, nickel, silver, and tin; in coarsely crystalline granite or other high-silica rock; in topaz-bearing tin-tungsten veins
Locality	United States, Germany, Australia, Bolivia, England
Etymology	Arabic, *bi ismid,* "having the properties of antimony"

Physical Properties of Bismuth

Cleavage	[0001] Perfect
Color	Silver white, pinkish white, red
Diaphaneity	Opaque
Fracture	Uneven
Habit	Granular, lamellar, platy
Hardness	2–2.5
Luster	Metallic
Specific Gravity	9.7–9.8, Average = 9.75
Streak	Silver white
Indicators	Tarnish, density, cleavage

Bismuth.

Bismuth has an exceptionally high resistance for a metal, and in fact is used in the electronics industry as a semi-conductor. High-purity bismuth produced in laboratories forms distinctive "hopper crystals" that are much prized by collectors. Bismuth can be found throughout the western United States and in Alabama, Connecticut, Georgia, Maine, Michigan, New Hampshire, South Carolina, South Dakota, Texas, Virginia, and Wisconsin.

Sulfur

Chemical Formula	S
Environment	Volcanic exhalations; bacterial reduction of sulfates
Locality	United States; Sicily, Italy; Chile; Poland
Etymology	Sanskrit, *sulvere,* "sulfur"; Latin, *sulphurium*

Physical Properties of Sulfur

Cleavage	[001] Imperfect, [110] Imperfect, [111] Imperfect
Color	Yellow, yellowish brown, yellowish gray, reddish, greenish
Density	2.05–2.09, Average = 2.06
Diaphaniety	Transparent to translucent

Sulfur.

Fracture	Sectile
Habit	Massive; reniform; stalactitic
Hardness	1.5–2.5
Luster	Resinous
Streak	White
Indicators	Color, odor, heat sensitivity, lack of good cleavage, crystal habit

Sulfur is quite common and can be found in every state except Arkansas, Delaware, Florida, Hawaii, Iowa, Kansas, Montana, North Dakota, Oklahoma, and Vermont.

Diamond

See listing under "Gemstones."

Graphite

Chemical Formula	C
Environment	Metamorphosed limestone; organic-rich shale; coal beds
Locality	New York, Texas, Russia, Mexico, Madagascar, India, Greenland
Etymology	Greek, *graphein,* "to write"

Graphite.

Physical Properties of Graphite

Cleavage	[0001] Perfect
Color	Iron black, dark gray, black, steel gray
Diaphaneity	Opaque
Fracture	Sectile
Habit	Earthy, foliated, tabular
Hardness	1.5–2
Luster	Submetallic
Specific Gravity	2.09–2.23, Average = 2.16
Streak	Black
Indicators	Softness, luster, density, streak

Carbon, the element that forms graphite, is one of the most common elements on Earth. Graphite can be found throughout New England, the western states, and Alabama, Arkansas, Georgia, Kansas, Maryland, Michigan, Minnesota, New Jersey, New York, North Carolina, Oklahoma, Pennsylvania, South Carolina, South Dakota, Tennessee, Virginia, and Wisconsin.

■ SULFIDES ■

Acanthite

Chemical Formula	Ag_2S
Environment	Low-temperature ore veins
Locality	Freiberg, Schneeberg, Annaberg, Germany
Etymology	Greek, *akanta,* "arrow"

Physical Properties of Acanthite

Cleavage	[001] Poor, [110] Poor
Color	Lead gray, gray, iron black
Diaphaneity	Opaque
Fracture	Sectile
Habit	Arborescent, blocky, skeletal
Hardness	2–2.5
Luster	Metallic
Specific Gravity	7.2–7.4, Average = 7.3
Streak	Shining black
Indicators	Crystal habit, density, softness, sectility, association with other silver sulfosalts, color

Acanthite. Lingqui County, Shanxi Province, China.

Acanthite occurs widely as an ore of silver throughout the western United States, most notably in Nevada's Comstock Lode, as well as in Connecticut, Georgia, Maine, Michigan, New Hampshire, New Jersey, New York, North Carolina, Pennsylvania, South Dakota, Tennessee, Texas, Virginia, and Wisconsin.

Chalcocite

Chemical Formula	Cu_2S
Environment	Secondary mineral in or near the oxidation zone of copper-sulfide deposits
Locality	United States; Cornwall, England; Italy; France; Spain
Etymology	Greek, *chalkos*, "copper"

Physical Properties of Chalcocite

Cleavage	[110] Indistinct
Color	Blue black, gray, black, black gray, steel gray
Diaphaneity	Opaque
Fracture	Conchoidal
Habit	Euhedral crystals, granular; massive
Hardness	2.5–3
Luster	Metallic
Specific Gravity	5.5–5.8, Average = 5.65
Streak	Grayish black
Indicators	Habit, streak, color

Chalcocite. 3.5 × 3.0 × 3.5 cm. This specimen, slightly larger than a thumbnail in total, is called a toenail. Bristol Mine, Hartford County, Connecticut.

Chalcocite is one of the most profitable ores of copper due to its high copper and the ease with which the copper and sulfur can be separated. It occurs widely throughout the Rocky Mountain states and most of the rest of the United States, with the exceptions of Arkansas, Florida, Hawaii, Kansas, Indiana, Mississippi, Nebraska, North Dakota, Ohio, and West Virginia. Connecticut has produced some of the most famously striking chalcocite crystals in the world.

Bornite

Chemical Formula	Cu_5FeS_4
Environment	Within igneous intrusions; primary and secondary mineral in veins of copper
Locality	United States; Cornwall, England; Germany
Etymology	Austrian mineralogist I. von Born (1742–1791)

Physical Properties of Bornite

Cleavage	[111] Imperfect
Color	Copper red, bronze brown, purple
Diaphaneity	Opaque
Fracture	Conchoidal
Habit	Granular, massive – granular, reniform
Hardness	3
Luster	Metallic
Magnetism	Magnetic after heating
Specific Gravity	4.9–5.3, Average = 5.09
Streak	Grayish black
Indicators	Lack of crystals, tarnish, streak

Bornite.

Bornite, sometimes called "peacock ore" because of its iridescent tarnish, is an important copper ore that is found widely throughout the western United States, New England, Delaware, Georgia, Hawaii, Maryland, Michigan, Missouri, New Jersey, New York, North Carolina, Oklahoma, Pennsylvania, South Carolina, South Dakota, Tennessee, Texas, Virginia, and Wisconsin.

Pentlandite

Chemical Formula	$(Fe,Ni)_9S_8$
Environment	Common sulfide phase in basic and ultra-basic intrusive igneous rocks
Locality	United States; Canada; Lillihammer, Norway; South Africa
Etymology	Irish natural historian J.B. Pentland (1797–1873).

Physical Properties of Pentlandite

Cleavage	None
Color	Bronze, brown
Diaphaneity	Opaque
Fracture	Conchoidal

Pentlandite.

Habit	Granular, granular, massive – granular
Hardness	3.5–4
Luster	Metallic
Specific Gravity	4.6–5, Average = 4.8
Streak	Greenish black
Indicators	Parting, streak, color

Isolated deposits of pentlandite occur in the western United States, Arkansas, Connecticut, Georgia, Hawaii, Maine, Maryland, Michigan, Minnesota, New Hampshire, New York, North Carolina, Virginia, and Wisconsin. The large pentlandite deposit at Sudbury, Ontario, is from a meteorite crater.

Galena

Chemical Formula	PbS
Environment	Veins of lead sulfide ore; within igneous and sedimentary rocks
Locality	United States, Mexico, Peru, Germany, England, Zambia
Etymology	Latin *galena*, used by Roman naturalist Pliny to describe lead ore

Galena.

Physical Properties of Galena

Cleavage	[001] Perfect, [010] Perfect, [100] Perfect
Color	Light lead gray, dark lead gray
Diaphaneity	Opaque
Fracture	Brittle
Habit	Euhedral crystals, massive – granular, massive
Hardness	2.5
Luster	Metallic
Specific Gravity	7.2–7.6, Average = 7.4
Streak	Grayish black
Indicators	Habit, cleavage, density

Galena is a very common mineral, and can be found in every U.S. state except Delaware, Florida, Hawaii, and North Dakota. Galena is the official state mineral of both Missouri and Wisconsin.

Sphalerite

Chemical Formula	(Zn,Fe)S
Environment	Sulfide ore veins, within all rock classes
Locality	United States, Australia, Europe, Burma, Peru
Etymology	Greek, *sphaleros*, "misleading"

Physical Properties of Sphalerite

Cleavage	[110] Perfect, [110] Perfect, [110] Perfect
Color	Brown, yellow, red, green, black
Diaphaneity	Translucent to transparent
Fracture	Uneven
Habit	Colloform; euhedral crystals; granular
Hardness	3.5–4
Luster	Resinous – greasy
Specific Gravity	3.9–4.2, Average = 4.05
Streak	Brownish white
Indicators	Habit, streak, cleavage, luster, twinning

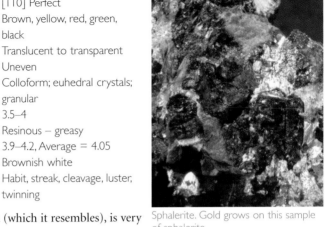

Sphalerite, like galena (which it resembles), is very common, occurring in every U.S. state except Delaware, Florida, Hawaii, and North Dakota.

Sphalerite. Gold grows on this sample of sphalerite.

Pyrrhotite

Chemical Formula	$Fe_{(1-x)}S$ (x=0–0.17)
Environment	Igneous and metamorphic rock
Locality	Tennessee; Ontario, Canada; Chihuahua, Mexico; Germany; Russia
Etymology	Greek, *pyrrhótes*, "redness"

Physical Properties of Pyrrhotite

Cleavage	[0001] Imperfect, [1120] Imperfect
Color	Bronze, bronze red, dark brown
Diaphaneity	Opaque
Fracture	Uneven
Habit	Massive – granular, platy, tabular
Hardness	3.5–4
Luster	Metallic
Magnetism	Naturally strong
Specific Gravity	4.58–4.65, Average = 4.61
Streak	Gray black
Indicators	Magnetism, habit, hardness, color

Pyrrhotite. Dal'negorsk, Russia.

Pyrrhotite is the most common magnetic mineral after magnetite. It is found in every U.S. state except Florida, Hawaii, Illinois, Iowa, Kentucky, Mississippi, Nebraska, North Dakota, Ohio, and West Virginia.

Nickeline

Chemical Formula	NiAs
Environment	Veins of ore with copper, nickel, and silver arsenides and sulfides
Locality	Ontario, Canada; Western Australia; Germany
Etymology	From its composition

Physical Properties of Nickeline

Cleavage	[1010] Imperfect, [0001] Imperfect
Color	Lead gray, grayish, copper, black
Diaphaneity	Opaque
Fracture	Uneven
Habit	Columnar, massive, reniform
Hardness	5.5
Luster	Metallic
Specific Gravity	7.78–7.8, Average = 7.79
Streak	Brownish black
Indicators	Color, density, streak, hardness, odor when heated

Nickeline occurs in Arizona, Colorado, Connecticut, Idaho, Maine, Michigan, Montana, Nevada, New Jersey, New Mexico, North Carolina, South Carolina, Texas, Utah, Washington, and Wisconsin. It is sometimes called niccolite, especially in Europe.

Covellite

Chemical Formula	CuS
Environment	Secondary mineral in the oxidation zone of sulfide copper deposits
Locality	Montana; Mount Vesuvius, Italy; Serbia; Germany; Austria
Etymology	Italian mineralogist N. Covelli (1790–1829)

Physical Properties of Covellite

Cleavage	[0001] Perfect
Color	Indigo blue, light blue, dark blue, black
Diaphaneity	Opaque
Fracture	Brittle
Habit	Foliated, platy
Hardness	1.5–2
Luster	Metallic
Specific Gravity	4.6–4.76, Average = 4.68
Streak	Black gray
Indicators	Habit, cleavage, iridescence, color

Covellite.

Covellite is somewhat rare, but widespread, occurring throughout the western states and in Alabama, Arkansas, Connecticut, Georgia, Kansas, Maine, Maryland, Massachusetts, Michigan, Missouri, New Hampshire, New Jersey, New York, North Carolina, Oklahoma,

Pennsylvania, Rhode Island, South Carolina, South Dakota, Tennessee, Texas, Virginia, and Wisconsin.

Cinnabar

Chemical Formula	HgS
Environment	Low-temperature hydrothermal solutions in veins
Locality	California; Nevada; Almaden, Spain; Italy; Slovenia; Peru; China
Etymology	Latin, *cinnabaris*

Physical Properties of Cinnabar

Cleavage	[1010] Perfect
Color	Lead gray, brown, brown pink, vermilion, gray
Diaphaneity	Transparent to translucent to opaque
Fracture	Brittle – sectile
Habit	Disseminated, drusy, massive
Hardness	2–2.5
Luster	Adamantine
Specific Gravity	8.1
Streak	Bright red
Indicators	Habit, density, cleavage, hardness, color

Cinnabar. Numerous very dark red cinnabar crystals grow out of a matrix or white dolomite crystals. Guizhou Province, China. Brought $5,290 at auction in February 2008.

Cinnabar is the most common ore of mercury. It occurs widely throughout the western United States, especially California, Oregon, Arizona, and Nevada, and also in Texas and Arkansas. Mercury is hghly toxic, so care should always be taken when handling cinnabar.

Millerite

Chemical Formula	NiS
Environment	Limestone and dolomite cavities
Locality	Mississippi River Valley; Western Australia; Germany; Quebec, Canada
Etymology	English mineralogist William Hallowes Miller (1801–1880)

Physical Properties of Millerite

Cleavage	[1011] Perfect, [0112] Perfect
Color	Bronze, greenish gray, gray, brass yellow
Diaphaneity	Opaque
Fracture	Uneven
Habit	Acicular, massive

Millerite. Halls Gap, Lincoln County, Kentucky.

Hardness	3–3.5
Luster	Metallic
Magnetism	Magnetic after heating
Specific Gravity	5.5
Streak	Greenish black
Indicators	Habit, color, luster

Millerite crystals tend to be dispersed throughout the ore mass in which they form, so specimen-quality occurrences are rare. In the United States, the best specimens are found in the Hall Gap area of Kentucky or in geodes in Indiana. Millerite is commonly found in iron-nickel meteorites.

Realgar

Chemical Formula	AsS
Environment	Associated with arsenic–antimony minerals. Common low-temperature hydrothermal vein mineral
Locality	United States, Iran, China, Japan, Switzerland
Etymology	Arabic, *rahj al ghar,* "powder of the mine"

Physical Properties of Realgar

Cleavage	[010] Good
Color	Aurora red, orange yellow, dark red
Diaphaneity	Transparent to translucent
Fracture	Sectile
Habit	Drusy, massive – granular, prismatic
Hardness	1.5–2
Luster	Submetallic
Specific Gravity	3.56
Streak	Orange
Indicators	Color, habit, hardness, luster

Realgar. Palomo Mine, Huancavelica Department, Peru

Realgar occurs across the western United States, especially in Nevada and Utah. It is unstable, altering to a yellow powder called pararealgar; this process is accelerated by exposure to light, so specimens must be stored in the dark.

Chalcopyrite

Chemical Formula	$CuFeS_2$
Environment	Common in sulfide veins; disseminated in igneous rocks
Locality	Worldwide
Etymology	Greek, *chalkos,* "copper" (i.e., "copper pyrite")

Physical Properties of Chalcopyrite

Cleavage	[112] Indistinct
Color	Brass yellow, honey yellow
Diaphaneity	Opaque
Fracture	Brittle
Habit	Drusy, euhedral crystals, striated
Hardness	3.5
Luster	Metallic
Magnetism	Magnetic after heating
Specific Gravity	4.1–4.3, Average = 4.19
Streak	Greenish black
Indicators	Habit, tarnish, hardness, brittleness

Chalcopyrite. Crystals to 2 cm. Huaron, Peru.

Chalcopyrite is very widespread; it is the most common ore of copper. It is found in almost every state except Florida, especially the Desert Southwest and the Pacific Northwest.

Orpiment

Chemical Formula	As_2S_3
Environment	Low-temperature hydrothermal veins, hot springs, common as an alteration product of arsenic minerals (e.g., realgar)
Locality	Worldwide
Etymology	Latin, *auripigmentum,* from its vivid golden color

Physical Properties of Orpiment

Cleavage	[010] Perfect
Color	Lemon yellow, brownish yellow, orange yellow
Diaphaneity	Transparent to translucent
Fracture	Sectile
Habit	Foliated, massive – fibrous, prismatic
Hardness	1.5–2
Luster	Pearly
Specific Gravity	3.49–3.56, Average = 3.52
Streak	Pale yellow
Indicators	Habit, cleavage, odor, color

Orpiment. Twin Creeks Mine, Humboldt County, Nevada.

Orpiment almost always occurs with realgar, and like realgar will deteriorate into a powder with exposure to light. Also like realgar, orpiment is highly toxic, so care should always be exercised when handling specimens. It occurs throughout the western United States, especially Nevada and Utah, as well as in Pennsylvania and New York.

Stibnite

Chemical Formula	Sb_2S_3
Environment	Found with metastibnite
Locality	United States, Canada, Mexico, Japan, China, Indonesia, Europe
Etymology	Greek, *stimmi* or *stibi*, "antimony"

Physical Properties of Stibnite

Cleavage	[010] Perfect
Color	Lead gray, bluish lead gray, steel gray, black
Diaphaneity	Opaque
Fracture	Conchoidal
Habit	Granular, prismatic, striated
Hardness	2
Luster	Metallic
Specific Gravity	4.63
Streak	Blackish gray
Indicators	Habit, hardness, flexibility

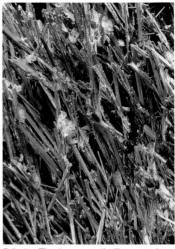

Stibnite. The long, needle-like crystals of this typical specimen show some minor barite association. Baia Sprie, Romania. This piece brought $747.50 at auction in February 2008.

Stibnite forms beautiful jutting clusters of crystals, but large deposits are rare. In the United States, notable occurrences are found in California, Nevada, and the Pacific Northwest.

Bismuthinite

Chemical Formula	Bi_2S_3
Environment	Low- to high-temperature hydrothermal vein deposits; tourmaline-bearing copper deposits in granite; recent volcanic exhalation deposits; some gold veins formed at high temperatures
Locality	United States, Canada, Mexico, Germany, England, Australia
Etymology	From its composition

Physical Properties of Bismuthinite

Cleavage	[010] Perfect
Color	Gray; silver white; tin white
Diaphaneity	Opaque
Fracture	Brittle – sectile
Habit	Granular, massive – lamellar, prismatic
Hardness	2
Luster	Metallic
Specific Gravity	6.8–7.2, Average = 7
Streak	Gray
Indicators	Habit, density, tarnish, hardness

Notable occurrences of bismuthinite in the United States include Arizona, California, Colorado, Connecticut, Nevada, New Mexico, and Utah, as well as some localities in Alabama, Alaska, Arkansas, Idaho, Maine, Michigan, Montana, New Hampshire, New York, North Carolina, Oregon, Pennsylvania, South Dakota, Texas, Washington, and Wyoming.

Pyrite

Chemical Formula	FeS_2
Environment	Deposits of sedimentary, magmatic, metamorphic, and hydrothermal rock
Locality	Worldwide
Etymology	Greek, *pyrites lithos*, "stone which strikes fire," from its ability to create sparks when striking iron

Physical Properties of Pyrite

Cleavage	[100] Poor, [110] Poor
Color	Pale brass yellow
Diaphaneity	Opaque
Fracture	Conchoidal
Habit	Drusy, stalactitic, striated
Hardness	6.5
Luster	Metallic
Magnetism	Magnetic after heating
Specific Gravity	5–5.02, Average = 5.01
Streak	Greenish black
Indicators	Habit, hardness, streak, luster, brilliance

Pyrite. This very sharp 4 cm cube of pyrite is growing out of a quartz matrix. Brought $805 at auction in early 2008.

Pyrite is the most common sulfide, and occurs throughout the Earth's crust in almost every environment. It can be found widely in every U.S. state.

Marcasite

Chemical Formula	FeS_2
Environment	Sedimentary, hydrothermal, and secondary mineral
Locality	Worldwide
Etymology	Arabic for pyrites

Physical Properties of Marcasite

Cleavage	[010] Indistinct
Color	Bronze, light brass yellow, tin white
Diaphaneity	Opaque
Fracture	Uneven
Habit	Globular, stalactitic, tabular
Hardness	6–6.5
Luster	Metallic
Magnetism	Magnetic after heating

Marcasite.

Specific Gravity	4.89
Streak	Gray brownish black
Indicators	Habit, smell, green tint

Marcasite occurs in every U.S. state except Florida, Hawaii, and South Carolina. Marcasite will very slowly oxidize when exposed to atmospheric moisture, deteriorating into a white powder and releasing sulfur, which gives off a characteristic smell.

Lollingite

Chemical Formula	$FeAs_2$
Environment	Mesothermal deposits associated with other sulfides; also within calcite gangue and in coarsely crystalline granite or other high-silica rock
Locality	United States; Lölling, Austria; Germany; Ontario, Canada; Scandinavia
Etymology	From Lölling, Austria

Physical Properties of Lollingite

Cleavage	[001] Distinct
Color	Silvery white, tarnish gray
Diaphaneity	Opaque
Fracture	Uneven
Habit	Massive – granular, prismatic, twinning common
Hardness	5
Luster	Metallic
Magnetism	Magnetic after heating
Specific Gravity	7.1–7.7, Average = 7.4
Streak	Grayish black
Indicators	Habit, color, streak, hardness

Lollingite is uncommon, and usually associated with arsenopyrite. In the United States it occurs primarily in Caifornia, Maine, New Hampshire, and South Dakota, though it can also be found in very isolated deposits in Alaska, Arizona, Colorado, Connecticut, Massachusetts, Nevada, New Jersey, New Mexico, New York, North Carolina, Utah, Virginia, Washington, and Wisconsin. Lollingite gives its name to a group of related minerals.

Cobaltite

Chemical Formula	$CoAsS$
Environment	High-temperature hydrothermal deposits, contact metamorphic rocks
Locality	United States, Mexico, Sweden, Norway, Germany, England
Etymology	German kobold or kobolt, "goblin"

Physical Properties of Cobaltite

Cleavage	[100] Good, [010] Good, [001] Good
Color	Reddish silver white, violet steel gray, black
Diaphaneity	Opaque
Fracture	Brittle
Habit	Granular, massive – granular, striated

Hardness	5.5
Luster	Metallic
Magnetism	Magnetic after heating
Specific Gravity	6.33
Streak	Grayish black
Indicators	Habit, cleavage, color, streak

Cobaltite is rare, although where it does occur it is an important ore of cobalt. It is found primarily in Arizona, California, Oregon, and especially Idaho, but it has also been known to occur in Colorado, Connecticut, Maine, Massachusetts, Missouri, Montana, Nevada, New Jersey, New Mexico, New York, North Carolina, Pennsylvania, Texas, Utah, Vermont, Virgina, Washington, and Wisconsin.

Cobaltite. Hakansboda, Sweden.

Arsenopyrite

Chemical Formula	FeAsS
Environment	High-temperature veins, coarsely crystalline granite or other high-silica rock in igneous veins, contact metamorphic rocks
Locality	World's most common arsenic-bearing mineral
Etymology	From its composition

Physical Properties of Arsenopyrite

Cleavage	[110] Distinct
Color	Tin white, light steel gray
Diaphaneity	Opaque
Fracture	Brittle
Habit	Euhedral crystals, prismatic, striated
Hardness	5
Luster	Metallic
Magnetism	Magnetic after heating
Specific Gravity	6.07
Streak	Black
Indicators	Habit, cleavage, garlic odor when fractured, color, luster

Arsenopyrite. A huge arsenopyrite crystal 3.5 cm long sitting on top of small transparent quartz crystals and small white calcite crystals.

Arsenopyrite is an important ore of arsenic, and its crystals make very attractive specimens for collectors. It occurs widely throughout New England, and the western states (where it is especially abundant), Alabama, Connecticut, Georgia, New Jersey, New York, North Carolina, South Dakota, and Virginia, as well as less frequently in Arkansas, Michigan, Missouri, Oklahoma, Pennsylvania, Rhode Island, South Carolina, Tennessee, and Texas.

Molybdenite

Chemical Formula	MoS_2
Environment	High-temperature hydro-thermal veins. Disseminated porphyritic deposits
Locality	Worldwide
Etymology	Greek, *molybdos*, "lead"

Physical Properties of Molybdenite

Cleavage	[0001] Perfect
Color	Black, lead gray, gray
Diaphaneity	Opaque
Fracture	Sectile
Habit	Disseminated, foliated, massive
Hardness	1
Luster	Metallic
Specific Gravity	5.5
Streak	Greenish gray
Indicators	Habit, hardness, cleavage, streak

Molybdenite.

Molybdenite is the only source for the element rhenium, which substitutes for a miniscule fraction of the molybdenum atoms. It is exceedingly common throughout the western United States, and is also found in New England as well as Alabama, Arkansas, Connecticut, Georgia, Iowa, Maryland, Michigan, Missouri, New Jersey, New York, North Carolina, Pennsylvania, South Carolina, South Dakota, Texas, Virgnia, and Wisconsin.

Calaverite

Chemical Formula	$AuTe_2$
Environment	Veins of low-temperature origin; moderate- to high-temperature deposits
Locality	Calaveras County, California; Canada; Romania; Australia
Etymology	From Calaveras County, California

Physical Properties of Calaverite

Cleavage	None
Color	Yellow, yellowish white
Diaphaneity	Opaque
Fracture	Brittle – conchoidal
Habit	Crystalline – fine, massive, striated
Hardness	2.5
Luster	Metallic
Specific Gravity	9.04
Streak	Green
Indicators	Habit, hardness, color, luster

Calaverite.

Calaverite occurs in Arizona, California, Colorado (where it is very widespread), Georgia, Nevada, New Mexico, North Carolina, South Dakota, Utah, Washington, and Wisconsin.

Sylvanite

Chemical Formula	$(Au,Ag)_2Te_4$
Environment	Low-temperature hydrothermal veins, moderate- and high-temperature deposits
Locality	Transylvania, Romania; United States; Canada; Australia
Etymology	From Transylvania

Physical Properties of Sylvanite

Cleavage	[010] Perfect
Color	Yellowish silver white, white
Diaphaneity	Opaque
Fracture	Uneven
Habit	Platy, prismatic, skeletal
Hardness	1.5–2
Luster	Metallic
Magnetism	Magnetic after heating
Specific Gravity	7.9–8.3, Average = 8.1
Streak	Steel gray
Indicators	Habit, hardness, color, luster

Sylvanite is the most common gold-bearing mineral. In the United States it occurs primarily in Colorado, as well as in Arizona, California, Idaho, Montana, Nevada, New Mexico, Oregon, South Dakota, Utah, and Washington.

Skutterudite

Chemical Formula	$(Co,Ni)As_3$
Environment	High-temperature veins, along with other nickel-cobalt minerals
Locality	New Jersey; Skutterud, Norway; Ontario, Canada
Etymology	From Skutterud, Norway

Physical Properties of Skutterudite

Cleavage	[100] Distinct, [111] Distinct
Color	White, light steel gray
Diaphaneity	Opaque
Fracture	Brittle
Habit	Colloform, granular; massive
Hardness	5.5–6
Luster	Metallic
Specific Gravity	6.1–6.9, Average = 6.5
Streak	Black
Indicators	Habit, color, streak

Skutterudite is found primarily in nickel and cobalt mining areas; in the United States. It occurs in Arizona, California, Colorado, Connecticut, Idaho, Michigan, Missouri, Nevada, New Jersey, New Mexico, Oregon, Utah, and Vermont.

Nickel-skutterudite

Chemical Formula	$(Co,Ni)As_3$
Environment	Veins of moderate-temperature ore
Locality	Schneeberg, Germany
Etymology	After skutterudite, rich with nickel

Physical Properties of Nickel-skutterudite

Cleavage	[001] Distinct, [111] Distinct, [011] Parting
Color	Gray, tin white, gray
Diaphaneity	Opaque
Fracture	Brittle – conchoidal
Habit	Crystalline – fine, granular, massive
Hardness	5.5–6
Luster	Metallic
Specific Gravity	6.5
Streak	Black
Indicators	Habit, color, streak

Nickel-skutterudite is found in Arizona, Connecticut, Michigan, Nevada, New Mexico, and Washington.

◼ SULFOSALTS ◼

Polybasite

Chemical Formula	$(Ag,Cu)_{16}Sb_2S_{11}$
Environment	Silver veins of low- to moderate-temperature origin
Locality	Worldwide
Etymology	Greek, poly, "many," and basis, "base"

Physical Properties of Polybasite

Cleavage	[001] Poor
Color	Black, dark ruby red
Diaphaneity	Opaque
Fracture	Uneven
Habit	Granular, massive – granular, pseudo hexagonal
Hardness	2.5–3
Luster	Submetallic
Specific Gravity	4.6–5, Average = 4.8
Streak	Reddish black
Indicators	Habit, density, hardness

Polybasite. Polybasite partly fills fractures in white, opaque quartz; in a few places finely crystalline chalcopyrite and in one place a little native silver are deposited on the polybasite. Nye County, Nevada. 1915.

Polybasite is very prevalent in Arizona, Colorado, Idaho, and Nevada; it is also found less commonly in Alaska, California, Massachusetts, Missouri, Montana, New Mexico, Oregon, South Dakota, Utah, Washington, and Wisconsin.

Enargite

Chemical Formula	Cu_3AsS_4
Environment	Moderate-temperature hydrothermal vein deposits. Low-temperature deposits (as a late-stage mineral)
Locality	Montana, Colorado, Utah, Mexico, Argentina, Peru, Chile, Philippines
Etymology	Greek *enarges*, "obvious"

Physical Properties of Enargite

Cleavage	[110] Perfect, [100] Distinct, [010] Distinct
Color	Steel gray, blackish gray, violet black
Diaphaneity	Opaque
Fracture	Uneven
Habit	Euhedral crystals, massive – granular, prismatic
Hardness	3
Luster	Metallic
Specific Gravity	4.4–4.5, Average = 4.45
Streak	Black
Indicators	Habit, streak, cleavage

Enargite.

Although enargite is generally rare, it occurs widely in Arizona, Colorado, Montana, Nevada, and Utah, as well as in California, Idaho, Kansas, Missouri, New Mexico, and Washington.

Stephanite

Chemical Formula	Ag_5SbS_4
Environment	Late-stage mineral in hydrothermal silver deposits
Locality	Nevada; Cornwall, England; Saxony, Germany; Chile; Mexico
Etymology	Austrian mining director and engineer Archduke Victor Stephan (1817–1867)

Physical Properties of Stephanite

Cleavage	[010] Imperfect, [021] Poor
Color	Lead gray, black
Diaphaneity	Opaque
Fracture	Subconchoidal
Habit	Massive, pseudo hexagonal, tabular

Stephanite.

Hardness	2–2.5
Luster	Metallic
Specific Gravity	6.2–6.3, Average = 6.25
Streak	Black
Indicators	Habit, density, hardness

Stephanite is found in Arizona, California, Colorado, Idaho, Montana, Nevada (where massive deposits occur in the Comstock Lode), New Mexico, Utah, and Washington.

TETRAHEDRITE GROUP

Tetrahedrite

Chemical Formula	$(Cu,Fe)_{12}Sb_4S_{13}$
Environment	Hydrothermal veins; low- to moderate-temperature contact metamorphic deposits
Locality	Saxony, Germany; Mexico; Australia
Etymology	From its crystal form

Physical Properties of Tetrahedrite

Cleavage	None
Color	Iron gray, black, steel gray
Diaphaneity	Opaque
Fracture	Uneven
Habit	Massive – granular, massive
Hardness	3.5–4
Luster	Metallic
Specific Gravity	4.6–5.2, Average = 4.9
Streak	Black
Indicators	Habit, color

Tetrahedrite.

Tetrahedrite occurs widely throughout the western United States—especially Arizona, Colorado, Idaho, Montana, and Nevada—as well as in Arkansas, Massachusetts, Michigan, Missouri, North Carolina, South Dakota, Texas, Virginia, Washington, and Wisconsin.

Tennantite

Chemical Formula	$(Cu,Fe)_{12}As_4S_{13}$
Environment	Hydrothermal veins, contact metamorphic deposits
Locality	Montana; Saxony, Germany; Cornwall, England; Switzerland; Namibia
Etymology	English chemist Smithson Tennant (1761–1815)

Physical Properties of Tennantite

Cleavage	None
Color	Steel gray, black
Diaphaneity	Opaque

Fracture	Hackly
Habit	Disseminated, massive – granular, massive
Hardness	3.5–4
Luster	Metallic
Specific Gravity	4.6–4.7, Average = 4.65
Streak	Reddish gray
Indicators	Habit, streak, color

Tennantite is much less common than tetrahedrite. In the United States it occurs most widely in Arizona and Colorado, and also in Alaska, California, Missouri, Montana, Nevada, New Mexico, Oregon, South Carolina, Texas, Utah, Virginia, Washington, and Wisconsin.

Tennantite.

Proustite

Chemical Formula	Ag_3AsS_3
Environment	Late-forming mineral in the oxidation and enriched zones of hydrothermal deposits, associated with other silver minerals and sulfides
Locality	Idaho; Saxony, Germany; Chañarcillo, Chile; Mexico
Etymology	French chemist J.L. Proust (1755–1826)

Physical Properties of Proustite

Cleavage	None
Color	Vermilion, reddish gray
Diaphaneity	Transparent to translucent
Fracture	Brittle – sectile
Habit	Blocky, crystalline – poor, massive
Hardness	2–2.5
Luster	Submetallic
Specific Gravity	5.5–5.6, Average = 5.55
Streak	Vermilion red
Indicators	Habit, density, color

Proustite is similar to pyrargyrite, and is often found with it, although proustite is much rarer. It occurs in Arizona, Colorado, Idaho, Montana, Nevada, New Mexico, Utah, and Washington.

Pyrargyrite

Chemical Formula	Ag_5SbS_3
Environment	Primary late-stage, low-temperature mineral formed by secondary enrichment.
Locality	United States; Saxony, Germany; Guanajuato, Mexico
Etymology	Greek, *pyr* and *argyros*, "fire-silver"

Physical Properties of Pyrargyrite

Cleavage	[1011] Poor
Color	Deep red, red gray
Diaphaneity	Opaque to translucent
Fracture	Brittle – conchoidal
Habit	Crystalline – poor, massive, prismatic
Hardness	2.5
Luster	Submetallic
Specific Gravity	5.85
Streak	Cherry red
Indicators	Habit, density, color

Pyrargyrite occurs across the Western United States and in South Dakota.

Pyrargyrite. Saxony, Germany.

Bournonite

Chemical Formula	PbCuSbS$_3$
Environment	Moderate-temperature hydrothermal veins
Locality	California; Cornwall, England; Harz, Germany; Romania; Mexico; Peru; Australia
Etymology	French mineralogist J.L. de Bournon (1751–1825)

Physical Properties of Bournonite

Cleavage	[010] Imperfect
Color	Gray, black, steel gray
Diaphaneity	Opaque
Fracture	Subconchoidal
Habit	Cog-wheel, platy, pseudo cubic
Hardness	3
Luster	Metallic
Specific Gravity	5.7–5.9, Average = 5.8
Streak	Gray
Indicators	Twinning, habit, color

Bournonite. Brought $2,127.50 at auction in early 2008.

Bournonite is not common in the United States, but can be found in Arizona, Colorado, Idaho, Nevada, New Mexico, Utah, and Washington.

Boulangerite

Chemical Formula	Pb$_5$Sb$_4$S$_{11}$
Environment	Low- to moderate-temperature hydrothermal veins

Locality	United States, France, Germany, Britain, Australia, China
Etymology	French mining engineer C.L. Boulanger (1810–1849)

Physical Properties of Boulangerite

Cleavage	[001] Indistinct, [010] Indistinct
Color	Lead gray, blue gray, gray
Diaphaneity	Opaque
Fracture	Brittle
Habit	Acicular, massive – fibrous, plumose
Hardness	2.5
Luster	Metallic
Specific Gravity	5.7–6.3, Average = 6
Streak	Reddish brown
Indicators	Habit, flexibility, color, luster

Boulangerite occurs in Colorado, Idaho, Montana, Nevada, North Carolina, South Dakota, Utah, Washington, and Wisconsin. A fine, feathery form is sometimes called "plumosite" (plumose = feathery).

Jamesonite

Chemical Formula	$Pb_4FeSb_6S_{14}$
Environment	Usually a late-stage hydrothermal mineral in low- to moderate-temperature lead-silver-zinc veins
Locality	South Dakota and Arkansas; Cornwall, England; Zacatecas, Mexico; Romania
Etymology	Scottish mineralogist R. Jameson (1774–1854)

Physical Properties of Jamesonite

Cleavage	[001] Perfect
Color	Lead gray, steel gray, dark lead gray
Diaphaneity	Opaque
Fracture	Brittle
Habit	Acicular, massive – fibrous, radial
Hardness	2.5
Luster	Metallic
Specific Gravity	5.5–5.63, Average = 5.56
Streak	Black, grayish
Indicators	Habit, brittleness, color, luster

Jamesonite.

Jamesonite occurs in Alaska, Arkansas, California, Colorado, Idaho, Nevada, South Dakota, Utah, Washington, and Wisconsin. Like boulangerite, it sometimes forms masses of feathery crystals.

Miargyrite

Chemical Formula	$AgSbS_2$
Environment	Low-temperature hydrothermal silver-bearing sulfide ores
Locality	United States, Mexico, Canada, Europe, South America, Australia, China, Japan
Etymology	Greek, *meyon,* "smaller," and *argyros,* "silver"

Physical Properties of Miargyrite

Cleavage	[010] Imperfect
Color	Steel gray, lead gray, blackish red, reddish gray
Diaphaneity	Translucent to subopaque
Fracture	Brittle
Habit	Disseminated, euhedral crystals, massive
Hardness	2–2.5
Luster	Submetallic
Specific Gravity	5.1–5.3, Average = 5.19
Streak	Cherry red
Indicators	Habit, streak, hardness, color, luster

Miargyrite.

Miargyrite occurs in California, Colorado, Idaho, and Nevada.

OXIDES AND HYDROXIDES

OXIDES

Cuprite

Chemical Formula	Cu_2O
Environment	Oxidation zone of copper deposits
Locality	Africa, Arizona, Europe, Chile
Etymology	Latin, *cuprum,* "copper"

Physical Properties of Cuprite

Cleavage	[111] Imperfect
Color	Brown red, purple red, red, black
Diaphaneity	Transparent to translucent
Fracture	Brittle – conchoidal
Habit	Capillary, massive – granular
Hardness	3.5–4
Luster	Adamantine

Cuprite on malachite.

Specific Gravity	6.1
Streak	Copper-red
Indicators	Color, form, hardness

Cuprite is a major ore of copper and is common worldwide. In the United States it can be found in Arizona, California, Colorado, Connecticut, Georgia, Idaho, Maine, Maryland, Massachusetts, Michigan, Missouri, Montana, Nevada, New Hampshire, New Jersey, New Mexico, North Carolina, Oklahoma, Oregon, Pennsylvania, South Carolina, South Dakota, Texas, Utah, Virginia, Washington, Winsconsin, and Wyoming. Large gem-quality crystals are extremely rare; almost every faceted cuprite specimen over one carat in weight came from a single deposit in Onganja, Namibia.

Zincite

Chemical Formula	(Zn,Mn)O
Environment	Metamorphosed weathered ore deposit
Locality	Sterling Hill and Franklin, New Jersey
Etymology	From its composition

Zincite.

Physical Properties of Zincite

Cleavage	[0001] Perfect
Color	Yellow, dark yellow, dark red, orange
Diaphaneity	Translucent to subtranslucent
Fracture	Subconchoidal
Habit	Disseminated, granular, massive – fibrous
Hardness	4–5
Luster	Submetallic
Specific Gravity	5.43–5.7, Average = 5.56
Streak	Yellowish orange
Indicators	Luster, color, streak

The only major source of zincite crystals is the Sterling Hill and Franklin mining area of New Jersey; the mineral is extremely rare elsewhere, especially in its crystal form.

Corundum   *See also listing under "Gemstones."*

Chemical Formula	Al_2O_3
Environment	Contact and regionally metamorphosed rock
Locality	North Carolina; Tchainit and Yakutia, Russia; Zimbabwe; India; Naxos, Greece
Etymology	Sanskrit, *kuruvinda*, "ruby"

Physical Properties of Corundum

Cleavage	None
Color	Blue, red, yellow, brown, gray
Diaphaneity	Transparent to translucent

Fracture	Tough
Habit	Euhedral crystals, prismatic, tabular
Hardness	9
Luster	Vitreous (glassy)
Specific Gravity	4–4.1, Average = 4.05
Streak	None
Indicators	Hardness, habit

Corundum is used as an industrial abrasive because if its hardness. Transparent specimens are used as gems—red varieties are called rubies, while all other colors are called sapphires. It is very widespread in Georgia, New York, and North Carolina, and occurs in lesser amounts in Alabama, Arizona, California, Colorado, Connecticut, Idaho, Michigan, Montana, Nevada, New Jersey, New Mexico, Pennsylvania, South Carolina, Utah, Virginia, Washington, Wyoming, and throughout New England.

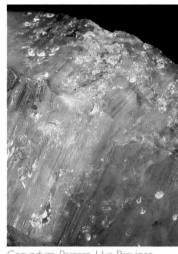

Corundum. Passaro, Uva Province, Sri Lanka.

Hematite
See also listing under "Gemstones."

Chemical Formula	Fe_2O_3
Environment	Magmatic, hydrothermal, metamorphic, and sedimentary rock
Locality	Minnesota and Michigan; Matto Grosso, Brazil; England; Australia
Etymology	Greek, *haimatites*, "bloodlike"

Physical Properties of Hematite

Cleavage	None
Color	Reddish gray, black, blackish red
Diaphaneity	Subtranslucent to opaque
Fracture	Conchoidal
Habit	Blocky, earthy, tabular
Hardness	6.5
Luster	Metallic
Magnetism	Magnetic after heating
Specific Gravity	5.3
Streak	Reddish brown
Indicators	Habit, streak, hardness

Hematite.

Hematite is a major ore of iron; it is very common, and occurs in a variety of forms. It occurs in every U.S. state except Florida and Delaware.

Ilmenite

Chemical Formula	$Fe^{2+}TiO_3$
Environment	Concentrated in placers as "black sand" deposits. Common accessory mineral in igneous and metamorphic rock
Locality	United States; Ilmen Mountains, Russia; South Africa; Canada; China; Norway
Etymology	After Ilmen Mountains, Russia

Physical Properties of Ilmenite

Cleavage	None
Color	Iron black, black
Diaphaneity	Opaque
Fracture	Conchoidal
Habit	Massive – lamellar, tabular
Hardness	5–5.5
Luster	Submetallic
Magnetism	Naturally weak
Specific Gravity	4.72
Streak	Brownish black
Indicators	Habit, density, lack of cleavage, luster

Ilmenite.

Ilmenite is the primary ore of titanium. It is found in all U.S. states except Delaware, Hawaii, Illinois, Iowa, Mississippi, Nebraska, North Dakota, and Ohio. It is especially prevalent in Arizona, Idaho, Nevada, North Carolina, South Carolina, Virginia, and New England.

Bixbyite

Chemical Formula	$(Mn,Fe)_2O_3$
Environment	Pneumatolytic, hydrothermal, and metamorphic rock
Locality	Utah; Siapa and Chhindwara, India; Australia; Mexico; Argentina; South Africa
Etymology	American mineralogist Maynard Bixby (1853–1935)

Physical Properties of Bixbyite

Cleavage	[111] Imperfect, [111] Imperfect, [111] Imperfect
Color	Black
Diaphaneity	Opaque
Fracture	Uneven

Bixbyite.

Habit	Crystalline – fine, massive – granular
Hardness	6–6.5
Luster	Metallic
Specific Gravity	4.95
Streak	Black
Indicators	Habit, density, hardness

Bixbyite is quite rare, but its striking crystals make it a very popular speciment for mineral collectors. In the United States it occurs only in Arizona, Arkansas, Nevada, New Mexico, Texas, and Utah.

Rutile

Chemical Formula	TiO_2
Environment	High-pressure and -temperature accessory mineral in igneous rocks. Common as detritus
Locality	United States; Binnental and Campolungo, Switzerland; Brazil
Etymology	Latin, *rutilus*, "reddish"

Physical Properties of Rutile

Cleavage	[110] Distinct
Color	Blood red, bluish, brownish yellow, brown red, violet
Diaphaneity	Transparent to translucent to opaque
Fracture	Uneven
Habit	Acicular, massive – granular, prismatic
Hardness	6–6.5
Luster	Adamantine
Specific Gravity	4.25
Streak	Grayish black
Indicators	Habit, streak, hardness, color, luster

Rutile. Spring Creek, Custer County, South Dakota.

Rutile has one of the highest refractive indexes of any mineral; microscopic inclusions of rutile in gemstones such as ruby and sapphire are responsible for chatoyance and asterism. It is common in the western United States, New England, North Carolina, South Carolina, and Virgina, and also occurs in Alabama, Arkansas, Connecticut, Florida, Georgia, Maryland, Michigan, Missouri, New Jersey, New York, Pennsylvania, South Dakota, Tennessee, Texas, and Wisconsin.

Pyrolusite

Chemical Formula	MnO_2
Environment	Sedimentary, hydrothermal, and secondary mineral
Locality	Worldwide

Etymology	Greek, *pyro*, "fire," and *louein*, "to wash," from its common use of removing the color imparted to glass by iron compounds

Physical Properties of Pyrolusite

Cleavage	[110] Perfect
Color	Steel gray, iron gray, bluish gray
Diaphaneity	Opaque
Fracture	Brittle
Habit	Dendritic, earthy, reniform
Hardness	6–6.5
Luster	Submetallic
Specific Gravity	4.4–5.06, Average = 4.73
Streak	Black
Indicators	Habit, luster, color, streak

Pyrolusite.

Pyrolusite is the most common manganese-bearing mineral and the most important ore of the element. It is found in every U.S. state except Delaware, Florida, Hawaii, Indiana, Kansas, Louisiana, Mississippi, and Ohio.

Cassiterite

Chemical Formula	SnO_2
Environment	Coarsely crystalline granite; alluvial placer deposits
Locality	Cornwall, England; Bolivia; Thailand; Malayasia; Indonesia; Russia
Etymology	Greek, *kassiteros*, "tin"

Physical Properties of Cassiterite

Cleavage	[100] Perfect, [110] Indistinct
Color	Brown, brownish black, colorless, green, gray
Diaphaneity	Transparent to translucent to opaque
Fracture	Irregular
Habit	Botryoidal, massive, prismatic
Hardness	6–7
Luster	Adamantine
Specific Gravity	6.8–7, Average = 6.9
Streak	Brownish white
Indicators	Habit, twinning, luster

Cassiterite. Pictured is a lustrous and fine example of a well-formed cassiterite crystal. Viloco Mine, La Paz Department, Bolivia.

Cassiterite is an important ore of tin. The best source of primary cassiterite is in Bolivia. In the United States it is common in California, Colorado, Maine, Nevada, New

Hampshire, North Carolina, South Carolina, South Dakota, Texas, and Virginia, and also occurs in Alabama, Alaska, Arizona, Connecticut, Florida, Georgia, Idaho, Massachusetts, Michigan, Missouri, Montana, New Mexico, Oregon, Pennsylvania, Utah, Washington, Wisconsin, and Wyoming.

Anatase

Chemical Formula	TiO_2
Environment	Usually secondary, from other titanium-bearing minerals. Common as detritus
Locality	United States, France, Switzerland, Brazil
Etymology	Greek, *anatasis*, "elongation"

Anatase. Unusually large (to 3 cm), these two anatase crystals grew parallel to each other and display tremendous luster. This specimen sold for $20,700 in early 2008.

Physical Properties of Anatase

Cleavage	[101] Perfect, [001] Distinct
Color	Black, reddish brown, yellowish brown, dark blue, gray
Diaphaneity	Transparent to translucent
Fracture	Conchoidal
Habit	Pyramidal, tabular
Hardness	5.5–6
Luster	Adamantine – resinous
Specific Gravity	3.9
Streak	Pale yellowish white
Indicators	Habit, luster, cleavage, streak

Anatase is a polymorph of rutile, and will revert into rutile above 915°C. It is found throughout New England and in Alabama, Arizona, Arkansas, California, Colorado, Georgia, Idaho, Kentucky, Missouri, Montana, Nevada, New Jersey, New Mexico, New York, North Carolina, Oregon, Pennsylvania, Texas, Utah, Virginia, Washington, and Wisconsin.

Brookite

Chemical Formula	TiO_2
Environment	Silica-bearing veins deposited by hot solutions
Locality	United States, Europe
Etymology	English mineralogist Henry James Brucke (1771–1857)

Physical Properties of Brookite

Cleavage	[120] Indistinct
Color	Brown, light brown, dark brown, dark reddish brown, orange
Diaphaneity	Transparent to translucent to opaque

Fracture	Subconchoidal
Habit	Platy, tabular
Hardness	5.5–6
Luster	Submetallic
Specific Gravity	4.1–4.14, Average = 4.11
Streak	Yellowish white
Indicators	Habit, luster, streak

Brookite is a polymorph of rutile, and will revert into rutile above 750°C. It occurs in Arizona, Arkansas, California, Colorado, Connecticut, Idaho, Maine, Massachusetts, Michigan, Montana, Nevada, New Hampshire, New Jersey, New Mexico, New York, North Carolina, Oklahoma, Oregon, Pennsylvania, Rhode Island, Utah, Virginia, Washington, and Wisconsin.

Brookite. These two perfectly formed large brookite crystals growing on a quartz matrix have great luster. This sample brought $1,265 at auction in early 2008.

Uraninite

Chemical Formula	UO_2
Environment	Coarsely crystalline granite and syenite rocks. Crusts of high-temperature hydrothermal veins. Quartz-pebble conglomerates
Locality	United States, Canada, Germany, France, England
Etymology	From its composition

Physical Properties of Uraninite

Cleavage	Poor
Color	Brownish black, gray, grayish black, black
Diaphaneity	Nearly opaque
Fracture	Brittle – conchoidal
Habit	Botryoidal, crystalline – coarse, dendritic
Hardness	5–6
Luster	Submetallic
Specific Gravity	6.5–10.95, Average = 8.72
Streak	Brownish black
Indicators	Luster, color, radioactivity

Uraninite.

Uraninite is the primary ore source for uranium, and also for radium, which occurs in trace amounts due to the radioactive decay of uranium. It is very common in Arizona, Colorado, and Utah, and can also be found in Alaska, California, Connecticut, Georgia, Idaho, Maine, Massachusetts, Michigan, Montana, Nevada, New Hampshire, New Jersey, New Mexico, New York, North Carolina, Oklahoma, Oregon, Pennsylvania, Rhode

Island, South Dakota, Texas, Virginia, Washington, and Wyoming. Especially high-grade uraninite occurs in northern Saskatchewan; in the Northwest Territories, it is found in large quantities in association with silver.

HYDROXIDES

Diaspore

Chemical Formula	AlO(OH)
Environment	Metamorphic and sedimentary bauxite ores
Locality	Worldwide
Etymology	Greek, *diaspora*, "to scatter," from its easy disintegration in flame

Physical Properties of Diaspore

Cleavage	[010] Perfect, [110] Good
Color	White, greenish gray, grayish brown, colorless, yellow
Diaphaneity	Transparent to subtranslucent
Fracture	Brittle – conchoidal
Habit	Disseminated, platy, tabular
Hardness	6.5–7
Luster	Vitreous – pearly
Specific Gravity	3.3–3.5, Average = 3.4
Streak	White
Indicators	Habit, hardness, cleavage

Diaspore (Burly Clay). Collected from Near Swiss, Missouri.

Especially large and well-formed crystals of diaspore are found in Hampden County, Massachusetts; the mineral also occurs in Arizona, California, Colorado, Connecticut, Georgia, Maine, Missouri, Nevada, North Carolina, Pennsylvania, South Carolina, Utah, Virginia, Washington, and Wisconsin. Diaspore, boehmite, and gibbsite constitute bauxite.

Goethite

Chemical Formula	$HFeO_2$
Environment	Iron ore deposits
Locality	Worldwide
Etymology	German poet J.W. Goethe (1749–1832)

Physical Properties of Goethite

Cleavage	[010] Perfect, [100] Distinct
Color	Brown, Reddish brown, yellowish brown, brownish yellow, ocher yellow
Diaphaneity	Subtranslucent to opaque
Fracture	Hackly
Habit	Acicular, radial, reniform
Hardness	5–5.5

Goethite. This goethite specimen displays iridescent, botryoidal crystals to 3 cm. Iron Mountain, Custer County, South Dakota.

Luster	Adamantine – silky
Specific Gravity	3.3–4.3, Average = 3.8
Streak	Yellowish brown
Indicators	Habit, streak, tarnish

Goethite occurs in every state except Delaware, Hawaii, Kansas, Mississippi, North Dakota, and West Virginia. It is especially common in Alabama, Georgia, Michigan, and Virginia.

Boehmite

Chemical Formula	AlO(OH)
Environment	Major part of most bauxite ores
Locality	United States, Jamaica, Surinam, Guyana, France, Hungary, Russia, Greece, Australia
Etymology	German geologist and paleontologist J. Bohm (1857–1938)

Physical Properties of Boehmite

Cleavage	[010] Good
Color	White, light yellow, yellowish green
Diaphaneity	Translucent
Fracture	Brittle
Habit	Massive, pistolitic
Hardness	3
Luster	Vitreous – pearly
Specific Gravity	3–3.07, Average = 3.03
Streak	White
Indicators	Association

Boehmite is found occasionally in Arizona, Arkansas, California, Colorado, Georgia, Montana, North Carolina, Pennsylvania, Utah, Virginia, and Washington. Boehmite is dimorphous with diaspore; with diaspore and gibbsite, it forms bauxite.

Manganite

Chemical Formula	MnO(OH)
Environment	Low-temperature hydrothermal or hot-spring manganese deposits
Locality	United States; Harz, Germany; Cornwall, England; France; United States; China
Etymology	From its composition

Physical Properties of Manganite

Cleavage	[010] Perfect
Color	Black, gray, grayish black
Diaphaneity	Opaque
Fracture	Brittle
Habit	Massive – fibrous, prismatic, pseudo orthorhombic
Hardness	4
Luster	Submetallic
Specific Gravity	4.3–4.4, Average = 4.34
Streak	Dark brown
Indicators	Habit, luster, striations

Manganite is widely found in formerly productive manganese regions of the Appalachian Mountains, from Virginia to Alabama. Well-crystallized manganite specimens are not common in the United States. However, attractive examples have been found in the Midvale mine (Rockbridge County, Virginia); the Powells Fort Mine (near Woodstock, Shenandoah County, Virginia); the Vesuvius mine (Augusta County, Virginia); in mines in Tennessee; and in Georgia (around Cartersville, Bartow County).

Brucite

Chemical Formula	Mg(OH)$_2$
Environment	Serpentine, chlorite or dolomitic schists, crystalline limestone (as an alteration product of periclase)
Locality	United States, Mexico, Canada, Europe, Africa, Australia
Etymology	American mineralogist A. Bruce (1777–1818)

Brucite.

Physical Properties of Brucite

Cleavage	[0001] Perfect
Color	Blue, gray, gray blue, yellow, white
Diaphaneity	Transparent
Fracture	Irregular
Habit	Fibrous, massive – lamellar, massive
Hardness	2.5–3
Luster	Vitreous – pearly
Specific Gravity	2.39–2.4, Average = 2.39
Streak	White
Indicators	Habit, luster, flexibility

Brucite often forms veins in chlorite and limestone. In the United States it occurs in Arkansas, California, Colorado, Maryland, Massachusetts, Michigan, Nevada, New Jersey, New Mexico, New York, North Carolina, Pennsylvania (especially Lancaster County), Texas, Utah, Vermont, Virginia, Washington, and Wisconsin.

Gibbsite

Chemical Formula	Al(OH)$_3$
Environment	Soil formed from aluminous rock in areas of heavy rainfall
Locality	United States, France, Germany, Hungary
Etymology	American collector G. Gibbs (1776–1833)

Physical Properties of Gibbsite

Cleavage	[001] Perfect
Color	Bluish, green, green white, gray, gray white
Diaphaneity	Translucent to transparent

Fracture	Tough
Habit	Earthy, spherical, stalactitic
Hardness	2.5–3
Luster	Vitreous – pearly
Specific Gravity	2.3–2.4, Average = 2.34
Streak	White
Indicators	Habit, hardness, clay smell

Gibbsite often forms layers in clays such as illite or kaolinite. It is found in Alabama, Arizona, Arkansas, Colorado, Connecticut, Georgia, Hawaii, Indiana, Iowa, Maine, Massachusetts, Michigan, Mississippi, Missouri, Montana, Nevada, New Mexico, New York, North Carolina, Oregon, Pennsylvania, Tennessee, Utah, Virginia, and Washington. Gibbsite, boehmite, and diaspore constitute bauxite.

Gibbsite.

MULTIPLE OXIDES

Spinel

See listing under "Gemstones."

Magnetite

Chemical Formula	Fe_3O_4
Environment	Common accessory mineral in igneous and metamorphic rocks. Also biologically produced by various organisms
Locality	Worldwide
Etymology	*Magnes,* the Greek shepherd who discovered the mineral when the iron tip of his staff stuck to a rock

Physical Properties of Magnetite

Cleavage	None
Color	Grayish black, iron black
Diaphaneity	Opaque
Fracture	Subconchoidal
Habit	Crystalline – fine, massive – granular, massive
Hardness	5.5–6
Luster	Metallic
Magnetism	Naturally strong
Specific Gravity	5.1–5.2, Average = 5.15
Streak	Black
Indicators	Magnetism, habit, streak

Magnetite. This magnetite specimen displays a group of cubic crystals up to 2 cm. Balmat, New York.

Magnetite is the most magnetic naturally occurring mineral on Earth. It occurs widely around the world and in every state except Delaware, Florida, Hawaii, North Dakota, and the Mississippi River basin states. It is especially common in mountainous areas, as magnetite occurs in practically all igneous and metamorphic rocks.

Franklinite

Chemical Formula	$(Zn,Mn,Fe^{2+})(Fe^{3+},Mn^{3+})2O_4$
Environment	Zinc-rich ore bodies weathered and later metamorphosed
Locality	Franklin, New Jersey; Germany; Sweden; Australia
Etymology	After Franklin, New Jersey

Franklinite.

Physical Properties of Franklinite

Cleavage	None
Color	Black, brownish black
Diaphaneity	Opaque
Fracture	Uneven
Habit	Crystalline – fine, euhedral crystals, massive
Hardness	5.5–6
Luster	Submetallic
Magnetism	Naturally weak
Specific Gravity	5.07–5.22, Average = 5.14
Streak	Reddish brown
Indicators	Habit, streak

Franklinite is a rare mineral. It can be found in California, Colorado, Nevada, New Mexico, and especially in New Jersey, where it is widely available in Franklin (which was also named after Benjamin Franklin), the "The Fluorescent Mineral Capital of the World"; the Franklin Furnace has produced more species of minerals and most notably more fluorescent minerals than any other location on Earth.

Chromite

Chemical Formula	$FeCr_2O_4$
Environment	Cumulate mineral found in iron- and magnesium-rich rocks with little or no silica, in layered intrusions. Also common in meteorites.
Locality	United States, South Africa, Turkey, France, Australia, Brazil
Etymology	From its composition

Physical Properties of Chromite

Cleavage	None
Color	Black, brownish black
Diaphaneity	Opaque
Fracture	Uneven

Habit	Granular, massive – granular, nuggets
Hardness	5.5
Luster	Metallic
Magnetism	Naturally weak
Specific Gravity	4.5–5.09, Average = 4.79
Streak	Brown
Indicators	Habit, streak, parting

Chromite is the only ore of chromium. About half of the world's output is mined in South Africa; in the Western Hemisphere it occurs primarily in Brazil and Cuba, although it is also found widely in California, Oregon, and Washington, as well as less commonly in Alabama, Alaska, Arizona, Arkansas, Colorado, Georgia, Idaho, Maine, Maryland, Michigan, Nevada, New York, North Carolina, Pennsylvania, Vermont, Virginia, and Wyoming.

Chrysoberyl   *See listing under "Gemstones."*

Pyrochlore

Chemical Formula	$(Na,Ca)_2Nb_2O_6(OH,F)$
Environment	Alkali-rich volcanic rock (nepheline-syenite)
Locality	Norway, Sweden, Russia, United States, Canada
Etymology	Greek *pyr,* "fire," and *chloros,* "green"

Pyrochlore.

Physical Properties of Pyrochlore

Cleavage	[1 1 1] Indistinct, [1 1 1] Indistinct, [1 1 1] Indistinct
Color	Brown, yellowish brown, yellow, greenish brown, reddish brown
Diaphaneity	Subtranslucent to opaque
Fracture	Uneven
Habit	Disseminated, granular
Hardness	5–5.5
Luster	Resinous – greasy
Specific Gravity	4.2–6.4, Average = 5.3
Streak	Yellowish brown
Indicators	Habit, luster, fracture, color, radioactivity

Pyrochlore usually forms beautiful, well-defined crystals, but these may sometimes seem amorphous due to damage from the decay of included radioactive elements. In the United States it occurs primarily in Arizona and Colorado, but also occasionally in Arkansas, California, Connecticut, Maryland, New Hampshire, New Mexico, Texas, Virginia, Wisconsin, and Wyoming.

Microlite

Chemical Formula	$(Na,Ca)_2 Ta_2 O_6 (O,OH,F)$
Environment	Granitic rocks
Locality	Sweden, Norway
Etymology	Greek *mikros*, "small," and *lithos*, "stone"

Physical Properties of Microlite

Cleavage	[1 1 1] Indistinct, [1 1 1] Indistinct, [1 1 1] Indistinct
Color	Yellowish brown, reddish brown, greenish brown, green, gray
Density	4.2–6.4, Average = 5.3
Diaphaniety	Subtranslucent to opaque
Fracture	Subconchoidal
Habit	Disseminated, pseudo octahedral
Hardness	5–5.5
Luster	Vitreous – resinous
Streak	Light yellow
Indicators	Habit, luster, fracture, color, radioactivity

Microlite. 1 mm crystal. Ipe Mine, Minas Gerais, Brazil.

Microlite forms a series with and exhibits many similarities to pyrochlore. In the United States it is found primarily in Colorado, Connecticut, and Maine, as well as in Arizona, California, Maryland, Massachusetts, Nevada, New Hampshire, New Mexico, North Carolina, Pennsylvania, South Dakota, Virginia, and Wisconsin.

Ferrotantalite

Chemical Formula	$FeTa_2O_6$
Environment	Accessory mineral in coarsely crystalline granite or other high-silica rock veins
Locality	Finland, United States, Australia
Etymology	Latin *ferrum*, "iron," and Greek *Tantalos,* legendary Phrygian king

Physical Properties of Ferrotantalite

Cleavage	[010] Distinct
Color	Brownish black, black
Diaphaneity	Opaque
Fracture	Brittle – conchoidal
Habit	Tabular, prismatic, equant, pyramidal, granular, massive
Hardness	6–6.5
Luster	Submetallic
Specific Gravity	8.2
Streak	Black brown
Indicators	Habit, streak, luster

Ferrotantalite occurs rarely in Colorado, New Hampshire, North Carolina, South Dakota, and Wisconsin.

Ferrocolumbite

Chemical Formula	$FeNb_2O_6$
Environment	In coarsely crystalline granite or other high-silica rock veins, and alluvial deposits
Locality	United States, Australia, Europe
Etymology	After its content (*niobium* being formerly known as *columbium,* and Latin *ferrum,* "iron")

Physical Properties of Ferrocolumbite

Cleavage	[010] Distinct
Color	Black, brownish black
Diaphaneity	Translucent to opaque
Fracture	Subconchoidal
Habit	Massive – granular, striated
Hardness	6
Luster	Submetallic
Specific Gravity	5.3–7.3, Average = 6.3
Streak	Blackish brown
Indicators	Habit, streak, luster

Ferrocolumbite is a rare mineral, found in Arizona, California, Colorado, Connecticut (where it was first discovered, in Haddam, Middlesex County), Georgia, Idaho, Maine, Massachusetts, Michigan, Nevada, New Hampshire, New York, North Carolina, Rhode Island, Texas, Virginia, and Wisconsin.

HALIDES

Halite

Chemical Formula	NaCl
Environment	Marine or continental deposits of inorganic chemical sediment evaporated from salty water; in sedimentary basins.
Locality	Worldwide
Etymology	Greek *halos,* "salt," and *lithos,* "rock"

Physical Properties of Halite

Cleavage	[100] Perfect, [010] Perfect, [001] Perfect
Color	White, clear, light blue, dark blue, pink
Diaphaneity	Transparent
Fracture	Brittle
Habit	Crystalline – coarse, euhedral crystals, granular
Hardness	2.5
Luster	Vitreous (glassy)

Halite.

Specific Gravity	2.17
Streak	White
Indicators	Taste, cleavage, habit

Halite, commonly called rock salt, is used to melt ice and snow on roadways in cold climates. It generally forms perfect cubic crystals, but can also form hopper crystals, which are very collectible. In Mulhouse, France, a silky purple and blue fibrous halite is found filling veins in rocks or other minerals.

Sylvite

Chemical Formula	KCl
Environment	Inorganic chemical sediment evaporated from salty water; in sedimentary basins; volcanic sublimate.
Locality	Worldwide
Etymology	Dutch chemist Sylvia de la Boe (1614–1672)

Physical Properties of Sylvite

Cleavage	[100] Perfect, [010] Perfect, [001] Perfect
Color	White, yellowish white, reddish white, bluish white, brownish white
Diaphaneity	Transparent
Fracture	Brittle – sectile
Habit	Euhedral crystals, fibrous, massive – granular
Hardness	2.5
Luster	Vitreous – greasy
Specific Gravity	1.99
Streak	White
Indicators	Taste, habit

Sylvite. Potash (Moab), Utah.

Sylvite is a major source of potassium for fertilizers. It is the official mineral of Saskatchewan, where the world's largest despoits were formed by evaporation of the prehistoric sea. It occurs hundreds of meters thick in former sea beds in Lousisiana, Texas, and Utah, and also in Alabama, Arizona. California, Colorado, Michigan, Nevada, New Mexico, New York, and North Dakota.

Chlorargyrite

Chemical Formula	AgCl
Environment	Oxidized silver deposits
Locality	New South Wales, Australia; United States; France; Italy; Germany; Bolivia, Chile
Etymology	Greek *chloros*, "pale green," and Latin *argentum*, "silver"

Physical Properties of Chlorargyrite

Cleavage	None
Color	Purplish gray, green, white, colorless
Diaphaneity	Transparent to translucent
Fracture	Sectile
Habit	Columnar, massive, cubic
Hardness	1–1.5
Luster	Adamantine – resinous
Specific Gravity	5.55
Streak	White
Indicators	Color, luster, ductility, habit

Chlorargyrite. This specimen of chlorargyrite (gray) with olivenite (green) was mined in Pershing County, Nevada.

Chlorargyrite rarely forms good crystals, and its color will darken to a brownish pruple with long-term exposure to light. It forms small but rich deposits of silver. It occurs widely throughout the western United States and less frequently in North Carolina, Oklahoma, South Dakota, and Virginia.

Bromargyrite

Chemical Formula	AgBr
Environment	Oxidized silver deposits
Locality	Mexico, Chile, United States, France, Germany
Etymology	Greek *bromos*, "stench," and Latin *argentum*, "silver"

Physical Properties of Bromargyrite

Cleavage	None
Color	Greenish brown, gray green, grayish yellow, yellow, olive green
Diaphaneity	Transparent to translucent
Fracture	Conchoidal – uneven
Habit	Columnar, massive, cubic
Hardness	1.5–2
Luster	Adamantine – greasy
Specific Gravity	5.8–6, Average = 5.9
Streak	Gray
Indicators	Color, luster, ductility, habit

Bromargyrite occurs in scattered deposits across the western United States.

Fluorite

Chemical Formula	CaF_2
Environment	Low-temperature vein deposits
Locality	Common worldwide
Etymology	From its composition containing fluorine (Latin *fluere*, "to flow")

Physical Properties of Fluorite

Cleavage	[I I I] Perfect, [I I I] Perfect, [I I I] Perfect
Color	White, yellow, green, red; blue
Diaphaneity	Transparent to subtrans-lucent
Fracture	Uneven
Habit	Crystalline – coarse, disseminated, massive – granular
Hardness	4
Luminescence	Fluorescent, short UV = blue, long UV = blue
Luster	Vitreous (glassy)
Specific Gravity	3.01–3.25, Average = 3.13
Streak	White
Indicators	Habit, hardness, fluorescence

Fluorite. This 6 cm specimen of fluorite was mined at the Denton Mine in Hardin County, Illinois.

Fluorite is one of the most popular minerals for collectors because it occurs in a wide variety of brilliant colors, and is frequently fluorescent (a phenomenon which takes its name from the mineral). In the United States it is found in Alaska, Arizona, Colorado, Illinois, Kentucky, Missouri, New Hampshire, New Mexico, New York, Ohio, Oklahoma, and Texas. It is the official mineral of Illinois, although the large deposits there have been worked out and production on an industrial scale has ceased.

Cryolite

Chemical Formula	Na_3AlF_6
Environment	Late-stage mineral in granitic pegmatites
Locality	Greenland, United States, Canada, Russia
Etymology	Greek *kryos*, "frost," and *lithos*, "stone"

Physical Properties of Cryolite

Cleavage	None
Color	Brownish black, colorless, gray, white, reddish brown
Diaphaneity	Transparent to translucent
Fracture	Uneven
Habit	Euhedral crystals, Massive – granular
Hardness	2.5–3
Luster	Vitreous – greasy
Specific Gravity	2.95–3, Average = 2.97
Streak	White
Indicators	Lack of taste, density, habit

Cryolite's refractive index is very close to that of water, so a clear specimen placed under-water will be all but invisible. It is a rare mineral that occurs in large quantities only on the western coast of Greenland. In the United States it can be found in parts of Colorado, Maine, Nevada, New Hampshire, New Mexico, Texas, Utah, and Virginia.

CARBONATES

Calcite

Chemical Formula	$CaCO_3$
Environment	Found in sedimentary, igneous, and metamorphic rocks
Locality	Common worldwide
Etymology	Latin *calx*, "lime"

Physical Properties of Calcite

Cleavage	[1011] Perfect, [1011] Perfect, [1011] Perfect
Color	Colorless, white, pink, yellow, brown
Diaphaneity	Transparent to translucent to opaque
Fracture	Brittle – conchoidal
Habit	Crystalline – coarse, massive, stalactitic
Hardness	3
Luminescence	Fluorescent
Luster	Vitreous (glassy)
Specific Gravity	2.71
Streak	White
Indicators	Habit, reaction to acid, hardness, birefrinegence

Calcite.

Calcite is one of the most common minerals, occurring practically everywhere in the world. It can be found in all 50 states. It is the primary component of most seashells. Calcite has two indexes of refraction; single crystals will exhibit a property called birefringence—objects seen through a clear speciment appear doubled. "Mexican onyx" is actually a banded calcite colored by impurities. Some varieties of calcite are popular for sculpture.

Magnesite

Chemical Formula	$MgCO_3$
Environment	Evaporite in sedimentary rocks
Locality	United States, Brazil, Spain, Austria
Etymology	Named for its composition

Physical Properties of Magnesite

Cleavage	[1011] Perfect, [1011] Perfect, [1011] Perfect
Color	Colorless, white, grayish white, yellowish white, brownish white
Diaphaneity	Transparent to translucent to opaque
Fracture	Brittle – conchoidal
Habit	Earthy; massive – fibrous, massive – granular
Hardness	4
Luster	Vitreous (glassy)

Specific Gravity	3
Streak	White
Indicators	Habit, reaction to acid

Magnesite is found in the United States in Alabama, Alaska, Arizona, California, Colorado, Connecticut, Delaware, Georgia, Idaho, Louisiana, Maine, Maryland, Massachusetts, Nevada, New Jersey, New Mexico, New York, North Carolina, Oregon, Pennsylvania, South Carolina, South Dakota, Tennessee, Texas, Utah, Vermont, Virginia, Washington, and Wisconsin.

Siderite

Chemical Formula	$FeCO_3$
Environment	Bedded biosedimentary deposits, occasionally appears in metamorphic and igneous rocks. Forms a series with rhodochrosite
Locality	Common worldwide
Etymology	Greek *sideros*, "iron"

Siderite.

Physical Properties of Siderite

Cleavage	[1011] Perfect, [1011] Perfect, [1011] Perfect
Color	Yellowish brown, brown, gray, yellowish gray, greenish gray
Diaphaneity	Translucent to subtranslucent
Fracture	Brittle – conchoidal
Habit	Botryoidal, massive, tabular
Hardness	3.5
Luster	Vitreous (Glassy)
Specific Gravity	3.96
Streak	White
Indicators	Habit, cleavage, color, density

Siderite is a common mineral, but collection-quality crystals are less so; when they are found, however, they often have a surface alteration that produces a beautiful iridescence. Siderite occurs in every U.S. state except Delaware, Florida, and Hawaii.

Rhodochrosite *See listing under "Gemstones."*

Smithsonite

Chemical Formula	$ZnCO_3$
Environment	Oxidized zinc-bearing ores
Locality	Namibia; Zambia; United States; Greece; Poland; Belgium
Etymology	English mineralogist James Smithson (1765–1829), financier of the Smithsonian Institution in Washington, DC

Physical Properties of Smithsonite

Cleavage	[1011] Perfect, [1011] Perfect, 1011 Perfect
Color	Grayish white, dark gray, green; blue, yellow
Diaphaneity	Subtransparent to translucent
Fracture	Brittle
Habit	Botryoidal, earthy, reniform
Hardness	4.5
Luster	Vitreous (glassy)
Specific Gravity	4.4–4.5, Average = 4.45
Streak	White
Indicators	Luster, habit, cleavage, hardness

Smithsonite. Gila County, Arizona.

Smithsonite is found in Arizona, Arkansas, California, Colorado, Idaho, Iowa, Kentucky, Missouri, Montana, Nevada, New Hampshire, New Jersey, New Mexico, Pennsylvania, Tennessee, Texas, Utah, Virginia, Washington, and Wisconsin.

Aragonite

Chemical Formula	$CaCO_3$
Environment	Ocean floor deposits; hot springs; volcanic cavities and caves
Locality	Aragon, Spain; worldwide
Etymology	After Aragon, Spain

Physical Properties of Aragonite

Cleavage	[010] Distinct
Color	Colorless, white, gray, yellowish white, reddish white
Diaphaneity	Transparent to translucent
Fracture	Subconchoidal
Habit	Columnar, fibrous, pseudo hexagonal
Hardness	3.5–4
Luster	Vitreous (glassy)
Specific Gravity	2.93
Streak	White
Indicators	Habit, cleavage, reaction to acid.

Aragonite. Aspen, Colorado.

Aragonite is unstable at normal temperatures and pressures, eventually converting to calcite, its polymorph. It occurs in Alabama, Arizona, Arkansas, California, Colorado, Connecticut, Georgia, Hawaii, Idaho, Illinois, Indiana, Iowa, Kentucky, Louisiana,

Maine, Maryland, Massachusetts, Michigan, Missouri, Montana, Nebraska, Nevada, New Hampshire, New Jersey, New Mexico, New York, North Carolina, North Dakota, Ohio, Oklahoma, Oregon, Pennsylvania, Rhode Island, South Dakota, Tennessee, Texas, Utah, Vermont, Virginia, Washington, West Virginia, Wisconsin, and Wyoming.

Witherite

Chemical Formula	$BaCO_3$
Environment	Low-temperature hydrothermal veins
Locality	Illinois, United States; Canada; United Kingdom; Germany
Etymology	English physician and mineralogist William Withering (1741–1799)

Physical Properties of Witherite

Cleavage	[010] Distinct
Color	Colorless, milky white, grayish white, pale yellowish white, pale brownish white
Diaphaneity	Subtransparent to translucent
Fracture	Subconchoidal
Habit	Columnar, pseudo hexagonal, reniform
Hardness	3–3.5
Luminescence	Fluorescent phosphorescent, short UV = bluish white, long UV = bluish white
Luster	Vitreous (glassy)
Specific Gravity	4.3
Streak	White
Indicators	Twinning, reaction to acid, fluorescence, phosphorescence

Witherite. 1.2 cm. Alston Moor, Cumbria, England.

Witherite is unusual in that it always forms twins. It is rare, occurring in Arizona, Arkansas, California, Illinois, Kentucky, Massachusetts, Michigan, Missouri, Montana, Nevada, New Mexico, New York, and Utah.

Strontianite

Chemical Formula	$SrCO_3$
Environment	Low-temperature hydrothermal deposits in limestone and marl, also forms geodes in limestone
Locality	Strontian, Scotland; Austria; Germany; France; Italy; China; United States
Etymology	After Strontian, Scotland

Physical Properties of Strontianite

Cleavage	[110] Good
Color	Colorless, greenish, gray, gray white, yellowish
Diaphaneity	Transparent to translucent

Fracture	Brittle – conchoidal
Habit	Columnar, massive – granular, pseudo hexagonal
Hardness	3.5
Luster	Vitreous (glassy)
Specific Gravity	3.78
Streak	White
Indicators	Habit, reaction to acid, density

Strontianite is rare, and crystals of strontianite are rarer still. In the United States it occurs in Alabama, Arizona, Arkansas, California, Colorado, Georgia, Illinois, Indiana, Kentucky, Louisiana, Maryland, Michigan, Mississippi, Missouri, Montana, Nevada, New Jersey, New Mexico, New York, Ohio, Oklahoma, Pennsylvania, South Dakota, Texas, Utah, Virginia, Washington, and Wisconsin.

Strontianite.

Cerussite

Chemical Formula	$PbCO_3$
Environment	Oxidized zones of base-metal deposits
Locality	Saxony, Germany; United States; Australia
Etymology	Latin *cerussa*, "white lead"

Physical Properties of Cerussite

Cleavage	[110] Distinct, [021] Distinct
Color	Colorless, white, gray, blue, green
Diaphaneity	Transparent to subtranslucent
Fracture	Brittle – conchoidal
Habit	Crystalline – coarse, massive – granular, reticulate
Hardness	3–3.5
Luster	Adamantine
Specific Gravity	6.58
Streak	White
Indicators	Twinning, luster, density

Cerussite. Pale white cerussite crystals are nestled on top of pale green needle-like pyromorphite crystals. Guangxi, China.

Cerussite, also called white lead, is a minor ore of lead, which produces its characteristic luster. It can form chevron, cyclic, or reticulated twins. In the United States it is extremely common in Arizona, Colorado, Idaho, Nevada, New Mexico, and Utah, and is also found in Alaska, Arkansas, California, Connecticut, Georgia, Illinois, Iowa, Kansas, Kentucky, Maine, Maryland, Massachusetts, Michigan, Missouri, Montana, New Hampshire, New Jersey, New York, North Carolina, Oklahoma, Oregon, Pennsylvania, Rhode Island, South Dakota, Tennessee, Texas, Vermont, Virginia, Washington, Wisconsin, and Wyoming.

Dolomite

Chemical Formula	$CaMg(CO_3)_2$
Environment	Common in sedimentary beds, metamorphic marbles, hydrothermal veins
Locality	Worldwide
Etymology	French mineralogist and geologist Deodat Guy Tancrede Gratet de Dolomieu (1750–1801)

Physical Properties of Dolomite

Cleavage	[1011] Perfect, [1011] Perfect, [1011] Perfect
Color	White, gray, reddish white, brownish white
Diaphaneity	Transparent to translucent
Fracture	Brittle – conchoidal
Habit	Blocky – rhombohedral, crystalline – coarse, massive
Hardness	3.5–4
Luster	Vitreous (glassy)
Specific Gravity	2.8–2.9, Average = 2.84
Streak	White
Indicators	Color, habit, hardness, density, luster

Dolomite.

Dolomite is very common worldwide, and is found in every U.S. state except Delaware, Florida, Hawaii, North Dakota, and South Carolina. It is generally difficult to distinguish from calcite, except for a distinctive pink variety, the color caused by manganese impurity.

Azurite

See listing under "Gemstones."

Malachite

See listing under "Gemstones."

Aurichalcite

Chemical Formula	$(Zn,Cu)_5(CO_3)_2(OH)_6$
Molecular Weight	546.71 gm
Environment	Secondary mineral in oxidized copper and zinc deposits
Locality	Greece, United States, Mexico, Namibia
Etymology	Greek *oreichalchos*, "mountain copper"

Physical Properties of Aurichalcite

Cleavage	[010] Perfect
Color	Pale green, sky blue, greenish blue
Diaphaneity	Transparent
Fracture	Uneven

Habit	Acicular, drusy, encrustations
Hardness	2
Luster	Pearly
Specific Gravity	3.64–3.9, Average = 3.77
Streak	Light blue
Indicators	Habit, color, hardness, reaction to acid

Aurichalcite typically occurs as a crust of acicular or feathery crystals. It can be found in Arizona, Arkansas, California, Colorado, Connecticut, Idaho, Kentucky, Maine, Massachusetts, Missouri, Montana, Nevada, New Hampshire, New Jersey, New Mexico, New York, North Carolina, Pennsylvania, Rhode Island, South Carolina, South Dakota, Texas, Utah, Vermont, Virginia, Wisconsin, and Wyoming.

Aurichalcite. Gila County, Arizona.

BORATES

Howlite

Chemical Formula	$Ca_2B_5SiO_9(OH)_5$
Environment	Secondary mineral in evaporite deposits
Locality	Canada; California, United States
Etymology	Canadian geologist Henry How (1828–1879)

Physical Properties of Howlite

Cleavage	None
Color	Colorless; white
Diaphaneity	Translucent
Fracture	Brittle – conchoidal
Habit	Earthy, massive, nodular
Hardness	2.5–3.5
Luster	Earthy (dull)
Specific Gravity	2.58
Streak	White
Indicators	Nodular habit, color, reaction to acid, luster, lack of cleavage

Howlite is found in only a few places worldwide, primarily in California—where nodules as large as 100 pounds have been found—and parts of Nevada. It can easily be dyed to very closely resemble turquoise, and a large fraudlent trade exists because howlite, though rare, is much less valuable than turquoise.

Boracite

Chemical Formula	$Mg_3B_7O_{13}Cl$
Environment	Evaporite deposits
Locality	Germany, France, England, United States, Bolivia
Etymology	From its composition

Physical Properties of Boracite

Cleavage	None
Color	Blue green, colorless, gray, yellow, white
Diaphaneity	Subtransparent to translucent
Fracture	Brittle – conchoidal
Habit	Crystalline – fine; disseminated
Hardness	7
Luster	Vitreous – adamantine
Specific Gravity	2.9
Streak	White
Indicators	Habit, color, cleavage, hardness

Boracite is uncommon in the United States, occurring only in Alabama and Louisiana.

Colemanite

Chemical Formula	$Ca_2B_6O_{11} \cdot 5H_2O$
Environment	Playa lakes and other evaporite deposits
Locality	California and Nevada, United States; Canada; Argentina; Turkey
Etymology	William T. Coleman, owner of the Death Valley, California, mine where the species was identified

Colemanite. California.

Physical Properties of Colemanite

Cleavage	[010] Perfect, [001] Distinct
Color	Colorless, gray, gray white, yellowish white, white
Diaphaneity	Transparent to translucent
Fracture	Brittle
Habit	Blocky, crystalline – coarse, massive – granular
Hardness	4.5
Luster	Vitreous (glassy)
Specific Gravity	2.42
Streak	White
Indicators	Habit, density, cleavage, hardness

Colemanite occurs widely in California, as well as in minor deposits in Arizona and Nevada.

Borax

Chemical Formula	$Na_2B_4O_7 \cdot 10H_2O$
Environment	Evaporite deposits, playa lakes, salt lakes

Locality	Turkey, United States, Chile, Tibet
Etymology	Arabic *buraq*, "white"

Physical Properties of Borax

Cleavage	[100] Perfect, [110] Perfect
Color	Blue, colorless, green, gray, gray white
Diaphaneity	Translucent to opaque
Fracture	Brittle – conchoidal
Habit	Massive, prismatic, tabular
Hardness	2–2.5
Luster	Greasy (oily)
Specific Gravity	1.7–1.72, Average = 1.71
Streak	White
Indicators	Habit, color, density, hardness

Borax.

Borax, like the less familiar borates, primarily forms evaporite deposits in playa lakes in arid regions such as Death Valley and Boron, California; in the United States it also occurs in similar parts of Nevada, New Mexico, and Oregon. Borax has a wide variety of industrial and commercial uses.

Kernite

Chemical Formula	$Na_2B_4O_6(OH)_2 \cdot 3H_2O$
Environment	Sedimentary basins and clay-shale deposits
Locality	Kern County, California; Argentina; Spain; Turkey
Etymology	After Kern County, California

Physical Properties of Kernite

Cleavage	[100] Perfect, [001] Perfect, [201] Good
Color	Colorless, white
Diaphaneity	Transparent to translucent
Fracture	Brittle
Habit	Acicular, crystalline – coarse; massive
Hardness	2.5–3
Luster	Vitreous – pearly
Specific Gravity	1.9–1.92, Average = 1.91
Streak	White
Indicators	Habit, density, cleavage, hardness

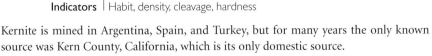

Kernite. Boron, California.

Kernite is mined in Argentina, Spain, and Turkey, but for many years the only known source was Kern County, California, which is its only domestic source.

Ulexite

Chemical Formula	$NaCaB_5O_9 \cdot 8H_2O$
Environment	Playa lakes and evaporite despoits
Locality	California, Nevada, Chile, Kazakhstan
Etymology	German chemist George Ludwig Ulex (1811–1883)

Physical Properties of Ulexite

Cleavage	[010] Perfect, [110] Perfect
Color	Colorless, white
Diaphaneity	Translucent
Fracture	Brittle
Habit	Acicular, capillary, fibrous
Hardness	2.5
Luster	Chatoyant
Specific Gravity	1.95–1.96, Average = 1.95
Streak	White
Indicators	Habit, density, light transmission

Ulexite.

Ulexite is commonly called television rock because the fibers transmit light well enough that when faces of a specimen are cut and polished perpendicular to the direction of the fibers, whatever image the specimen rests on will be reproduced clearly on the top surface. Ulexite is found in the United States in California, Nevada, and Oklahoma.

■ SULFATES ■

Thenardite

Chemical Formula	Na_2SO_4
Environment	Salt lakes, evaporite deposits, efflorescences in arid regions
Locality	North America, Europe, Asia
Etymology	French chemist Louis Jacques Thenard (1777–1826)

Physical Properties of Thenardite

Cleavage	[010] Perfect
Color	White, grayish white, yellowish white, reddish white, brownish white
Diaphaneity	Transparent
Fracture	Splintery
Habit	Encrustations, prismatic, tabular
Hardness	2.5
Luminescence	Fluorescent

Thenardite. Borax Lake, California.

Luster	Vitreous – greasy
Specific Gravity	2.67–2.7, Average = 2.68
Streak	White
Indicators	Habit, cleavage, salty taste, fluorescence

Thenardite occurs in the United States in Arizona, California, Colorado, Hawaii, Missouri, Nevada, New Mexico, North Dakota, Ohio, Oklahoma, Utah, Virginia, and Washington. Specimens should be stored in closed containers because the mineral will absorb water from the atmosphere and gradually convert into a related but distinct hydrous mineral, mirabilite ($Na_2SO_4 \cdot 10H_2O$).

Barite

Chemical Formula	$BaSO_4$
Environment	Sedimentary rocks, as a gangue mineral in metallic ore deposits
Locality	Worldwide
Etymology	Greek *baryos*, "heavy"

Physical Properties of Barite

Cleavage	[010] Perfect, [210] Perfect, [010] Imperfect
Color	White, yellowish white, grayish white, brownish white, dark brown
Diaphaneity	Transparent to translucent to opaque
Fracture	Uneven
Habit	Massive – fibrous, prismatic, tabular
Hardness	3–3.5
Luminescence	Phosphorescent
Luster	Vitreous (glassy)
Specific Gravity	4.48
Streak	White
Indicators	Habit, density

Barite.

Barite typically forms clusters of parallel tabular crystals, but is sometimes found in balded masses known as "desert roses." Barite is a common mineral, occurring in every U.S. state except Delaware, Florida, Hawaii, Mississippi, and North Dakota.

Celestine

Chemical Formula	$SrSO_4$
Environment	Bedded sedimentary rocks, primarily in deposits of gypsum, halite, or limestone
Locality	United States, Canada, Mexico, Europe, China, Australia
Etymology	Latin *coelestis*, "celestial"

Physical Properties of Celestine

Cleavage	[001] Perfect, [210] Good
Color	Blue, brown, colorless, green, gray
Diaphaneity	Transparent to subtranslucent
Fracture	Brittle – conchoidal
Habit	Crystalline – coarse, granular, massive
Hardness	3–3.5
Luster	Vitreous (glassy)
Specific Gravity	3.9–4, Average = 3.95
Streak	White
Indicators	Habit, color

Celestite. This pale colored celestite specimen was collected at Put-in-Bay, Lake Erie, Ohio.

Celestine (also incorrectly called celestite) is the most common strontium-bearing mineral. It sometimes forms pale sky-blue crystals (for which it is named), which are highly prized by collectors. It occurs in the United States in Alabama, Arizona, Arkansas, California, Colorado, Connecticut, Illinois, Indiana, Iowa, Kansas, Kentucky, Louisiana, Michigan, Mississippi, Missouri, Nebraska, Nevada, New Jersey, New Mexico, New York, North Carolina, Ohio, Oklahoma, Pennsylvania, South Dakota, Tennessee, Texas, Utah, Virginia, Washington, West Virginia, and Wisconsin.

Anglesite

Chemical Formula	$PbSO_4$
Environment	Oxidized lead deposits
Locality	Anglesey, Wales; Italy; United States; Mexico; Namibia; Australia
Etymology	After the island of Anglesey, Wales

Physical Properties of Anglesite

Cleavage	[001] Good, [210] Distinct
Color	Blue, colorless, green, gray, yellow
Diaphaneity	Transparent to translucent
Fracture	Brittle – conchoidal
Habit	Granular, stalactitic
Hardness	2.5–3
Luster	Adamantine
Specific Gravity	6.3
Streak	White
Indicators	Habit, density, luster, color

Anglesite.

Anglesite generally occurs as isolated crystals formed by the oxidation of galena, although in Australia and Mexico it is known to form large masses on its own. In the United States it is found in Alabama, Arizona, Arkansas, California, Colorado, Connecticut, Georgia, Idaho, Illinois, Iowa, Kentucky, Maine, Maryland, Massachusetts, Michigan, Missouri, Montana, Nevada, New Hampshire, New Jersey, New Mexico, New York, North Carolina, Oklahoma, Pennsylvania, Rhode Island, South Dakota, Tennessee, Texas, Utah, Virginia, Washington, Wisconsin, and Wyoming.

Anhydrite

Chemical Formula	$CaSO_4$
Environment	Sedimentary evaporite deposits, and as a gangue in ore veins; often interbedded with halite
Locality	Worldwide
Etymology	Greek *anhydros,* "waterless"

Physical Properties of Anhydrite

Cleavage	[010] Perfect, [100] Perfect, [001] Good
Color	Colorless, white, bluish white, violet white, dark gray
Diaphaneity	Transparent to subtransparent to translucent
Fracture	Brittle – conchoidal
Habit	Massive – fibrous, massive – granular, plumose
Hardness	3.5
Luster	Vitreous – pearly
Specific Gravity	2.96–2.98, Average = 2.97
Streak	White
Indicators	Habit, cleavage, density

Anhydrite is a common mineral formed usually by the loss of water from gypsum ($CaSO_4 \cdot 2H_2O$), hence the name. Good crystal specimens are generally rare except in Mexico and Peru. It is found in the United States in Alabama, Alaska, Arizona, Arkansas, California, Colorado, Connecticut, Florida, Idaho, Indiana, Iowa, Kentucky, Louisiana, Maine, Massachusetts, Michigan, Mississippi, Missouri, Montana, Nevada, New Jersey, New Mexico, New York, North Carolina, Ohio, Pennsylvania, South Dakota, Texas, Utah, Virginia, Washington, West Virginia, and Wisconsin.

Glauberite

Chemical Formula	$Na_2Ca(SO_4)_2$
Environment	Salt-lake and ocean deposits; evaporite beds in arid regions
Locality	United States, Chile, Austria, Germany, Italy, Spain, China, Australia
Etymology	After "Glauber's Salt" (sodium sulfate)

Physical Properties of Glauberite

Cleavage	[001] Perfect
Color	Colorless, gray, gray white, yellow, yellowish white
Diaphaneity	Transparent to translucent
Fracture	Brittle – conchoidal
Habit	Prismatic, tabular

Glauberite.

Hardness	2.5–3
Luster	Vitreous (glassy)
Specific Gravity	2.7–2.85, Average = 2.77
Streak	White
Indicators	Habit, hardness, cleavage, salty taste

Glauberite is found in the United States in Arizona, California, Nevada, New Jersey, New Mexico, North Dakota, Texas, and Utah.

Gypsum

Chemical Formula	$CaSO_4 \cdot 2H_2O$
Environment	Sedimentary evaporite deposits
Locality	Worldwide. Crystals exceeding 10 meters long are found in the Naica mine in Chihuahua, Mexico
Etymology	Greek gyps, "burned"

Gypsum. Red River flood plain, Winnipeg, Manitoba, Canada.

Physical Properties of Gypsum

Cleavage	[010] Perfect, [100] Distinct, [011] Distinct
Color	White, colorless, yellowish white, greenish white, brown
Diaphaneity	Transparent to translucent
Fracture	Fibrous
Habit	Crystalline – coarse, massive – fibrous, tabular
Hardness	2
Luster	Pearly
Specific Gravity	2.3
Streak	White
Indicators	Habit, cleavage, hardness

Gypsum is a very common mineral, occurring in several forms. It is used in making drywall for construction, plaster of Paris, as an additive in Portland cement, even as a food additive and source of dietary calcium (for instance, in tofu, where it functions as a coagulant, and in snack foods such as Twinkies). Individual crystals as large as 10 meters long have been found in Kalimantan, Indonesia. It is found in every state except Alaska, Delaware, Minnesota, and South Carolina.

Selenite. Selenite is a colorless transparent variety of gypsum that forms large, often perfect, crystals. When free of inclusions or imperfections they can appear glassy. Selenite is a popular crystal for

Selenite. This group of randomly oriented selenite prisms displays "fish tail" terminations. Grown in the caves of the silver mines of Chihuahua, Mexico, this specimen measures 11" high by 11" wide by 7" deep.

collections. (Named from the Greek, from its pearly luster ("moon light") on cleavage fragments.)

Alabaster. Alabaster is a massive form of fine-grained gypsum. It has been popular for thousands of years as a carving medium. In ancient times both gypsum and calcite were referred to as alabaster, but today only the gypsum form is given that name. Though the translucent pure-white alabaster is the most widely known, gypsum alabaster can be gray, green, yellow, orange, pink, red, brown, gold, or even black. (Named after Alabastron, Egypt, an ancient source of calcite alabaster.)

Chalcanthite

Chemical Formula	$CuSO_4 \cdot 5H_2O$
Environment	Oxidized zone of copper deposits in arid environments
Locality	United States, Mexico, Chile, Europe, Australia
Etymology	Greek *chalkos*, "copper," and *anthos*, "flower"

Physical Properties of Chalcanthite

Cleavage	[110] Imperfect, [110] Indistinct, [111] Indistinct
Color	Green, green blue, light blue, dark blue
Diaphaneity	Subtransparent to translucent
Fracture	Conchoidal
Habit	Encrustations, reniform, stalactitic
Hardness	2.5
Luster	Vitreous (glassy)
Specific Gravity	2.12–2.3, Average = 2.21
Streak	White
Indicators	Color, habit, density, solubility

Because chalcanthite is water-soluble, it is typically found in arid regions. In the United States, it occurs in Alabama, Alaska, Arizona, California, Colorado, Connecticut, Idaho, Maryland, Massachusetts, Michigan, Missouri, Montana, Nevada, New Jersey, New Mexico, North Carolina, Oklahoma, Oregon, Pennsylvania, South Carolina, South Dakota, Tennessee, Texas, Utah, Virginia, Washington, Wisconsin, and Wyoming. It is highly sought by collectors because of its rich color and striking crystals, but should be kept in sealed containers because it will absorb moisture from the atmostphere and disintegrate; also, it is easily grown artificially, so specimens should be examined closely.

Melanterite

Chemical Formula	$FeSO_4 \cdot 7H_2O$
Environment	Secondary mineral formed by the oxidation of iron sulfides
Locality	Europe, United States, Mexico, Argentina, Bolivia, Australia
Etymology	Greek *melas*, "black"

Physical Properties of Melanterite

Cleavage	[001] Perfect, [110] Distinct
Color	Green, yellow green, brownish black, bluish green, greenish white
Diaphaneity	Subtransparent to translucent
Fracture	Conchoidal
Habit	Capillary, efflorescences, encrustations

Hardness	2
Luster	Vitreous (glassy)
Specific Gravity	1.89–1.9, Average = 1.89
Streak	White
Indicators	Habit, density, solubility, color

Like chalcanthite, melanterite is water-soluble, and so specimens in collections need to be protected from the atmosphere. It is found in Alabama, Alaska, Arizona, Arkansas, California, Colorado, Connecticut, Georgia, Idaho, Indiana, Iowa, Kentucky, Maine, Maryland, Massachusetts, Michigan, Missouri, Montana, Nevada, New Hampshire, New Jersey, New Mexico, New York, North Carolina, Ohio, Oklahoma, Oregon, Pennsylvania, Rhode Island, South Dakota, Tennessee, Texas, Utah, Vermont, Virginia, Washington, West Virginia, and Wisconsin.

Epsomite

Chemical Formula	$MgSO_4 \cdot 7H_2O$
Environment	Efflorescences on calcareous or dolomitic cave walls, salt-lake deposits
Locality	North America, Europe, Argentina, Bolivia, Chile, Peru, China, Australia
Etymology	After Epsom, Surrey, England

Physical Properties of Epsomite

Cleavage	[010] Perfect, [101] Distinct
Color	Colorless, white, yellowish white, greenish white, pinkish white
Diaphaneity	Transparent to translucent
Fracture	Brittle
Habit	Acicular, encrustations, fibrous
Hardness	2–2.5
Luster	Vitreous (glassy)
Specific Gravity	1.67–1.68, Average = 1.67
Streak	White
Indicators	Habit, density, solubility, taste

Epsomite is commonly known as the household chemical Epsom salt. It occurs widely in the United States, in Alabama, Arizona, California, Colorado, Connecticut, Georgia, Idaho, Illinois, Indiana, Kentucky, Michigan, Missouri, Montana, Nevada, New Jersey, New Mexico, New York, Ohio, Oklahoma, Oregon, Pennsylvania, South Dakota, Tennessee, Texas, Utah, Virginia, Washington, Wisconsin, and Wyoming.

Brochantite

Chemical Formula	$Cu(SO_4)(OH)_6$
Environment	Secondary mineral forming in rapidly oxidizing copper sulfide deposits or arid regions
Locality	Chile, United States, United Kingdom, Italy, Romania, Zaire, Russia
Etymology	French geologist and mineralogist A.J.M. Brochant de Villiers (1772–1840)

Physical Properties of Brochantite

Cleavage	[100] Perfect
Color	Green; emerald green; black

Diaphaneity	Transparent to translucent
Fracture	Brittle – conchoidal
Habit	Acicular, drusy, prismatic
Hardness	3.5–4
Luster	Vitreous – pearly
Specific Gravity	3.97
Streak	Pale green
Indicators	Habit, hardness, cleavage, color

Brochantite is widely available in Arizona, and also occurs in Alabama, Arkansas, California, Colorado, Connecticut, Georgia, Idaho, Maine, Maryland, Massachusetts, Michigan, Missouri, Montana, Nevada, New Hampshire, New Jersey, New Mexico, New York, North Carolina, Oklahoma, Pennsylvania, Texas, Utah, Virginia, and Washington. It is a pseudomorph of azurite and malachite.

Brochantite. La Farola Mine, Tierra Amarilla, Chile.

Antlerite

Chemical Formula	$Cu_3(SO_4)(OH)_4$
Environment	Secondary mineral in oxidized zones of carbonate-poor copper deposits
Locality	Antler Mine, Arizona, and many other locations in the United States; Mexico; Chile; Europe; Australia
Etymology	After Antler Mine, Arizona

Physical Properties of Antlerite

Cleavage	[010] Perfect
Color	Green, light green, emerald green, black, black green
Diaphaneity	Translucent
Fracture	Uneven
Habit	Acicular, concretionary, reniform
Hardness	3
Luster	Vitreous (glassy)
Specific Gravity	3.9
Streak	Pale green
Indicators	Habit, hardness, cleavage, color

Antlerite is common in Arizona, and also occurs in Alabama, Alaska, California, Colorado, Montana, Nevada, New Jersey, New Mexico, Utah, and Virginia. It is closely related to and very similar in appearance to brochantite, but much less common

Linarite

Chemical Formula	$PbCu(SO_4)(OH)_2$
Environment	Secondary mineral in the oxidized zones of lead deposits
Locality	Linares Plateau, Spain; France; Germany; Austria; Italy; Ireland; Japan; Australia; United States
Etymology	After Linares Plateau, Spain

Physical Properties of Linarite

Cleavage	[100] Perfect, [001] Distinct
Color	Sky blue, deep blue
Diaphaneity	Transparent to translucent
Fracture	Conchoidal
Habit	Encrustations, platy, prismatic
Hardness	2.5
Luster	Vitreous (glassy)
Specific Gravity	5.3–5.5, Average = 5.4
Streak	Light blue
Indicators	Habit, color, lack of reaction to acid

Linarite forms very small but intensely blue crystals. In the United States it can be found in Arizona, Arkansas, California, Colorado, Connecticut, Georgia, Idaho, Maine, Massachusetts, Missouri, Montana, Nevada, New Hampshire, New Jersey, New Mexico, New York, North Carolina, Pennsylvania, Utah, and Virginia.

Jarosite

Chemical Formula	$KFe_3^{3+}(SO_4)_2(OH)_6$
Environment	Secondary mineral in the oxidized zones of sulfide deposits
Locality	Barranco del Jaroso, Spain; Germany; United Kingdom; United States; Brazil; Bolivia; Namibia
Etymology	After Barranco del Jaroso, Spain

Jarosite.

Physical Properties of Jarosite

Cleavage	[0001] Distinct
Color	Brown, yellow, yellow brown, light yellow
Diaphaneity	Translucent
Fracture	Uneven
Habit	Crystalline – fine, fibrous, massive
Hardness	2.5–3.5
Luster	Vitreous (glassy)
Specific Gravity	2.9–3.3, Average = 3.09
Streak	Yellow
Indicators	Habit, color, hardness

Jarosite is a rare mineral, occurring in the United States in parts of Alabama, Arizona, California, Colorado, Connecticut, Georgia, Idaho, Illinois, Iowa, Missouri, Montana, Nevada, New Mexico, New York, Oregon, Pennsylvania, Rhode Island, South Dakota, Texas, Utah, Vermont, Virginia, Washington, and Wisconsin.

Cyanotrichite

Chemical Formula	$Cu_4Al_2SO_4(OH)_{12} \cdot 2H_2O$
Environment	Formed in the oxidized zones of copper ores
Locality	South Africa, Argentina, France, United Kingdom, Germany, United States
Etymology	Greek *kyaneos,* "blue," and *triches,* "hair"

Physical Properties of Cyanotrichite

Cleavage	None
Color	Sky blue, light blue, dark blue
Diaphaneity	Translucent
Fracture	Uneven
Habit	Acicular, drusy; spherical
Hardness	2
Luster	Silky
Specific Gravity	2.74–2.95, Average = 2.84
Streak	Pale blue
Indicators	Habit, color

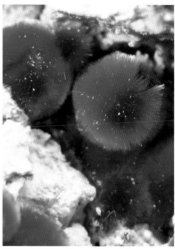

Cyanotrichite. Grand View Mine, Coconino County, Arizona.

Cyanotrichite is a very rare mineral but a very desirable crystal for collections due to its bright blue color and tufting acicular habit. It is found in parts of Arizona, Colorado, Idaho, Nevada, New Mexico, and Utah.

PHOSPHATES

Triphylite

Chemical Formula	$LiFePO_4$
Environment	Found in granitic pegmatites
Locality	United States, Brazil, Argentina, Europe, Japan, South Africa, Namibia
Etymology	Greek *tri,* "three," and *fylon,* "family"

Physical Properties of Triphylite

Cleavage	[001] Perfect, [110] Good
Color	Gray, bluish gray, brownish, blackish
Diaphaneity	Transparent to translucent
Fracture	Uneven
Habit	Massive – granular, prismatic
Hardness	4–5
Luster	Greasy (oily)

Triphylite. Chandlers Hill, New Hampshire.

Specific Gravity	3.4–3.6, Average = 3.5
Streak	Grayish white
Indicators	Color, cleavage, density

Triphylite is uncommon, and rarely forms good crystals. It occurs widely in Maine, New Hampshire, and South Dakota, and also in Alabama, Arizona, California, Colorado, Connecticut, Massachusetts, New York, and Wisconsin. It forms a series with and is very similar to lithiophilite.

Lithiophilite

Chemical Formula	$LiMnPO_4$
Environment	Found in granitic pegmatites
Locality	United States, Brazil, Argentina, Europe, Madagascar, South Africa, Namibia
Etymology	From its composition and from the Greek *philos*, "loving"

Physical Properties of Lithiophilite

Cleavage	[100] Perfect, [010] Very Good, [011] Imperfect
Color	Brown, yellowish brown, salmon, brownish, blackish
Diaphaneity	Transparent to translucent
Fracture	Conchoidal – uneven
Habit	Prismatic
Hardness	4–5
Luster	Vitreous – resinous
Specific Gravity	3.34
Streak	Gray white
Indicators	Color, cleavage, density

Like triphylite, with which it forms a series, lithiophilite is uncommon and rarely forms good crystals. It was first discovered in Fairfield County, Connecticut, and is also found in Alabama, Arizona, California, Colorado, Idaho, Maine, Massachusetts, New Hampshire, New Mexico, South Dakota, and Wisconsin.

Beryllonite

Chemical Formula	$NaBePO_4$
Environment	Found in granitic and alkalic pegmatites
Locality	Brazil, United States, Canada, Sweden, Finland, United Kingdom, Portugal, Pakistan
Etymology	From its composition

Physical Properties of Beryllonite

Cleavage	[010] Perfect, [100] Good
Color	Colorless, white, light yellow
Diaphaneity	Transparent to translucent
Fracture	Brittle – conchoidal
Habit	Tabular, equant, massive
Hardness	5.5–6
Luster	Vitreous – pearly
Specific Gravity	2.8

Streak	White
Indicators	Habit, color, hardness, locality

Beryllonite is very rare, and is found in few places in the world. It was discovered in Maine, where it occurs most widely; it can also be found in Nevada, New Hampshire, and New Mexico.

Purpurite

Chemical Formula	$MnPO_4$
Environment	Forms an alteration of lithiophylite in complex granitic pegmatites
Locality	United States, Germany, Portugal, South Africa
Etymology	Latin purpureus, "purple red"

Physical Properties of Purpurite

Cleavage	[100] Perfect, [001] Perfect
Color	Brownish black, violet, dark pink, dark red, reddish purple
Diaphaneity	Subtranslucent to opaque
Fracture	Brittle – uneven
Habit	Massive – granular
Hardness	4–5
Luster	Earthy (dull)
Specific Gravity	3.4
Streak	Red
Indicators	Color, lack of crystals, luster

Purpurite. White Elephant Mine, Custer County, South Dakota.

Purpurite forms by alteration of lithiophilite, of which it is a pseudomorph. It is very rare; in the United States it occurs in Arizona, California, Colorado, Connecticut, Maine, Massachusetts, New Hampshire, North Carolina, South Dakota, and Wisconsin.

Monazite

Chemical Formula	$(Ce,La,Nd,Th)PO_4$
Environment	Forms as an accessory mineral in granitic pegmatites
Locality	Worldwide
Etymology	Greek monazeis, "to be alone" (from its isolated crystals)

Physical Properties of Monazite

Cleavage	[001] Distinct, [100] Indistinct
Color	Brown, colorless, greenish, gray white, yellow
Diaphaneity	Subtransparent to subtranslucent
Fracture	Conchoidal
Habit	Crystalline – fine, twinning common
Hardness	5–5.5
Luster	Adamantine – resinous
Specific Gravity	4.8–5.5, Average = 5.15
Streak	Grayish white
Indicators	Habit, color, cleavage, density, hardness, radioactivity

Monazite has at least four different kinds, but these differences depend only on the relative amounts of cerium, lanthanum, neodymium, and thorium; all forms exhibit similar properties. It occurs in Arizona, Arkansas, California Colorado, Connecticut, Maine, Michigan, Nevada, New Hampshire, New Jersey, New Mexico, Mew York, North Carolina, Pennsylvania, Rhode Island, South Dakota, Texas, Virginia, Washington, and Wisconsin.

Hureaulite

Chemical Formula	$Mn_5(PO_3OH)_2(PO_4)_2 \cdot 4(H_2O)$
Environment	Forms as an alteration of triphylite in pegmatite
Locality	Les Hureaux, Limousin, France; Germany; Portugal; United States; Brazil
Etymology	After Les Hureaux, France

Hureaulite. Tip Top Mine, Custer County, South Dakota.

Physical Properties of Hureaulite

Cleavage	[100] Good
Color	Red, white, grayish white, yellowish white, reddish white
Diaphaneity	Transparent to translucent
Fracture	Brittle – uneven
Habit	Compact, fibrous, massive
Hardness	5
Luster	Vitreous – greasy
Specific Gravity	3.18
Streak	White
Indicators	Color, habit

Hureaulite is rare, but its small crystals form clusters which are very popular with collectors. It occurs in Alabama, Arizona, California, Connecticut, Maine, Nevada, New Hampshire, North Carolina, South Dakota, and Wisconsin.

Roselite

Chemical Formula	$Ca_2(Co,Mg)(AsO_4)_2 \cdot 2(H_2O)$
Environment	Oxidized zone of cobalt arsenide-rich ore veins.
Locality	Germany, Morocco, Chile, Canada
Etymology	Gustav Rose (1798–1873), professor of mineralogy, University of Berlin

Roselite. Bou Azzer, Morocco.

Physical Properties of Roselite

Cleavage	[010] Perfect
Color	Dark rose red, pink
Diaphaneity	Transparent to translucent
Fracture	Uneven
Habit	Drusy, botyroidal, spherical

Hardness	3.5
Luster	Vitreous (glassy)
Specific Gravity	3.69
Streak	Light red
Indicators	Color, habit, streak, cleavage, density

Roselite has not been found in the United States.

Phosphophyllite

Chemical Formula	$Zn_2(Fe,Mn)(PO_4)_2 \cdot 4H_2O$
Environment	Secondary mineral in zoned granitic pegmatites
Locality	Germany, Sweden, Czech Republic, United States, Bolivia, Australia
Etymology	After its composition and from the Greek *fyllon*, "leaf"

Physical Properties of Phosphophyllite

Cleavage	[100] Perfect, [010] Distinct, [102] Distinct
Color	Blue green, colorless, light green
Diaphaneity	Transparent
Fracture	Uneven
Habit	Drusy
Hardness	3–3.5
Luster	Vitreous (glassy)
Specific Gravity	3.1
Streak	White
Indicators	Habit, cleavage, color

Phosphophyllite is rare but very sought after by collectors because of its delicate color. The best gem-quality specimens came from Bolivia, but it is no longer mined there. In the United States it is found in Maine, New Hampshire, North Carolina, South Dakota, and Virginia.

Autunite

Chemical Formula	$Cu(UO_2)_2(PO_4)_2 \cdot 10{-}12H_2O$
Environment	Secondary mineral formed in oxidized zones of uraninite
Locality	Autun and many other locations in France; Germany; Austria; Italy; Portugal; Spain; Madagascar; United Kingdom; United States
Etymology	After Autun, France

Physical Properties of Autunite

Cleavage	[001] Perfect, [100] Poor, [010] Poor
Color	Yellow, pale yellow, lemon yellow, greenish yellow, pale green
Diaphaneity	Transparent to translucent
Fracture	Uneven
Habit	Foliated, micaceous, tabular
Hardness	2–2.5
Luminescence	Fluorescent, short UV = yellow, long UV = yellow
Luster	Vitreous – Pearly
Specific Gravity	3.1–3.2, Average = 3.15
Streak	Pale yellow
Indicators	Color, habit, fluorescence, radioactivity

Autunite is one of the more attractive radioactive minerals. It should be stored in a sealed container to minimize water loss, as it will convert to meta-autunite-I if it dehydrates. It is most common in France and Germany. In the United States it is found in Alabama, Arizona, Califirnia, Colorado, Connecticut, Idaho, Maine, Maryland, Massachusetts, Montana, Nebraska, Nevada, New Hampshire, New Jersey, New Mexico, New York, North Carolina, Oklahoma, Pennsylvania, Rhode Island, South Dakota, Texas, Utah, Virginia, Washington, and Wyoming.

Torbernite

Chemical Formula	$Cu(UO_2)_2(PO_4)_2 \cdot 8-12H_2O$
Environment	Secondary mineral in copper-bearing uranium deposits
Locality	United States, Mexico, Zaire, South Africa, Namibia, Gabon, Europe, Japan, Australia
Etymology	Swedish chemist Tornbern Bergmann (1735–1784)

Physical Properties of Torbernite

Cleavage	[001] Perfect, [100] Distinct
Color	Green, grass green, leek green, apple green, siskin green
Diaphaneity	Transparent to subtranslucent
Fracture	Brittle
Habit	Earthy, foliated, tabular
Hardness	2–2.5
Luminescence	Fluorescent and radioactive, short UV = yellow, long UV = yellow
Luster	Vitreous – pearly
Specific Gravity	3.2
Streak	Pale green
Indicators	Color, habit, non-fluorescence, radioactivity

Torbernite. Cunha Baixa Mine, Magualde, Viseu District, Portugal.

Torbernite is a popular uranium-bearing mineral for collectors, but, like autunite, it should be stored in a sealed container to minimize water loss. In the United States it is found in Alabama, Arizona, California, Colorado, Connecticut, Idaho, Maine, Maryland, Massachusetts, Missouri, Montana, Nevada, New Hampshire, New Mexico, New York, North Carolina, Oklahoma, Oregon, Pennsylvania, South Dakota, Texas, Utah, and Washington.

Carnotite

Chemical Formula	$K_2(UO_2)2V_2 O_8 \cdot 3(H_2 O)$
Environment	Occurs as crusts and flakes in sandstone
Locality	Worldwide
Etymology	French chemist M.A. Carnot (1839–1920)

Physical Properties of Carnotite

Cleavage	[001] Perfect
Color	Yellow, golden yellow, greenish yellow
Diaphaneity	Translucent to opaque

Fracture	Uneven
Habit	Earthy, encrustations, platy
Hardness	2
Luminescence	Radioactive
Luster	Pearly
Specific Gravity	3.7–4.7, Average = 4.2
Streak	Light yellow
Indicators	Color, density, habit, non-fluorescence, radioactivity

Carnotite is not common, but is an important uranium ore nonetheless. It was discovered in Colorado, where it occurs widely, as it does in Arizona and Utah, and also occurs in California, Idaho, Maine, Nebraska, Nevada, New Mexico, Oklahoma, Oregon, Pennsylvania, South Dakota, Texas, and Wyoming.

Carnotite. Happy Jack Mine, White County, Utah.

Vivianite

Chemical Formula	$Fe_3(PO_4)_2 \cdot 8H_2O$
Environment	Common secondary mineral in metallic ore deposits and pegmatites; sedimentary authigenic mineralization associated with organic materials
Locality	Worldwide
Etymology	English mineralogist J.G. Vivian (1785–1855)

Physical Properties of Vivianite

Cleavage	[010] Perfect
Color	Colorless, green, blue, dark green, dark bluish green
Diaphaneity	Transparent to translucent to opaque
Fracture	Sectile
Habit	Concretionary, divergent, earthy
Hardness	1.5–2
Luster	Vitreous – pearly
Specific Gravity	2.6–2.7, Average = 2.65
Streak	Bluish white
Indicators	Color, habit, flexible crystals

Vivianite. Cigana Mine, Galileia, Minas Gerais, Brazil.

Vivianite is often found inside fossilized seashells and makes an attractive specimen, but it darkens almost to black on prolonged exposure to light, so it should not be kept on display. It occurs throughout the United States in Alabama, Arkansas, California, Colorado, Connecticut, Delaware, Florida, Georgia, Idaho, Indiana, Kentucky, Louisiana, Maine, Maryland, Massachusetts, Michigan, Missouri, Montana, Nebraska, Nevada, New

Hampshire, New Jersey, New Mexico, New York, North Carolina, Ohio, Oklahoma, Pennsylvania, South Dakota, Utah, Virginia, Washington, and Wisconsin.

Erythrite

Chemical Formula	$Co_3(AsO_4)_2 \cdot 8H_2O$
Environment	Secondary mineral in oxidized zones of cobalt deposits
Locality	Germany, France, Austria, Canada, United States, Japan, Morocco
Etymology	Greek *erythros*, "red"

Physical Properties of Erythrite

Cleavage	[010] Perfect
Color	Colorless, violet red, light pink, purple red
Diaphaneity	Transparent to subtranslucent
Fracture	Sectile
Habit	Divergent, prismatic, striated
Hardness	1.5–2
Luster	Pearly
Specific Gravity	3.06–3.18, Average = 3.12
Streak	Pinkish red
Indicators	Color, flexible crystals

Erythrite. These 0.5 mm erythrite crystals were collected at Bou Azzer, Morocco.

Erythrite occurs in Arizona, California, Colorado, Connecticut, Georgia, Idaho, Michigan, Missouri, Nevada, New Jersey, New Mexico, New York, Oregon, Pennsylvania, Texas, Utah, Virginia, Washington, Wisconsin, and Wyoming.

Annabergite

Chemical Formula	$Ni_3(AsO_4)_2 \cdot 8H_2O$
Environment	Oxidation zone of nickel-copper-arsenic deposits
Locality	Annaberg, Germany; Europe; Morocco; Australia; United States
Etymology	After Annaberg, Germany

Physical Properties of Annabergite

Cleavage	[010] Perfect
Color	Apple green, greenish white, gray, yellow green, white
Diaphaneity	Transparent to subtransparent to translucent
Fracture	Brittle
Habit	Earthy, encrustations, massive
Hardness	2
Luster	Pearly
Specific Gravity	3–3.1, Average = 3.05
Streak	Light green
Indicators	Color, hardness, flexible crystals

Annabergite occasionally forms very small crystals, but is usually found as a powdery crust. In the United States it occurs in Arizona, California, Colorado, Connecticut, Idaho,

Michigan, Missouri, Montana, Nevada, New Jersey, New Mexico, North Carolina, Texas, Utah, and Washington.

Variscite

Chemical Formula	$AlPO_4 \cdot 2H_2O$
Environment	Deposit from high-phosphate waters acting on aluminous rocks
Locality	Germany, France, Poland, United Kingdom, Australia, United States
Etymology	After Variscia, the ancient name of Vogtland, Germany

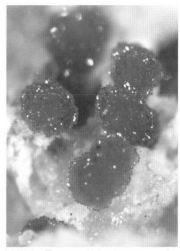

Physical Properties of Variscite

Cleavage	[010] Perfect
Color	Blue green, colorless, green, light green
Diaphaneity	Transparent to translucent
Fracture	Conchoidal
Habit	Encrustations, massive, reniform
Hardness	4–5
Luster	Earthy (Dull)
Specific Gravity	2.5–2.52, Average = 2.5
Streak	White
Indicators	Color, habit, density, luster

Variscite. These variscite 1 mm crystals were collected at Boa Vista, Galileia, Minas Gerais, Brazil.

Variscite is sometimes confused with turquoise, although variscite tends to be greener. It is rare, and can be found in Alabama, Arizona, Arkansas, California, Georgia, Idaho, Nevada, New Mexico, North Carolina, Pennsylvania, South Carolina, South Dakota, Tennessee, Texas, Utah, Virginia, and Wisconsin.

Strengite

Chemical Formula	$FePO_4 \cdot 2H_2O$
Environment	Secondary mineral formed by alteration of iron-bearing phosphates; forms a series with variscite
Locality	United States, Australia, Brazil, France, Germany, Portugal, United Kingdom, Sweden, South Africa, Rwanda, Senegal
Etymology	German mineralogist Johann August Streng (1830–1897)

Physical Properties of Strengite

Cleavage	[010] Good, [001] Poor
Color	Colorless, pale violet, deep violet, red, carmine red

Strengite. Stewart Mine, San Diego County, California.

Diaphaneity	Transparent to translucent
Fracture	Brittle – conchoidal
Habit	Botryoidal, radial, spherical
Hardness	3.5
Luster	Vitreous (glassy)
Specific Gravity	2.87
Streak	White
Indicators	Color, habit, luster

Strengite is very rare, and specimens are usually small, making the mineral most suitable for micromount collections. Specimens can occasionally be found in Alabama, Arizona, Arkansas, California, Colorado, Connecticut, Georgia, Idaho, Maine, Nevada, New Hampshire, New Mexico, North Carolina, Pennsylvania, South Carolina, South Dakota, Utah, and Virginia.

Scorodite

Chemical Formula	$FeAsO_4 \cdot 2H_2O$
Environment	Forms in the oxidation zones of iron-rich arsenide deposits and in gossans; forms a series with mansfieldite
Locality	Mexico, United States, Brazil, United Kingdom, Namibia
Etymology	Greek *skorodon*, "garlic" (from its odor when heated)

Physical Properties of Scorodite

Cleavage	[201] Imperfect, [100] Poor, [001] Poor
Color	Yellowish green, pale leek green, liver brown, blue green, black green
Diaphaneity	Subtransparent to translucent
Fracture	Splintery
Habit	Earthy, fibrous, granular
Hardness	3.5–4
Luster	Vitreous – greasy
Specific Gravity	3.1–3.3, Average = 3.2
Streak	Greenish white
Indicators	Color, luster, non-fluorescence, habit, garlic smell when heated

Scorodite. Gold Hill, Utah.

Scorodite occurs in Alabama, Alaska, Arizona, California, Colorado, Connecticut, Georgia, Idaho, Montana, Nevada, New Hampshire, New Jersey, New Mexico, New York, North Carolina, Oregon, South Dakota, Texas, Utah, Virginia, Washington, and Wyoming.

Conichalcite

Chemical Formula	$CaCu(AsO_4)(OH)$
Environment	Oxidation zone of copper ores
Locality	North America, Chile, Europe, Zaire
Etymology	Greek *konis*, "powder," and *chalkos*, "copper"

Physical Properties of Conichalcite

Cleavage	None
Color	Yellow green, emerald green
Diaphaneity	Subtranslucent
Fracture	Brittle – uneven
Habit	Fibrous, massive, reniform
Hardness	4.5
Luster	Vitreous – greasy
Specific Gravity	4.1
Streak	Light green
Indicators	Habit, color, density

Conichalcite. These small dark conichalcite crystals were collected at Mammoth Mine, Tintic District, Utah.

Conichalcite is found in Arizona, California, Colorado, Idaho, Michigan, Montana, Nevada, New Jersey, New Mexico, Pennsylvania, South Dakota, Utah, Virginia, and Washington.

Austinite

Chemical Formula	$CaZnAsO_4OH$
Environment	Oxidized zone of arsenic-rich base-metal deposits
Locality	United States, Mexico, Germany, Morocco, Namibia
Etymology	American mineralogist Austin Flint Rogers (1877–1957)

Physical Properties of Austinite

Cleavage	[110] Good
Color	Brown, colorless, green, yellowish white, white
Diaphaneity	Transparent to translucent
Fracture	Brittle – uneven
Habit	Acicular, bladed, drusy, fibrous
Hardness	4–4.5
Luster	Subadamantine
Specific Gravity	4.13

Austinite. Mina Ojuela, Mapimi, Durango, Mexico.

Streak	White
Indicators	Habit, cleavage, color, luster, density, non-fluorescence

Austinite is very rare. It occurs most often in Nevada, and also in Arizona, California, Colorado, New Jersey, New Mexico, Utah, and Washington.

Descloizite

Chemical Formula	$PbZnVO_4OH$
Environment	Occurs as a secondary mineral in the oxidation zone of base-metal deposits; forms a series with mottramite
Locality	Namibia, Zaire, Austria, Germany, Mexico, United States
Etymology	Alfred Lewis Oliver Legrand Des Cloizeaux (1817–1897), professor of mineralogy, University of Paris

Descloizite. Richmond Sitting Bull Mine, Lawrence County, South Dakota.

Physical Properties of Descloizite

Cleavage	None
Color	Dark brownish black, dark reddish brown, orange red, reddish brown, black
Diaphaneity	Transparent to opaque
Fracture	Brittle
Habit	Encrustations, plumose, tabular
Hardness	3.5
Luster	Greasy (oily)
Specific Gravity	6.1–6.2, Average = 6.15
Streak	Light brownish green
Indicators	Color, habit, density

Descloizite is found in Arizona, California, Colorado, Idaho, Montana, Nevada, New Jersey, New Mexico, Pennsylvania, South Dakota, Texas, Utah, and Washington.

Mottramite

Chemical Formula	$PbCuVO_4OH$
Environment	Secondary mineral in the oxidation zone of base-metal deposits; forms a series with descloizite
Locality	Mottram, England; Europe; United States; Mexico; Chile; Namibia, South Africa; Australia
Etymology	After Mottram, England

Physical Properties of Mottramite

Cleavage	None
Color	Brown, brown red, brownish black, green, dark green

Diaphaneity	Transparent to opaque
Fracture	Brittle
Habit	Encrustations, plumose, radial
Hardness	3.5
Luster	Greasy (oily)
Specific Gravity	5.9–6, Average = 5.95
Streak	Light brownish green
Indicators	Color, habit, density

Mottramite. Tsumeb Mine, Tsumeb, Namibia.

Mottramite is the copper analog of descloizite, with which it forms a series. It occurs in Arizona, California, Idaho, Michigan, Montana, Nevada, New Mexico, Pennsylvania, South Dakota, Texas, Utah, and Washington.

Herderite

Chemical Formula	$CaBePO_4F$
Environment	Occurs in granitic pegmatites; forms a series with hydroxylherderite, for which it is often mistaken
Locality	Germany, Russia, Brazil, United States
Etymology	Siegmund August Wolfgang von Herder (1776–1838), German mining official

Physical Properties of Herderite

Cleavage	[110] Indistinct
Color	White, yellowish white, greenish white
Diaphaneity	Transparent to translucent
Fracture	Subconchoidal
Habit	Prismatic, twinning is common
Hardness	5
Luster	Vitreous (glassy)
Specific Gravity	3
Streak	White
Indicators	Habit, color, fluorescence, hardness

Herderite is rare; in the United States it is found only in California, Connecticut, Maine, New Hampshire, and North Carolina. It often forms very striking twins.

Brazilianite

Chemical Formula	$NaAl_3(PO_4)_2(OH)_4$
Environment	In phosphate-rich igneous pegmatites
Locality	Brazil, United States
Etymology	After Brazil

Physical Properties of Brazilianite

Cleavage	[010] Good
Color	Colorless, greenish yellow, yellow green, light yellow

Diaphaneity	Transparent
Fracture	Conchoidal
Habit	Euhedral crystals, spherical
Hardness	5.5
Luster	Vitreous (glassy)
Specific Gravity	2.98
Streak	White
Indicators	Color, habit, density, cleavage

Brazilianite is one of only a few gem-quality phosphate minerals, and one of the hardest; it is often cut and faceted when found in sufficient size. It is rare, however, occurring in the United States only in Arizona, Connecticut, Maine, New Hampshire, and South Dakota.

Brazilianite. Marcel Telirio Mine, Linopolis, Minas Gerais, Brazil.

Amblygonite

Chemical Formula	$(Li,Na)Al(PO_4)(F,OH)$
Environment	In phosphate-rich igneous pegmatites
Locality	Brazil, United States, Namibia, Madagascar, France
Etymology	Greek *amblys,* "blunt," and *goni,* "angle"

Physical Properties of Amblygonite

Cleavage	[100] Perfect, [110] Good, [011] Distinct
Color	White, yellow, gray, bluish gray, greenish gray
Diaphaneity	Transparent to subtransparent to translucent
Fracture	Uneven
Habit	Columnar, euhedral crystals, prismatic
Hardness	5.5–6
Luster	Vitreous – pearly
Specific Gravity	2.98–3.11, Average = 3.04
Streak	White
Indicators	Density, cleavage

Amblygonite occurs in Arizona, California, Colorado, Connecticut, Maine, Massachusetts, New Hampshire, New Mexico, North Carolina, South Dakota, Wisconsin, and Wyoming. Gem-quality specimens are found in Brazil and Burma.

Olivenite

Chemical Formula	Cu_2AsO_4OH
Environment	In the oxidized zone of arsenic-bearing copper deposits
Locality	Austalia, Chile, Austria, France, Germany, Italy, Hungary, Spain, United Kingdom, United States
Etymology	German *olivenerz,* "olive"

Physical Properties of Olivenite

Cleavage	[110] Indistinct, [010] Indistinct, [110] Indistinct
Color	Olive green, yellowish brown, dirty white, blackish green, liver brown

Diaphaneity	Subtransparent to translucent to opaque
Fracture	Brittle – conchoidal
Habit	Prismatic, radial, reniform
Hardness	3
Luster	Vitreous – greasy
Specific Gravity	4.1–4.4, Average = 4.25
Streak	Yellowish green
Indicators	Color, habit, density

Olivenite occurs in Arizona, California, Colorado, Idaho, Michigan, Montana, Nevada, New Mexico, North Carolina, South Dakota, and Utah.

Olivenite. Majuba Hill Mine, Pershing County, Nevada.

Libethenite

Chemical Formula	Cu_2PO_4OH
Environment	Secondary mineral in the oxidized zone of copper ore
Locality	L'ubietová, Slovakia; worldwide
Etymology	After L'ubietová, Slovakia (*Libethen* in German)

Physical Properties of Libethenite

Cleavage	[100] Indistinct, [010] Indistinct
Color	Green, dark green, blackish green, light olive green, dark olive green
Diaphaneity	Translucent to subtranslucent
Fracture	Brittle
Habit	Drusy, globular, prismatic
Hardness	4
Luster	Vitreous – greasy
Specific Gravity	3.6–4, Average = 3.8
Streak	Light green
Indicators	Color, streak, habit

Libethenite is isostructural with olivenite and adamite. It is found in the United States in Arizona, California, Colorado, Idaho, Montana, Nevada, New Mexico, North Carolina, Pennsylvania, South Dakota, Utah, and Virginia.

Adamite

Chemical Formula	$Zn2(AsO4)(OH)$
Environment	Secondary mineral in arsenic-bearing zinc deposits
Locality	Chile, Mexico, United States, Europe
Etymology	French mineralogist Gilbert Joseph Adam (1795–1881)

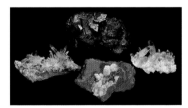

Adamite.

Physical Properties of Adamite

Cleavage	[101] Good, [010] Poor
Color	Yellow, green, violet, pink, yellowish green
Diaphaneity	Subtransparent
Fracture	Brittle

Habit	Drusy, encrustations, tabular
Hardness	3.5
Luminescence	Fluorescent and phosphorescent.
Luster	Vitreous – resinous
Specific Gravity	4.3–4.5, Average = 4.4
Streak	White
Indicators	Habit, color, luster, fluorescence

Adamite exhibits a bright green fluorescence that makes it a very popular mineral for collectors. In the United States it occurs in Arizona, California, Colorado, Montana, Nevada, New Jersey, New Mexico, South Dakota, and Utah.

Augelite

Chemical Formula	$Al_2PO_4(OH)_3$
Environment	Formed by hydrogen metamorphism of phosphate-bearing rock; occurs in some high-temperature hydrothermal ores
Locality	Sweden, Bolivia, United States
Etymology	Greek for "luster"

Physical Properties of Augelite

Cleavage	[110] Perfect, [201] Good
Color	Colorless, yellow, yellow green, white, light blue
Diaphaneity	Transparent to translucent
Fracture	Conchoidal
Habit	Tabular, platy, equant
Hardness	4.5–5
Luster	Vitreous – pearly
Specific Gravity	2.696
Streak	White
Indicators	Habit, color, cleavage

Augelite is found in Arizona, California, Connecticut, Maine, Nevada, New Hampshire, South Dakota, and Virginia.

Apatite

Chemical Formula	$Ca_5(PO_4)_3(OH,F,Cl)$
Environment	Apatite is now a group name for a series of related minerals: fluoroapatite, chloroapatite, and hydroxylapatite
Locality	Common worldwide
Etymology	Greek apatao, "I am misleading"

Physical Properties of Apatite

Cleavage	[0001] Indistinct, [1010] Indistinct
Color	White, yellow, green, red, blue
Diaphaneity	Transparent to translucent
Fracture	Conchoidal
Habit	Colloform, earthy, massive – granular

Hardness	5
Luster	Vitreous (glassy)
Specific Gravity	3.16–3.22, Average = 3.19
Streak	White
Indicators	Habit, color, hardness

Apatite group minerals occur widely in all types of rock, but usually just as small, scattered grains; good crystals are less common, but they can be found in some metamorphic rocks. Apatite is a major component of tooth enamel. Apatites occur in Alabama, Alaska, Arizona, Arkansas, California, Colorado, Connecticut, Delaware, Florida, Georgia, Idaho, Indiana, Kansas, Kentucky, Louisiana, Maine, Maryland, Massachusetts, Michigan, Missouri, Montana, Nebraska, Nevada, New Hampshire, New Jersey, New Mexico, New York, North Carolina, Oregon, Pennsylvania, South Carolina, South Dakota, Tennessee, Texas, Utah, Vermont, Virginia, Washington, Wisconsin, and Wyoming.

Apatite. This large crystal of gemmy apatite collected at Cerro de Mercado, Durango, Mexico, is 4 cm and sits on a calcite matrix.

Pyromorphite

Chemical Formula	$Pb_5(PO_4)_3CL$
Environment	Secondary mineral in the oxidized zones of lead ores
Locality	United States, Mexico, Germany, France, Austria, United Kingdom, Australia
Etymology	Greek *pyr*, "fire," and *morfe*, "form" (from the recrystallization of the molten mineral)

Physical Properties of Pyromorphite

Cleavage	[1011] Imperfect
Color	Green, yellow, brown, grayish white, yellowish red
Diaphaneity	Subtransparent to subtranslucent
Fracture	Brittle
Habit	Globular, prismatic, reniform
Hardness	3.5–4
Luster	Adamantine – resinous
Specific Gravity	6.7–7, Average = 6.85
Streak	White
Indicators	Habit, color, lack of transparency

Pyromorphite. Daoping Mine, Guilin Prefecture, Guangxi Zhuang, China.

Pyromorphite is isostructural with apatite, and forms a series with mimetite and vanadinite. It readily forms crystals, sometimes with a unique barrel shape. Pyromorphite is found in Alaska, Arizona, California, Colorado, Connecticut, Georgia, Idaho, Illinois, Kentucky, Maine, Massachusetts, Missouri, Montana, Nevada, New Hampshire, New Jersey, New Mexico, New York, North Carolina, Oklahoma, Pennsylvania, Rhode Island, South Carolina, South Dakota, Texas, Utah, Virginia, Washington, and Wisconsin.

Mimetite

Chemical Formula	$Pb_5(AsO_4)_3CL$
Environment	Secondary mineral in the oxidized zones of lead ores, or where lead and arsenic occur together
Locality	Namibia, Mexico, United States, United Kingdom, France, Germany, Italy, Greece, Australia
Etymology	Greek *mimethes*, "imitator" (for its resemblance to pyromorphite)

Mimetite. San Francisco Mine, Sonora, Mexico.

Physical Properties of Mimetite

Cleavage	[1011] Imperfect
Color	White, yellow, orange, brown, red
Diaphaneity	Subtransparent to translucent
Fracture	Brittle – conchoidal
Habit	Globular, prismatic, reniform
Hardness	3.5–4
Luster	Adamantine – resinous
Specific Gravity	7.1–7.24, Average = 7.17
Streak	White
Indicators	Habit, luster, color

The best prismatic crystals of mimetite occur in Saxony, Germany, and Cornwall, England. In the United States it is found in Arizona, California, Colorado, Connecticut, Idaho, Maine, Massachusetts, Missouri, Montana, Nevada, New Jersey, New Mexico, North Carolina, Pennsylvania, South Dakota, Texas, Utah, and Washington.

Vanadinite

Chemical Formula	$Pb_5(VO_4)_3CL$
Environment	In the oxidized zones of lead ores
Locality	Mexico, United States, Namibia, Zambia, South Africa
Etymology	After its composition

Physical Properties of Vanadinite

Cleavage	None
Color	Brown, brownish yellow, brown red, colorless, yellow

Diaphaneity	Subtranslucent to opaque
Fracture	Brittle – conchoidal
Habit	Globular, nodular, prismatic
Hardness	3.5–4
Luster	Adamantine
Specific Gravity	6.8–7.1, Average = 6.94
Streak	Brownish yellow
Indicators	Color, habit, luster, density

Vanadinite occurs worldwide, but is fairly uncommon. In the United States it occurs in Arizona, California, Colorado, Idaho, Montana, Nevada, New Jersey, New Mexico, New York, Pennsylvania, South Dakota, Texas, Utah, Virginia, and Wisconsin.

Vanadinite.

Lazulite

Chemical Formula	$MgAl_2(PO_4)_2(OH)_2$
Environmant	Within metamorphic rocks, border zones of complex granitic pegmatites, and alluvial deposits; forms a series with scorzalite
Locality	Austria, Switzerland, Brazil, United States, Canada
Etymology	Arabic azul, "sky," and Greek lithos, "stone"

Physical Properties of Lazulite

Cleavage	[110] Good, [101] Indistinct
Color	Blue, blue green, light blue, black blue
Diaphaneity	Subtranslucent to opaque
Fracture	Uneven
Habit	Massive – granular, pyramidal
Hardness	5–6
Luster	Vitreous (glassy)
Specific Gravity	3–3.1, Average = 3.05
Streak	White
Indicators	Color, habit

Lazulite is a rare mineral that is very similar in appearance to, and often confused with, lazurite and azurite. It forms a series with scorzalite. It is found in Arizona, California, Colorado, Connecticut, Georgia, Maine, Missouri, Nevada, New Hampshire, New Jersey, New Mexico, North Carolina, South Carolina, South Dakota, Vermont, Virginia, and Wisconsin.

Scorzalite

Chemical Formula	$(Fe,Mg)Al_2(PO_4)_2(OH)_2$
Environment	Secondary mineral in granitic pegmatites; forms a series with lazulite
Locality	Brazil, United States, Japan, Sweden
Etymology	Brazilian mineralogist Everisto Pena Scorza (1899–1969)

Physical Properties of Scorzalite

Cleavage	[110] Good
Color	Dark blue, greenish blue

Diaphaneity	Subtranslucent to opaque
Fracture	Uneven
Habit	Granular, massive – granular
Hardness	5.5–6
Luster	Vitreous – dull
Specific Gravity	3.27
Streak	White
Indicators	Color, habit, density

Scorzalite forms a series with Lazulite, but is much rarer. It is found in Arizona, California, Colorado, Connecticut, Maine, New Hampshire, and South Dakota.

Childrenite

Chemical Formula	$FeAlPO_4(OH)_2 \cdot H_2O$
Environment	Forms by alteration of granitic phosphates in the presence of aluminum; forms a series with eosphorite
Locality	United Kingdom, United States, Brazil
Etymology	English chemist and mineralogist John George Children (1777–1852)

Physical Properties of Childrenite

Cleavage	[100] Poor
Color	White, yellowish brown, brownish black
Diaphaneity	Translucent
Fracture	Conchoidal – uneven
Habit	Platy, prismatic, tabular
Hardness	4.5–5
Luster	Vitreous – resinous
Specific Gravity	3.18–3.25, Average = 3.21
Streak	White
Indicators	Habit, color, density

Childrenite. Siglo XX Mine, Llallagua, Potosi Department, Bolivia.

Childrenite is so rare that it is not entirely understood; it probably forms by alteration of lithiophilite or triphilite, but this is not certain. Childrenite forms a series with eosphorite. It occurs in Maine, New Hampshire, North Carolina, and South Dakota.

Eosphorite

Chemical Formula	$MnAlPO_4(OH)_2 \cdot H_2O$
Environment	Forms by alteration of granitic phosphates in the presence of aluminum; forms a series with childrenite
Locality	United States, Brazil, Germany
Etymology	Greek for "dawn-bearing" (from the pink color)

Physical Properties of Eosphorite

Cleavage	[100] Indistinct
Color	Light pink, yellow brown, light brown, light yellow, colorless
Diaphaneity	Transparent to translucent
Fracture	Conchoidal – uneven
Habit	Massive – fibrous, prismatic; striated
Hardness	5
Luster	Vitreous – resinous
Specific Gravity	3.06–3.1, Average = 3.08
Streak	White
Indicators	Habit, color, density

Eosphorite. These sparkling, transparent cinnamon-colored sprays of eosphorite prisms densely coat the matrix they grow on. Jequitinhonha River, Taquaral, Itinga, Minas Gerais, Brazil. Brought $322 at auction in early 2008.

Eosphorite is more common than childrenite, with which it forms a series. It occurs in Arizona, California, Connecticut, Maine, New Hampshire, North Carolina, and South Dakota.

Wardite

Chemical Formula	$NaAl_3(PO_4)_2(OH)_4 \cdot 2H_2O$
Environment	Forms by alteration of amblygonite in pegmatites and phosphate deposits
Locality	United States, Brazil, Canada
Etymology	American mineral dealer and collector Henry Augustus Ward (1834–1906)

Physical Properties of Wardite

Cleavage	[001] Perfect
Color	Blue green, colorless, white, light green
Diaphaneity	Transparent to translucent
Fracture	Conchoidal
Habit	Encrustations, fibrous, radial
Hardness	5
Luster	Vitreous (glassy)
Specific Gravity	2.81–2.87, Average = 2.84
Streak	White
Indicators	Color, habit, nonfluorescence

Wardite is one of only a very few minerals with tetragonal tetrahedral symmetry, and is therefore much sought after for collections. It occurs in California, Connecticut, Idaho, Maine, Nevada, New Hampshire, South Dakota, and Utah.

Legrandite

Chemical Formula	$Zn_2(AsO_4)(OH) \cdot H_2O$
Environment	Secondary mineral in zinc ores
Locality	Mexico, Germany, Greece, Japan
Etymology	Belgian mining engineer M. Legrand

Physical Properties of Legrandite

Cleavage	[100] Imperfect
Color	Yellow, yellowish orange
Diaphaneity	Translucent
Fracture	Brittle – conchoidal
Habit	Crystalline – fine, prismatic
Hardness	4–5
Luster	Vitreous (glassy)
Specific Gravity	4
Streak	White
Indicators	Color, luster, density, habit

Legrandite is very rare and highly prized by collectors. In the United States it is found only in the famed Franklin mining district of New Jersey.

Legrandite. Flor de Pena, Lampoz, Nuevo Leon, Mexico.

Turquoise   *See listing under "Gemstones."*

Wavellite

Chemical Formula	$Al_3(PO_4)_2(OH,F)_3 \cdot 5H_2O$
Environment	Secondary mineral in aluminum-bearing metamorphic and phosphate rocks
Locality	England, United States, Bolivia, Australia
Etymology	English physician William Wavell (died 1829)

Physical Properties of Wavellite

Cleavage	[110] Perfect, [101] Good
Color	Blue, brown, brownish black, colorless, green
Diaphaneity	Translucent
Fracture	Fibrous
Habit	Radial, stalactitic, stellate
Hardness	3.5–4
Luster	Vitreous – pearly
Specific Gravity	2.3–2.4, Average = 2.34
Streak	White
Indicators	Habit, color, hardness

Wavellite. Mauldin Mountain, Montgomery County, Arkansas.

Wavellite forms interesting clusters of radiating "starburst" crystals. It is found in Alabama, Arizona, Arkansas, California, Florida, Georgia, Missouri, Montana, Nevada, New Mexico, New York, North Carolina, Oklahoma, Pennsylvania, Rhode Island, South Carolina, Tennessee, Texas, Utah, Vermont, Virginia, and Wisconsin.

MOLYBDATES AND TUNGSTATES

Wolframite *Wolframite Series*

Chemical Formula	(Fe,Mn)WO4
Environment	High-temperature hydrothermal veins and pneumatolytically altered greisens; granitic pegmatites
Locality	Germany, Portugal, Russia, Australia, Thailand, Korea, Bolivia, United States, China
Etymology	German *Wolfram* (the name for tungsten)

Wolframite. Minor amounts of siderite grow on this lustrous wolframite crystal collected at Minas de Panasqueira, Beira Baixa Province, Portugal. It brought $3,450 at auction in February 2008.

Physical Properties of Wolframite

Cleavage	[010] Perfect
Color	Brownish black, iron black
Diaphaneity	Opaque
Fracture	Brittle
Habit	Lamellar, massive – granular, prismatic
Hardness	4.5
Luster	Submetallic
Specific Gravity	7.1–7.5, Average = 7.3
Streak	Reddish brown
Indicators	Habit, color, density, luster, cleavage

The wolframite series are the most important ores of tungsten, which is used in making cutting and grinding tools. Sixty precent of the world's tungsten reserves are in China. In the United States wolframite can be found in Alaska, Arizona, California, Colorado, Connecticut, Idaho, Maine, Missouri, Montana, Nevada, New Hampshire, New Mexico, North Carolina, Rhode Island, South Dakota, Texas, Utah, Virgnia, Washington, and Wyoming.

Huebnerite *Wolframite Series*

Chemical Formula	$MnWO_4$
Environment	High-temperature hydrothermal veins and pneumatolytically altered greisens; granitic pegmatites
Locality	China, Russia, France, United Kingdom, United States, Peru, Bolivia
Etymology	German mineralogist Adolph Hübner

Physical Properties of Huebnerite

Cleavage	[010] Perfect
Color	Brown, reddish brown, brownish black
Diaphaneity	Transparent to translucent
Fracture	Brittle

Habit	Lamellar; massive – granular; prismatic
Hardness	4.5
Luster	Submetallic
Specific Gravity	7.2–7.1, Average = 7.15
Streak	Reddish brown
Indicators	Habit, color, density, luster, cleavage

Huebnerite, also spelled hübnerite, is the manganese-rich member of the wolframite series. It is found in Arizona, California, Colorado, Connecticut, Idaho, Maine, Massachusetts, Missouri, Montana, Nevada, New Jersey, New Mexico, North Carolina, South Dakota, Texas, Utah, Virginia, and Washington.

Huebnerite. Gladstone, Colorado.

Ferberite *Wolframite Series*

Chemical Formula	FeWO4
Environment	High-temperature hydrothermal veins and pneumatolytically altered greisens; granitic pegmatites
Locality	China, United States, Russia, Korea, United Kingdom, Bolivia
Etymology	Amateur mineralogist Moritz Rudolph Ferber (1805–1875)

Physical Properties of Ferberite

Cleavage	[010] Perfect, [100] Parting, [102] Parting
Color	Black
Diaphaneity	Nearly opaque
Fracture	Brittle – uneven
Habit	Lamellar, massive – granular, prismatic
Hardness	4.5
Luster	Submetallic
Specific Gravity	7.5–7.4, Average = 7.45
Streak	Brownish black
Indicators	Habit, color, density, luster, cleavage

Ferberite (with quartz). Yaogangxian Mine, Hunan, China.

Ferberite is the iron-rich member of the wolframite series. It is found in Arizona, Arkansas, California, Colorado, Connecticut, Idaho, Maine, Michigan, Montana, Nevada, New Mexico, North Carolina, South Dakota, Utah, and Washington.

Scheelite

Chemical Formula	$CaWO_4$
Environment	Contact metamorphic tactites; high-temperature hydrothermal veins; granitic pegmatites
Locality	Brazil, Australia, Austria, Bolivia, Burma, England, Finland, France, Italy, Japan, Sri Lanka, Switzerland, United States, China, Korea
Etymology	Swedish chemist Karl Wilhelm Scheele (1742–1786)

Physical Properties of Scheelite

Cleavage	[010] Distinct
Color	Colorless, white, pale yellow, brownish yellow, reddish yellow
Diaphaneity	Transparent to translucent
Fracture	Uneven
Habit	Columnar, disseminated, massive – granular
Hardness	4–5
Luminescence	Fluorescent, short UV = bright bluish white
Luster	Vitreous (glassy)
Specific Gravity	5.9–6.12, Average = 6.01
Streak	White
Indicators	Habit, color, density, luster, fluorescence

Scheelite. Two scheelite crystals sit on a matrix of muscovite mica. The crystals form nearly perfect octahedrons up to 6 cm. This specimen sold for $4,140 in early 2008.

Scheelite is an important tungsten ore, especially in the United States where it occurs in abundance, especially in the western states. Its fluorescence makes it popular among collectors. It is found in Alabama, Alaska, Arizona, California, Colorado, Connecticut, Georgia, Idaho, Maine, Massachusetts, Michigan, Missouri, Montana, Nevada, New Hampshire, New Jersey, New Mexico, New York, North Carolina, Oregon, Rhode Island, South Dakota, Texas, Utah, Virginia, Washington, Wisconsin, and Wyoming.

Powellite

Chemical Formula	$CaMoO_4$
Environment	Contact metamorphic tactites; high-temperature hydrothermal veins; granitic pegmatites
Locality	United States, United Kingdom, Sweden, Norway, Russia, India
Etymology	American geologist John Westly Powell (1834–1902)

Physical Properties of Powellite

Cleavage	[111] Distinct
Color	Blue, brown, green yellow, greenish blue, gray

Diaphaneity	Transparent
Fracture	Brittle – conchoidal
Habit	Crystalline – coarse, granular
Hardness	3.5
Luster	Adamantine – resinous
Specific Gravity	4.34
Streak	Light yellow
Indicators	Habit, color, fluorescence, cleavage

Powellite forms a series with scheelite. It was discovered in Idaho, and also occurs in Arizona, California, Colorado, Connecticut, Georgia, Idaho, Maine, Michigan, Montana, Nevada, New Hampshire, New Jersey, New Mexico, North Carolina, Oregon, Rhode Island, Texas, Utah, and Washington.

Wulfenite

Chemical Formula	$PbMoO_4$
Environment	Secondary mineral in oxidized zones of lead deposits; forms a series with stolzite
Locality	Austria, Germany, France, Italy, United Kingdom, Morocco, Namibia, Mexico, United States
Etymology	Austrian mineralogist Franz Xaver von Wulfen (1728–1805)

Wulfenite. This 2 mm crystal of wulfenite was collected at Whim Creek, Western Australia, Australia.

Physical Properties of Wulfenite

Cleavage	[101] Imperfect
Color	Orange yellow, waxy yellow, yellowish gray, olive green, brown
Diaphaneity	Subtransparent to subtranslucent
Fracture	Brittle – conchoidal
Habit	Massive – granular, tabular
Hardness	3
Luster	Resinous – greasy
Specific Gravity	6.5–7, Average = 6.75
Streak	Yellowish white
Indicators	Habit, color, density, luster

Wulfenite generally forms tabular crystals and has a bright color, making it very popular for collections. It occurs in Arizona, Arkansas, California, Colorado, Connecticut, Idaho, Maine, Massachusetts, Montana, Nevada, New Hampshire, New Jersey, New Mexico, New York, Pennsylvania, Rhode Island, South Dakota, Texas, Utah, Virginia, Washington, and Wyoming.

SILICATES

NEOSILICATES

Phenakite

Chemical Formula	Be_2SiO_4
Environment	Forms in granitic pegmatites and schists
Locality	Russia, Brazil, United States, Norway
Etymology	Greek *phenakos*, "deceiver" (from its similarity to quartz when colorless)

Physical Properties of Phenakite

Cleavage	[1120] Distinct
Color	Colorless, wine yellow, yellow, pink, pinkish red
Diaphaneity	Transparent to subtranslucent
Fracture	Brittle – conchoidal
Habit	Granular, massive – fibrous
Hardness	7.5–8
Luster	Vitreous (glassy)
Specific Gravity	2.97–3, Average = 2.98
Streak	White
Indicators	Habit, hardness

Phenakite is rare, but often occurs with precious gems like topaz, emerald, and chrysoberyl; phenakite is often used as a gemstone itself. It occurs in Alaska, Colorado, Connecticut, Idaho, Maine (where especially large crystals are found), Massachusetts, Nevada, New Hampshire, North Carolina, Oregon, Texas, Virginia, and Wisconsin.

Willemite

Chemical Formula	Zn_2SiO_4
Environment	Secondary alteration product of sphalerite in hydrothermal veins
Locality	United States, Canada, Belgium, Greenland
Etymology	Honorific of Willem I, king of the Netherlands (1772–1843)

Physical Properties of Willemite

Cleavage	[0001] Poor, [1120] Poor
Color	White, yellow, green, reddish brown, black
Diaphaneity	Transparent to translucent to opaque
Fracture	Uneven
Habit	Massive – granular, massive, prismatic
Hardness	5.5
Luminescence	Fluorescent, short UV = green
Luster	Vitreous – resinous
Specific Gravity	3.9–4.2, Average = 4.05
Streak	White
Indicators	Fluorescence, luster, cleavage, habit

Willemite almost always fluoresces bright green no matter what its actual color, and is therefore very popular as a collection specimen. It is widespread throughout Arizona and occurs in especially large quantities in the Franklin mining district of New Jersey; it is also found in California, Colorado, Idaho, Montana, Nevada, New Mexico, New York, Oklahoma, and Utah.

Fayalite

Olivine Group. See also listing under "Gemstones."

Chemical Formula	Fe_2SiO_4
Molecular Weight	203.78 gm
Environment	Ultramafic igneous rocks
Locality	Fayal Island, Azores; Portugal; worldwide
Etymology	After Fayal Islands

Physical Properties of Fayalite

Cleavage	[010] Indistinct
Color	Brown black, black
Diaphaneity	Transparent to translucent
Fracture	Conchoidal
Habit	Granular, massive – granular
Hardness	6.5
Luster	Vitreous (glassy)
Specific Gravity	4.39
Streak	White
Indicators	Color, hardness, environment, lack of cleavage

Fayalite is the iron-rich member of the olivine series, the gemstone variety is called peridot. It occurs in Arizona, California, Colorado, Georgia, Hawaii, Idaho, Maine, Massachusetts, Michigan, Nevada, New Hampshire, New Jersey, New Mexico, New York, North Carolina, Oregon, Pennsylvania, Rhode Island, Texas, Vermont, Virginia, Washington, and Wisconsin.

Forsterite

Olivine Group. See also listing under "Gemstones."

Chemical Formula	Mg_2SiO_4
Environment	Ultramafic igneous rocks and dolomitic marble
Locality	Common worldwide
Etymology	German naturalist Johann Forster (1739–1806)

Physical Properties of Forsterite

Cleavage	[001] Good, [010] Distinct
Color	Colorless, green, yellow, yellow green, white
Diaphaneity	Transparent
Fracture	Conchoidal
Habit	Crystalline – fine, tabular
Hardness	6–7
Luster	Vitreous (glassy)
Specific Gravity	3.21–3.33, Average = 3.27
Streak	White
Indicators	Color, hardness, environment, lack of cleavage

Forsterite is the magnesium-rich member of the olivine series; its gemstone variety is peridot. It occurs in Alaska, Arizona, Arkansas, California, Colorado, Connecticut, Hawaii, Idaho, Kansas, Louisiana, Maine, Maryland, Massachusetts, Michigan, Missouri, Montana, Nevada, New Jersey, New Mexico, New York, North Carolina, Pennsylvania, Rhode Island, South Dakota, Texas, Utah, Vermont, Virginia, Washington, Wisconsin, and Wyoming.

Tephroite

Olivine Group. See also listing under "Gemstones."

Chemical Formula	Mn_2SiO_4
Environment	Occurs through contact metamorphism of manganese-bearing rocks
Locality	United States, United Kingdom, Austria, Sweden, Japan
Etymology	Greek *tephros*, "ash gray"

Physical Properties of Tephroite

Cleavage	[010] Indistinct
Color	Gray, olive green, bluish green, red, reddish brown
Diaphaneity	Transparent to translucent
Fracture	Brittle – conchoidal
Habit	Granular, massive – granular, prismatic
Hardness	6.5
Luster	Vitreous – greasy
Specific Gravity	4.11–4.39, Average = 4.25
Streak	Gray
Indicators	Habit, cleavage, environment

Tephroite is a manganese-bearing member of the olivine series. It occurs in Arizona, California, Colorado, Connecticut, Massachusetts, New Jersey (especially in the Franklin mining district), North Carolina, Rhode Island, Texas, Virginia, and Washington.

Pyrope
Garnet Group. See listing under "Gemstones."

Almandine
Garnet Group. See listing under "Gemstones."

Spessartine
Garnet Group. See listing under "Gemstones."

Andradite
Garnet Group. See listing under "Gemstones."

Grossular
Garnet Group. See listing under "Gemstones."

Uvaroite
Garnet Group. See listing under "Gemstones."

Zircon
See listing under "Gemstones."

Sillimanite

Chemical Formula	Al_2SiO_5
Environment	Metamorphosed peri-aluminous sedimentary rocks
Locality	Common worldwide
Etymology	American chemist and mineralogist B. Silliman (1779–1824)

Physical Properties of Sillimanite

Cleavage	[010] Perfect
Color	Bluish, brownish greenish, colorless, gray, gray green
Diaphaneity	Transparent to translucent
Fracture	Splintery
Habit	Acicular, fibrous, prismatic
Hardness	7
Luster	Vitreous (glassy)
Specific Gravity	3.24
Streak	White
Indicators	Habit, color, brittleness

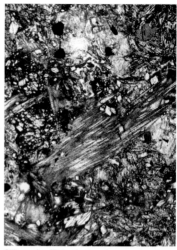

Sillimanite. This photomicrograph of sillimanite schist shows diamond-shaped crystals and fibers of sillimanite. Pend Oreille County, Washington.

Sillimanite is a polymorph of andalusite and kyanite. It is the official mineral of Delaware, and also occurs in Alabama, Arizona, Colorado, Connecticut, Florida, Georgia, Idaho, Kansas, Maine, Maryland, Massachusetts, Michigan, Montana, Nevada, New Hampshire, New Jersey, New Mexico, New York, North Carolina, Pennsylvania, Rhode Island, South Carolina, South Dakota, Texas, Vermont, Virginia, Washington, Wisconsin, and Wyoming.

Andalusite

Chemical Formula	Al_2SiO_4
Environment	Metamorphosed peri-aluminous sedimentary rocks
Locality	Andalucia, Spain; Austria; United States; China
Etymology	After Andalucia, Spain

Physical Properties of Andalusite

Cleavage	[110] Distinct, [100] Indistinct, [010] Poor
Color	Dark green, gray, brown, red, green
Diaphaneity	Transparent to translucent
Fracture	Splintery
Habit	Blocky, euhedral crystals, prismatic
Hardness	6.5–7
Luster	Vitreous (glassy)
Specific Gravity	3.13–3.17, Average = 3.15
Streak	White
Indicators	Habit, color, hardness

Andalusite is a polymorph of kyanite and sillimanite. It exhibits strong pleochroism. It is found in Alabama, Arizona, California, Colorado, Connecticut, Georgia, Idaho, Maine, Massachusetts, Michigan, Montana, Nevada, New Hampshire, New Jersey, New Mexico, North Carolina, Pennsylvania, South Carolina, South Dakota, Texas, Utah, Vermont, Virginia, Washington, Wisconsin, and Wyoming.

Kyanite

Chemical Formula	Al_2SiO_5
Environment	Metamorphosed peri-aluminous sedimentary rocks
Locality	Common worldwide
Etymology	Greek *kyanos*, "blue"

Physical Properties of Kyanite

Cleavage	[100] Perfect, [010] Imperfect
Color	Blue, white, gray, green, lack
Diaphaneity	Translucent to transparent
Fracture	Brittle
Habit	Columnar, fibrous
Hardness	4 parallel to long axis, 7 perpendicular to long axis
Luster	Vitreous – pearly
Specific Gravity	3.56–3.67, Average = 3.61
Streak	White
Indicators	Habit, color, luster, unusual hardness

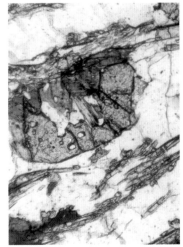

Kyanite. This specimen has nicely contrasting blue blades of kyanite that have intergrown with black biotite. It sold in early 2008 for $126.50.

Kyanite is a polymorph of andalusite and sillimanite. Kyanite exhibits an unusually great difference in hardness across different axes, a property known as anisotropism. It occurs in Alabama, Arizona, California, Colorado, Connecticut, Delaware, Florida, Georgia, Idaho, Maine, Maryland, Massachusetts, Michigan, Montana, Nevada, New Hampshire, New Jersey, New Mexico, North Carolina, Pennsylvania, Rhode Island, South Carolina, South Dakota, Tennessee, Utah, Vermont, Virginia, Washington, Wisconsin, and Wyoming.

Staurolite

Chemical Formula	$(Fe,Mg)_2(Al_9Si,Al)_4O_{20}(O,OH)_4$
Environment	Metamorphosed peri-aluminous sedimentary rocks
Locality	Common worldwide
Etymology	Greek *stauros*, "cross," and *lithos*, "stone"

Physical Properties of Staurolite

Cleavage	[010] Distinct
Color	Brownish yellow, brownish black, yellow brown, dark brown, reddish brown
Diaphaneity	Translucent to opaque
Fracture	Subconchoidal
Habit	Tabular, twinning common
Hardness	7–7.5

Staurolite.

Luster	Vitreous – dull
Specific Gravity	3.65–3.77, Average = 3.71
Streak	Gray
Indicators	Color, twinning, habit

Staurolite characteristically forms cross-shaped twins, a property from which its name is derived. It is the official mineral of Georgia, and also occurs in Alabama, Arizona, California, Colorado, Connecticut, Florida, Idaho, Maine, Maryland, Massachusetts, Michigan, Minnesota, Nevada, New Hampshire, New Jersey, New Mexico, North Carolina, Oklahoma, Pennsylvania, Rhode Island, South Carolina, South Dakota, Tennessee, Texas, Utah, Vermont, Virginia, Washington, and Wisconsin.

Topaz

See listing under "Gemstones."

Chondrodite

Chemical Formula	$(Mg,Fe)_5(SiO_4)_2(F,OH)_2$
Environment	Contact metamorphic rocks
Locality	Worldwide
Etymology	Greek *chondros*, "grain"

Physical Properties of Chondrodite

Cleavage	[100] Good
Color	Yellow, orange, brownish white, reddish white, greenish white
Diaphaneity	Transparent to translucent
Fracture	Conchoidal
Habit	Crystalline – fine, massive – granular
Hardness	6–6.5
Luster	Vitreous – greasy
Specific Gravity	3.1–3.2, Average = 3.15
Streak	Gray
Indicators	Habit, color, luster, cleavage

Chondrodite is rare, and is never found anywhere in abundance. In the United States it occurs in Arizona, California, Colorado, Connecticut, Georgia, Idaho, Massachusetts, Nevada, New Jersey, New Mexico, New York, Pennsylvania, and Washington.

Titanite

Chemical Formula	$CaTiSiO_5$
Environment	Accessory mineral in intermediate and felsic plutonic rocks and pegmatites; also occurs in gneisses, schists, and some skarns
Locality	Worldwide
Etymology	After its composition

Physical Properties of Titanite

Cleavage	[110] Distinct, [100] Imperfect, [112] Imperfect
Color	Reddish brown, gray, yellow, green, red
Diaphaneity	Transparent to translucent to opaque
Fracture	Subconchoidal
Habit	Crystalline – fine, massive – lamellar

Hardness	5–5.5
Luster	Adamantine – resinous
Specific Gravity	3.4–3.56, Average = 3.48
Streak	Reddish white
Indicators	Habit, luster, hardness, color

Titanite (formerly also called sphene) is an important ore of titanium and can also make a beautiful gemstone when clear–it has greater fire than diamond–but its use is limited by its relative softness and brittleness. It occurs in Alabama, Alaska, Arizona, Arkansas, California, Colorado, Connecticut, Georgia, Idaho, Maine, Maryland, Massachusetts, Michigan, Missouri, Montana, Nevada, New Hampshire, New Jersey, New Mexico, New York, Oklahoma, Oregon, Pennsylvania, Rhode Island, South Carolina, South Dakota, Texas, Utah, Vermont, Virginia, Washington, Wisconsin, and Wyoming.

Titanite. Large, twinned sphene crystals are growing out of a pale white feldspar matrix. Capelinha, Minas Gerais, Brazil.

Dumortierite

Chemical Formula	$Al_7O_3(BO_3)(SiO_4)_3$
Environment	Pegmatitic, pneumatolytic, and metamorphic rocks
Locality	Austria, Germany, Madagascar, Russia, Sweden, United States
Etymology	French paleontologist M.E. Dumortier (1803–1873)

Physical Properties of Dumortierite

Cleavage	[100] Good, [110] Indistinct
Color	Blue, brown, violet, greenish blue, pink
Diaphaneity	Transparent to translucent
Fracture	Fibrous
Habit	Columnar, fibrous, prismatic
Hardness	8.5
Luster	Vitreous (Glassy)
Specific Gravity	3.3–3.4, Average = 3.34
Streak	White
Indicators	Hardness, color, density, fluorescence

Dumortierite is pleochroic, and is sometimes used as imitation lapis lazuli for carvings. It occurs in Arizona, California, Colorado, Maine, Montana, Nevada, New Mexico, New York, North Carolina, Pennsylvania, Utah, and Washington.

Datolite

Chemical Formula	$CaBSiO_4(OH)$
Environment	Secondary mineral in basaltic rocks
Locality	United States, Canada, Mexico, Austria, Germany, Italy, Sweden, Norway
Etymology	Greek *dateisthai*, "to divide"

Physical Properties of Datolite

Cleavage	None
Color	Brown, colorless, yellow, white, light green
Diaphaneity	Transparent to translucent
Fracture	Brittle
Habit	Granular, porcelainous, prismatic
Hardness	5.5
Luster	Vitreous (glassy)
Specific Gravity	2.8–3, Average = 2.9
Streak	White
Indicators	Habit, lack of cleavage, hardness, color

Datolite is a popular mineral for collections, especially crystals from the Lake Superior region, which are unusually fine-grained and exhibit color banding. It is found in Arizona, California, New York, Pennsylvania, and Washington.

SOROSILICATES

Hemimorphite

Chemical Formula	$Zn_4Si_2O_7(OH)_2 \cdot H_2O$
Environment	Secondary mineral in the oxidized zones of zinc ore deposits
Locality	Russia, Zambia, Mexico, United States, United Kingdom, France, Austria, Germany, Italy, Norway, Japan, Australia
Etymology	Named for the hemimorphic nature of the crystals

Hemimorphite.

Physical Properties of Hemimorphite

Cleavage	[110] Perfect
Color	Brown, colorless, greenish gray, yellow brown, white
Diaphaneity	Transparent to translucent
Fracture	Conchoidal
Habit	Botyroidal, massive, stalactitic
Hardness	5
Luster	Vitreous (glassy)
Specific Gravity	3.4–3.5, Average = 3.45
Streak	White
Indicators	Habit, color, density, luster

Hemimorphite gets its name from its hemimorphic crystals—which means that the crystals terminate differently on each end; the bottom is rather blunt, while the top forms a pyramid. It occurs in Arizona, Arkansas, California, Colorado, Connecticut, Idaho, Illinois, Iowa, Kansas, Kentucky, Maine, Maryland, Massachusetts, Missouri,

Montana, Nevada, New Hampshire, New Jersey, New Mexico, New York, North Carolina, Ohio, Oklahoma, Pennsylvania, Rhode Island, South Dakota, Tennessee, Texas, Utah, Virginia, Washington, Wisconsin, and Wyoming.

Ferroaxinite

Chemical Formula	$Ca_2FeAl_2(BO_3)Si_4O_{12}(OH)$
Environment	Contact metamorphic rocks and hydrothermal and alpine veins
Locality	United States, Mexico, Brazil, Switzerland, United Kingdom, France, Slovakia, Japan
Etymology	Greek *acine*, "ax" (for the acute shape of typical crystals), and Latin *ferrum*, "iron"

Physical Properties of Ferroaxinite

Cleavage	[100] Distinct, [001] Poor, [110] Poor
Color	Brown, purplish blue, gray, greenish yellow
Diaphaneity	Transparent to subtranslucent
Fracture	Brittle – conchoidal
Habit	Lamellar, massive – granular
Hardness	6.5–7
Luster	Vitreous (glassy)
Specific Gravity	3.27–3.29, Average = 3.28
Streak	White
Indicators	Habit, hardness, color

Ferroaxinite is the iron-rich member of the axinite group, which tends to form unusual spatula-shaped crystals that are popular among collectors. It can be found in California, Connecticut, Maine, Montana, Nevada, New Jersey, North Carolina, Pennsylvania, Rhode Island, Vermont, Virginia, and Washington.

Lawsonite

Chemical Formula	$CaAl_2Si_2O_7(OH)_2 \cdot H_2O$
Environment	A crystalline schist associated with serpentine, and as a secondary mineral in altered gabbros and diorites
Locality	United States, Italy
Etymology	Scottish-American geologist Andrew Cowper Lawson (1861–1952)

Physical Properties of Lawsonite

Cleavage	[010] Perfect, [001] Perfect, [110] Poor
Color	Colorless, white, gray, blue, pinkish
Diaphaneity	Translucent to transparent
Fracture	Brittle – uneven
Habit	Prismatic, tabular
Hardness	7.5
Luster	Vitreous – greasy
Specific Gravity	3.09
Streak	White
Indicators	Color, hardness, cleavage

Lawsonite forms under high-pressure, low-temperature conditions, and is therefore a useful index mineral, indicating the degree of metamorphism its parent rock has undergone. It is found in Arizona, California, and Washington.

Danburite

Chemical Formula	$CaB_2(SiO_4)_2$
Environment	Within granite and in contact metamorphic carbonates
Locality	Connecticut, United States; Mexico; Japan; Russia; Burma; Madagascar
Etymology	After Danbury, Connecticut

Physical Properties of Danburite

Cleavage	[001] Poor
Color	Colorless, white, gray, brownish white, straw yellow
Diaphaneity	Transparent to translucent
Fracture	Subconchoidal
Habit	Disseminated, euhedral crystals, prismatic
Hardness	7
Luminescence	Fluorescent
Luster	Vitreous – greasy
Specific Gravity	2.97–3.02, Average = 2.99
Streak	White
Indicators	Habit, cleavage, hardness

Danburite was discovered in Danbury, Connecticut (hence its name), and can also be found in Alabama, Arizona, California, Louisiana, Montana, New York, Texas, Utah, and Washington.

Clinozoisite

Chemical Formula	$Ca_2Al_3(SiO_4)_3(OH)$
Environment	Regional and contact metamorphic calcium-rich rocks; also an alteration of plagioclase feldspars
Locality	Austria, Italy, Sweden, Mexico, United States, China
Etymology	After its resemblance to zoisite and its monoclinic crystal form

Clinozoisite.

Physical Properties of Clinozoisite

Cleavage	[001] Perfect
Color	Colorless, green, gray, yellow green, light yellow
Diaphaneity	Transparent to translucent
Fracture	Uneven
Habit	Fibrous, massive – granular, prismatic
Hardness	7
Luster	Vitreous (glassy)

Specific Gravity	3.3–3.4, Average = 3.34
Streak	Grayish white
Indicators	Cleavage, habit, color, hardness

Clinozoisite occurs in Alabama, Alaska, Arizona, California, Colorado, Connecticut, Georgia, Idaho, Maine, Maryland, Massachusetts, Michigan, Missouri, Nevada, New Hampshire, New Jersey, New Mexico, New York, North Carolina, Oregon, Pennsylvania, Rhode Island, South Carolina, Utah, Vermont, Virginia, Washington, Wisconsin, and Wyoming.

Epidote

Chemical Formula	$Ca_2Al_2(Fe,Al)SiO_4(Si_2O_7)O(OH)$
Environment	Regional and contact metamorphic rocks; also an alteration of plagioclase feldspars
Locality	Common worldwide
Etymology	Greek *epidosis*, "addition"

Epidote.

Physical Properties of Epidote

Cleavage	[001] Perfect
Color	Yellowish green, brownish green, black, yellow, gray
Diaphaneity	Transparent to translucent to opaque
Fracture	Regular
Habit	Fibrous, massive, prismatic
Hardness	7
Luster	Vitreous (glassy)
Specific Gravity	3.3–3.6, Average = 3.45
Streak	Grayish white
Indicators	cleavage, habit, color, hardness

Epidote is strongly pleochroic and forms very striking crystals, often with a unique pistachio green color. It is widespread, and can be found in Alabama, Alaska, Arizona, California, Colorado, Connecticut, Georgia, Hawaii, Idaho, Iowa, Maine, Maryland, Massachusetts, Michigan, Minnesota, Missouri, Montana, Nevada, New Hampshire, New Jersey, New Mexico, New York, North Carolina, Oklahoma, Oregon, Pennsylvania, Rhode Island, South Carolina, South Dakota, Tennessee, Texas, Utah, Vermont, Virginia, Washington, West Virginia, Wisconsin, and Wyoming.

Zoisite   *See listing under "Gemstones."*

Pumpellyite

Chemical Formula	$Ca_2MgAl_2(SiO_4)(Si_2O_7)(OH)_2 \cdot H_2O$
Environment	Low-temperature metamorphic basaltic rock
Locality	Michigan, United States; Belgium; Japan
Etymology	American geologist R. Pumpelly (1837–1923)

Physical Properties of Pumpellyite

Cleavage	[001] Good, [100] Good
Color	Blue green, olive green, brown
Diaphaneity	Translucent
Fracture	Subconchoidal
Habit	Fibrous, massive — lamellar, spherical
Hardness	5.5
Luster	Vitreous (glassy)
Specific Gravity	3.2
Streak	White
Indicators	Habit, color, luster

Pumpellyite was discovered in Michigan and can also be found in California, Maine, New Jersey, North Carolina, and Pennsylvania.

Pumpellyite variety chlorastrolite. This gem variety, commonly known as "greenstone," occurs as amygdule fillings in basalt. Isle Royale, Lake Superior District, Michigan.

Vesuvianite

Chemical Formula	$Ca_{10}Mg_2Al_4(SiO_4)_5(Si_2O_7)_2(OH)_4$
Environment	Metamorphic limestone rocks and alpine veins
Locality	Mount Vesuvius, Italy; Canada; United States; Mexico; Russia; Norway; Sweden; Switzerland
Etymology	After Mount Vesuvius

Physical Properties of Vesuvianite

Cleavage	[110] Indistinct, [100] Indistinct, [001] Indistinct
Color	Blue, brown, green, yellow, white
Diaphaneity	Subtransparent to subtranslucent
Fracture	Subconchoidal
Habit	Columnar, granular, massive
Hardness	6.5
Luster	Vitreous — resinous
Specific Gravity	3.35–3.45, Average = 3.4
Streak	White
Indicators	Habit, color, cleavage

A blue variety of vesuvianite known as cyprine is found in Franlkin, New Jersey; a massive green variety is found in California and so is called Californite. In addition to these locations, vesuvianite also occurs in Alabama, Alaska, Arizona, Arkansas, Colorado, Connecticut, Georgia, Idaho, Maine, Maryland, Massachusetts, Missouri, Montana, Nevada, New Hampshire, New Mexico, New York, North Carolina, Pennsylvania, Rhode Island, Texas, Utah, Vermont, Virginia, Washington, and Wisconsin.

CYCLOSILICATES

Benitoite

Chemical Formula	$BaTiSi_3O_9$
Environment	Forms in compact veins from hydrothermal solutions in fractures in serpentine

Locality	Benitoite Mine, San Benito, California, United States
Etymology	After Benitoite Mine

Physical Properties of Benitoite

Cleavage	[1011] Poor
Color	Blue, purple, pink, white, colorless
Diaphaneity	Transparent to translucent
Fracture	Conchoidal
Habit	Tabular
Hardness	6–6.5
Luminescence	Fluorescent, short UV = blue
Luster	Vitreous (glassy)
Specific Gravity	3.6
Streak	White
Indicators	Habit, fluorescence, color

Benitoite. This is the state mineral of California. Benitoite Gem Mine, San Benito County, California.

Benitoite's rich color and clarity make it suitable for use as a gemstone but its rarity limits its application. It is found in California, and occasionally in Arkansas.

Beryl

See listing under "Gemstones."

Dioptase

Chemical Formula	$CuSiO_2(OH)_2$
Environment	Secondary mineral in the oxidized zones of copper deposits
Locality	Namibia, Zaire, Russia, United States, Chile
Etymology	Greek *dia*, "through," and *optomai*, "vision"

Physical Properties of Dioptase

Cleavage	[1011] Good
Color	Dark blue green, emerald green, turquoise
Diaphaneity	Transparent to translucent
Fracture	Conchoidal
Habit	Cryptocrystalline, crystalline – coarse, massive
Hardness	5
Luster	Vitreous (glassy)
Specific Gravity	3.28–3.35, Average = 3.31
Streak	Green
Indicators	Habit, color, hardness

Dioptase.

Dioptase is one of few minerals that compares with the deep green color of emerald; however, it is much softer than emerald, and so is rarely used as a gemstone. It is prevalent in Arizona, and is also found in California, Michigan, Nevada, New Jersey, New Mexico, and Pennsylvania.

Cordierite
See listing under "Gemstones."

Dravite
Tourmaline Group. See also listing under "Gemstones."

Chemical Formula	$NaMg_3Al_6(BO_3)_3Si_6O_{18}(OH)_4$
Environment	Contact-metamorphic aureolesin, magnesian, or dolomitic limestones.
Locality	Drava River, Austria; Norway; Sweden; Brazil; Africa; Australia
Etymology	After the Drava River

Physical Properties of Dravite

Cleavage	[1011] Indistinct
Color	Black, green, red, blue, white
Diaphaneity	Transparent to translucent to opaque
Fracture	Subconchoidal
Habit	Columnar, divergent, massive
Hardness	7–7.5
Luster	Vitreous – resinous
Specific Gravity	2.98–3.2, Average = 3.09
Streak	Colorless
Indicators	Habit, triangular cross section, color

Dravite occurs in Alabama, Arizona, California, Colorado, Connecticut, Georgia, Idaho, Maine, Maryland, Massachusetts, Nevada, New Hampshire, New Jersey, New Mexico, New York, North Carolina, Pennsylvania, Rhode Island, Texas, Vermont, Virginia, and Washington.

Schorl
Tourmaline Group. See also listing under "Gemstones."

Chemical Formula	$NaFe_3Al_6(BO_3)_3Si_6O_{18}(OH)_4$
Environment	Granites, pegmatites, gabbros, and hydrothermal veins
Locality	Common worldwide
Etymology	Village of Zschorlau (formerly Schorl), Germany

Schorl.

Physical Properties of Schorl

Cleavage	[1011] Indistinct
Color	Black, brownish black, bluish black
Diaphaneity	Opaque
Fracture	Brittle – Conchoidal
Habit	Acicular, prismatic, striated
Hardness	7.5
Luminescence	Piezoelectric
Luster	Vitreous (glassy)
Specific Gravity	3.1–3.2, Average = 3.15
Streak	Brown
Indicators	Habit, triangular cross section, color

Schorl is the most common member of the tourmaline group, accounting for as much as 95% of all tourmaline. It is found in Alabama, Arizona, California, Colorado, Connecticut, Delaware, Georgia, Idaho, Maine, Maryland, Massachusetts, Michigan, Montana, Nevada, New Hampshire, New Jersey, New Mexico, New York, North Carolina, Pennsylvania, Rhode Island, South Carolina, South Dakota, Texas, Utah, Vermont, Virginia, Washington, Wisconsin, and Wyoming.

INOSILICATES

Enstatite

Chemical Formula	$Mg_2Si_2O_6$
Environment	Mafic magmatic rocks
Locality	Common worldwide
Etymology	Greek *enstates*, "opponent"

Physical Properties of Enstatite

Cleavage	[110] Distinct, [010] Distinct
Color	White, yellowish green, brown, greenish white, gray
Diaphaneity	Translucent to opaque
Fracture	Brittle
Habit	Lamellar, massive – fibrous
Hardness	5.5
Luster	Vitreous – pearly
Specific Gravity	3.1–3.3, Average = 3.2
Streak	Gray
Indicators	Color, habit, hardness, cleavage, luster

Enstatite.

Enstatite forms a series with hypersthene and ferrosilite. A bronze variety with a submetallic luster is called bronzite; an emerald green variety is called chrome enstatite and is sometimes used as a gemstone. Enstatite is found in Alabama, Arizona, California, Colorado, Connecticut, Delaware, Georgia, Hawaii, Idaho, Kansas, Kentucky, Louisiana, Maine, Maryland, Massachusetts, Michigan, Montana, Nevada, New Mexico, New York, North Carolina, Oregon, Pennsylvania, Rhode Island, South Carolina, South Dakota, Texas, Utah, Vermont, Virginia, Washington, Wisconsin, and Wyoming.

Diopside

Chemical Formula	CaMgSi2O6
Environment	Igneous and metamorphic rocks
Locality	Common worldwide
Etymology	Greek *dis*, "two," and *opsis*, "opinion"

Physical Properties of Diopside

Cleavage	[110] Distinct/good
Color	Blue, brown, colorless, green, gray
Diaphaneity	Transparent to translucent
Fracture	Brittle – conchoidal
Habit	Blocky, granular, prismatic

Hardness	6
Luster	Vitreous (glassy)
Specific Gravity	3.25–3.55, Average = 3.4
Streak	White green
Indicators	Habit, color, fracture, cleavage

Diopside occurs in several gemmy varieties: star diopside is rutilated and exhibits asterism; chrome diopside has a rich green color caused by the chromium content; a rare deep blue variety called violan is found in Italy. In the United States, diopside is found in Alaska, Arizona, Arkansas, California, Colorado, Connecticut, Delaware, Georgia, Hawaii, Idaho, Kansas, Kentucky, Louisiana, Maine,

Diopside.

Maryland, Massachusetts, Michigan, Minnesota, Montana, Nevada, New Hampshire, New Jersey, New Mexico, New York, North Carolina, Oklahoma, Oregon, Pennsylvania, Rhode Island, South Carolina, South Dakota, Tennessee, Texas, Utah, Vermont, Virginia, Washington, Wisconsin, and Wyoming.

Hedenbergite

Chemical Formula	$CaFeSi_2O_6$
Environment	Contact metamorphic rocks and skarns
Locality	North America, Europe, China, Greenland, Japan
Etymology	Swedish mineralogist M.A.L. Hedenberg

Physical Properties of Hedenbergite

Cleavage	[110] Distinct/good
Color	Brownish green, gray green, grayish black, dark green, black
Diaphaneity	Transparent to translucent to opaque
Fracture	Brittle – conchoidal
Habit	Crystalline – fine, granular, lamellar
Hardness	5–6
Luster	Vitreous – pearly
Specific Gravity	3.55
Streak	White green
Indicators	Habit, color, fracture, cleavage

Hedenbergite. Light colored limestone altered to irregular dark mass of hedenbergite (pyroxene) by contact metamorphism near Hanover, Grant County, New Mexico.

Good crystals of hedenbergite are rare, but its tendency to form clusters of radiating prisms makes it highly prized for mineral collections. It is found in is found in Alabama, Alaska, Arizona, Arkansas, California, Colorado, Connecticut, Idaho, Massachusetts, Michigan,

Nevada, New Hampshire, New Jersey, New Mexico, New York, North Carolina, Oregon, South Dakota, Tennessee, Texas, Utah, Vermont, Virginia, Washington, and Wisconsin.

Augite

Chemical Formula	$(Ca,Na)(Mg,Fe,Al,Ti)$ $(Al,Si)_2O_6$
Environment	Within basic igneous and metamorphic rocks
Locality	Common worldwide
Etymology	Greek *auge*, "luster"

Augite.

Physical Properties of Augite

Cleavage	[110] Perfect, [010] Indistinct
Color	Brown green, green, light brown, dark brown, black
Diaphaneity	Translucent to opaque
Fracture	Brittle – conchoidal
Habit	Columnar, granular, massive – fibrous
Hardness	5–6.5
Luster	Vitreous – resinous
Specific Gravity	3.2–3.6, Average = 3.4
Streak	Greenish gray
Indicators	Habit, color, parting, cleavage

Augite is found in Alabama, Arizona, Arkansas, California, Colorado, Connecticut, Georgia, Idaho, Indiana, Kansas, Louisiana, Maine, Massachusetts, Michigan, Minnesota, Missouri, Montana, Nevada, New Hampshire, New Jersey, New Mexico, New York, North Carolina, Oklahoma, Oregon, Pennsylvania, Rhode Island, South Carolina, South Dakota, Tennessee, Texas, Utah, Vermont, Virginia, Washington, West Virginia, and Wisconsin.

Jadeite   *See listing under "Gemstones."*

Aegirine

Chemical Formula	$NaFe^{3+}Si_2O_6$
Environment	In alkali igneous nepheline syenites, pegmatites, and carbonatites
Locality	Norway, Greenland, Canada, United States, Russia, Nigeria
Etymology	After the Teutonic god of the sea

Physical Properties of Aegirine

Cleavage	[110] Distinct/good
Color	Green, greenish black, reddish brown, black
Diaphaneity	Subtransparent to translucent to opaque
Fracture	Brittle
Habit	Acicular

Hardness	6–6.5
Luster	Vitreous – resinous
Specific Gravity	3.5–3.54, Average = 3.52
Streak	Yellowish gray
Indicators	Habit, density, cleavage, color, hardness

Aegirine forms a series with augite. Its tall crystals with steep pyramidal tops are highly prized by collectors. It is found in Alaska, Arizona, Arkansas, California, Colorado, Illinois, Indiana, Kansas, Louisiana, Maine, Massachusetts, Michigan, Minnesota, Montana, Nevada, New Hampshire, New Jersey, New Mexico, North Carolina, Oklahoma, Oregon, Rhode Island, South Dakota, Tennessee, Texas, Utah, Vermont, Virginia, Washington, and Wisconsin.

Spodumene

Chemical Formula	LiAlSi$_2$O$_6$
Environment	Lithium-rich granitic pegmatites
Locality	United States, Afghanistan, Pakistan, Brazil, Madagascar
Etymology	Greek *spodoumenos,* "burnt to ash" (from its ashy color)

Physical Properties of Spodumene

Cleavage	[110] Perfect, [100] Good
Color	Grayish white, pink, violet, emerald green, yellow
Diaphaneity	Transparent to translucent
Fracture	Splintery
Habit	Bladed, prismatic
Hardness	6.5–7
Luster	Vitreous (glassy)
Specific Gravity	3.1–3.2, Average = 3.15
Streak	White
Indicators	Habit, color, fracture, cleavage

Spodumene. Pictured are five stones, all of the kunzite variety. They sold at auction in early 2008 for $1,150.

Spodumene is an ore of lithium. Its two gem varieties, pink to lilac kunzite and green hiddenite, are pleochroic and highly sought after by collectors. Spodumene is found in Alabama, Arizona, California, Colorado, Connecticut, Georgia, Maine, Massachusetts, Michigan, New Hampshire, New Mexico, New York, North Carolina, South Dakota, Utah, Virginia, Wisconsin, and Wyoming.

Shattuckite

Chemical Formula	Cu$_5$(SiO$_3$)$_4$(OH)$_2$
Environment	Occurs as an alteration of malachite
Locality	Shattuck mine, Arizona, United States; Namibia; Zaire
Etymology	After Shattuck mine, Arizona

Physical Properties of Shattuckite

Cleavage	[010] Perfect, [100] Perfect
Color	Blue, dark blue, green
Diaphaneity	Transparent to translucent
Fracture	Uneven
Habit	Fibrous; granular
Hardness	3.5
Luster	Vitreous (glassy)
Specific Gravity	3.8
Streak	Pale blue
Indicators	Color, habit, density

Shattuckite is very rare, and is a pseudomorph of malachite. It was discovered in Arizona, where it is most prevalent; it is also found in Nevada and New Mexico.

Shattuckite. Morenci Mine, Greenlee County, Arizona.

Wollastonite

Chemical Formula	CaSiO₃
Environment	High-temperature metamorphic siliceous carbonates, igneous rocks, skarn
Locality	China, Canada, United States, United Kingdom, Sweden, Japan
Etymology	English mineralogist and chemist W.H. Wollaston (1766–1828)

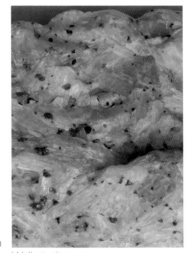

Physical Properties of Wollastonite

Cleavage	[100] Perfect, [102] Good, [001] Good
Color	White, yellow, gray, red, brown
Diaphaneity	Subtransparent to translucent
Fracture	Splintery
Habit	Massive – fibrous, radial
Hardness	5
Luster	Vitreous – silky
Specific Gravity	2.8–2.9, Average = 2.84
Streak	White
Indicators	Habit, cleavage, hardness

Wollastonite.

Wollastonite is used in ceramics, plastics, and paint because of its high brightness and whiteness. It is found in Arizona, Arkansas, California, Colorado, Connecticut, Idaho, Iowa, Kansas, Maine, Massachusetts, Michigan, Montana, Nevada, New Jersey, New

Mexico, New York, North Carolina, Oregon, Pennsylvania, South Dakota, Texas, Utah, Virginia, Washington, and Wisconsin.

Pectolite

Chemical Formula	$NaCa_2Si_3O_8(OH)$
Environment	Within basaltic rocks
Locality	United States, United Kingdom, Italy, Canada, Russia, Sweden, Norway
Etymology	Greek *pektos*, "compacted," and *lithos*, "stone"

Physical Properties of Pectolite

Cleavage	[001] Perfect, [100] Perfect
Color	White, gray, light pink, light green
Diaphaneity	Subtranslucent to translucent to opaque
Fracture	Splintery
Habit	Acicular, globular, radial
Hardness	5
Luminescence	Triboluminescent.
Luster	Vitreous – silky
Specific Gravity	2.86
Streak	White
Indicators	Habit, brittleness, cleavage

Pectolite is common worldwide. In the United States it is found in Arizona, Arkansas, California, Connecticut, Kansas, Maine, Massachusetts, Nevada, New Jersey, New Mexico, New York, Pennsylvania, Virginia, Washington, Wisconsin, and Wyoming.

Rhodonite   *See listing under "Gemstones."*

Babingtonite

Chemical Formula	$Ca_2(Fe++,Mn)Fe+++Si_5O_{14}$ (OH)
Environment	Associated with zeolites
Locality	India, United Kingdom, Italy, United States, Sweden, Poland
Etymology	Irish physicist and mineralogist W. Babington (1757–1833)

Physical Properties of Babingtonite

Cleavage	[100] Perfect, [001] Perfect
Color	Brownish black, greenish black, black
Diaphaneity	Transparent to Translucent
Fracture	Conchoidal
Habit	Drusy, radial
Hardness	5.5–6
Luster	Vitreous (glassy)
Specific Gravity	3.4
Streak	Brown
Indicators	Habit, color, luster

Babington. These large black crystals of babingtonite, at up to 2.5 cm, are as large as they come. Hongxi, Meigu, Sichuan Province, China.

Babingtonite occurs in Arizona, Connecticut, Maine, Massachusetts, Michigan, New Hampshire, New Jersey, New York, North Carolina, Pennsylvania, Rhode Island, and Virginia.

Tremolite   *See also listing for nephrite under "Gemstones."*

Chemical Formula	$Ca_2Mg_5Si_8O_{22}(OH)_2$
Environment	Occurs through contact metamorphism of calcium-rich rocks
Locality	Tremola Valley, Switzerland; Italy; Finland; France; Tanzania; Canada; United States
Etymology	After Tremola Valley, Switzerland

Physical Properties of Tremolite

Cleavage	[110] Perfect, [010] Distinct
Color	Brown, colorless, gray, white, light green
Diaphaneity	Transparent to translucent
Fracture	Subconchoidal
Habit	Columnar, massive – fibrous, massive – granular
Hardness	5–6
Luminescence	Fluorescent, short UV = yellow, long UV = pink
Luster	Vitreous – pearly
Specific Gravity	2.9–3.2, Average = 3.05
Streak	White
Indicators	Fibrousness, color, cleavage, habit, hardness

Tremolite is perhaps best known for its fibrous variety, asbestos. A green variety is called nephrite, which is one of two minerals (the other being jadeite) that are commonly called jade, a popular gemstone for carving. Tremolite occurs in Alabama, Arizona, Arkansas, California, Colorado, Delaware, Georgia, Idaho, Maine, Maryland, Massachusetts, Michigan, Missouri, Montana, Nevada, New Hampshire, New Jersey, New Mexico, New York, North Carolina, Oregon, Rhode Island, South Carolina, South Dakota, Tennessee, Texas, Utah, Vermont, Virginia, Washington, Wisconsin, and Wyoming.

Actinolite   *See also listing for nephrite under "Gemstones."*

Chemical Formula	$Ca_2(Mg,Fe)_5Si_8O_{22}(OH)_2$
Environment	Common in metamorphic rocks
Locality	Common worldwide
Etymology	Greek *aktinos*, "ray" (from its fibrous nature)

Physical Properties of Actinolite

Cleavage	[110] Perfect, [110] Perfect
Color	Green, Green black, Gray green, Black.
Diaphaneity	Translucent to transparent
Fracture	Splintery
Habit	Bladed, Fibrous, Radial
Hardness	5.5
Luster	Vitreous (glassy)
Specific Gravity	2.98–3.1, Average = 3.04

Actinolite. This fibrous spray of actinolite grows alongside phlogopite crystals.

Streak	White
Indicators	Toughness, fibrousness, color, habit, hardness

Actinolite is part of a series with tremolite; as with tremolite, a green variety of actinolite is called nephrite, more commonly known as jade. Actinolite occurs in Alabama, Alaska, Arizona, Arkansas, California, Colorado, Connecticut, Georgia, Idaho, Maine, Maryland, Massachusetts, Michigan, Missouri, Montana, Nebraska, Nevada, New Hampshire, New Jersey, New Mexico, New York, North Carolina, Oregon, Pennsylvania, Rhode Island, South Dakota, Tennessee, Texas, Utah, Vermont, Virginia, Washington, Wisconsin, and Wyoming.

Magnesiohornblende   *Hornblende series*

Chemical Formula	$Ca_2[Mg_2(Al,Fe^{3+})]Si_7AlO_{22}(OH)_2$
Environment	Common in igneous and metamorphic rocks
Locality	Common worldwide
Etymology	From its composition and its relationship to hornblende

Hornblende.

Physical Properties of Magnesiohornblende

Cleavage	[110] Perfect
Color	Brown, green, greenish brown, greenish black, dark green
Diaphaneity	Translucent to opaque
Fracture	Subconchoidal
Habit	Columnar, massive – fibrous, massive – granular
Hardness	5–6
Luster	Vitreous – pearly
Specific Gravity	3–3.47, Average = 3.23
Streak	White
Indicators	Habit, color, cleavage

Hornblendes are not often included in specimen collections, because they tend be dark and uninteresting, and rarely form good crystals. Magnesiohornblende is found in Arizona, Colorado, Maine, Massachusetts, Montana, Nevada, New Jersey, New Mexico, New York, North Carolina, Oregon, Rhode Island, and Vermont.

Ferrohornblende   *Hornblende series*

Chemical Formula	$Ca_2[Fe^{4+}(Al,Fe^{3+})]Si_7AlO_{22}(OH)_2$
Environment	Within granites, granodiorites, metabasalts, and schists; forms a series with magnesiohornblende
Locality	Common worldwide
Etymology	After its composition and its relationship to hornblende

Physical Properties of Ferrohornblende

Cleavage	[110] Perfect
Color	Brown, green, greenish brown, black
Diaphaneity	Translucent to opaque
Fracture	Subconchoidal
Habit	Columnar, massive – fibrous, massive – granular
Hardness	5–6
Luster	Vitreous – pearly
Specific Gravity	3–3.47, Average = 3.23
Streak	White
Indicators	Habit, color, cleavage

Ferrohornblende is found in Arizona, Arkansas, Colorado, Connecticut, Georgia, Maine, Maryland, Massachusetts, Michigan, Nevada, New Jersey, New Mexico, New York, Rhode Island, Vermont, Virginia, Washington, and Wisconsin.

Pargasite

Chemical Formula	$NaCa_2(Mg,Fe)_4Al(Si_6Al_2)O_{22}(OH)_2$
Environment	Occurs in metamorphic rocks
Locality	Pargas, Finland; Norway; Sweden; Greenland; Canada; United States; Pakistan
Etymology	After Pargas, Finland

Physical Properties of Pargasite

Cleavage	[110] Perfect, [010] Perfect
Color	Bluish green, brown, grayish black, light brown, dark green
Diaphaneity	Transparent to translucent
Fracture	Brittle – uneven
Habit	Tabular
Hardness	6
Luster	Vitreous (glassy)
Specific Gravity	3.069–3.181, Average = 3.12
Streak	White
Indicators	Habit, fracture, luster

Pargasite occurs in Arizona, California, Colorado, Connecticut, Maine, Maryland, Massachusetts, Michigan, Nevada, New Hampshire, New Jersey, New Mexico, New York, North Carolina, Rhode Island, South Dakota, Utah, Virginia, and Washington.

Glaucophane

Chemical Formula	$Na_2(Mg_3Al_2)Si_8O_{22}(OH)_2$
Environment	Formed in high-temperature and -pressure metamorphic subduction zones
Locality	Common worldwide
Etymology	Greek *glaukos*, "blue," and *fanos*, "appearing"

Physical Properties of Glaucophane

Cleavage	[110] Good, [001] Good
Color	Gray, bluish black, lavender blue, azure blue
Diaphaneity	Translucent
Fracture	Brittle – conchoidal
Habit	Columnar, Granular, massive – fibrous
Hardness	6–6.5
Luster	Vitreous – pearly
Specific Gravity	3–3.15, Average = 3.07
Streak	Grayish blue
Indicators	Habit, color, luster

Glaucophane is found in California, Colorado, Idaho, Massachusetts, New York, South Dakota, Vermont, and Washington.

Glaucophane.

Riebeckite

Chemical Formula	$Na_2Fe_3^{2+}Fe_2^{3+}Si_8O_{22}(OH)_2$
Environment	Within magmatic metamorphic rocks
Locality	Yemen, Zimbabwe, South Africa, Madagascar, Kazakhstan, Ukraine, Norway, Greenland
Etymology	German explorer Emil Riebeck (1853–1885)

Physical Properties of Riebeckite

Cleavage	[110] Perfect
Color	Blue, black, dark green
Diaphaneity	Translucent to subtranslucent to opaque
Fracture	Brittle – uneven
Habit	Fibrous, massive – fibrous, striated
Hardness	4
Luster	Vitreous – silky
Specific Gravity	3.4
Streak	Greenish brown
Indicators	Habit, color, streak, cleavage, hardness

Riebeckite occurs in Alaska, Arizona, Arkansas, California, Colorado, Idaho, Maine, Maryland, Massachusetts, Michigan, Missouri, Montana, Nevada, New Hampshire, New Jersey, New Mexico, New York, North Carolina, Oklahoma, Pennsylvania, Rhode Island, South Carolina, Texas, Utah, Virginia, and Washington.

Inesite

Chemical Formula	$Ca_2Mn_7Si_{10}O_{28}(OH)_2 \cdot 5H_2O$
Environment	Within hydrothermally altered manganese-rich rocks
Locality	Australia, United States, Mexico, Indonesia, Sweden
Etymology	Greek ines, "flesh fibers"

Physical Properties of Inesite

Cleavage	[010] Perfect, [100] Good
Color	Brown, brown, pink, orange
Diaphaneity	Translucent
Fracture	Brittle – uneven
Habit	Massive – fibrous, radial, spherical
Hardness	6
Luster	Vitreous (glassy)
Specific Gravity	3.029–3.1, Average = 3.06
Streak	White
Indicators	Habit, color, luster

Inesite is uncommon, but its very attractive rose-colored chisel-shaped crystals are popular for collections when they can be found. In the United States it occurs only in California, Colorado, and Washington.

Inesite. Fengjashan Mine, Huangshi Prefecture, Hubei Province, China.

Neptunite

Chemical Formula	$KNa_2Li(Fe^{2+},Mn)_2Ti_2Si_8O_{24}$
Environment	Within natrolite embedded in serpentinite rock
Locality	California and New Mexico, United States; Greenland; Russia
Etymology	After Neptune, Roman god of the sea (because it was found with aegirine, named for his Scandinavian counterpart)

Physical Properties of Neptunite

Cleavage	[110] Good
Color	Black, red
Diaphaneity	Translucent
Fracture	Conchoidal
Habit	Crystalline – coarse, prismatic, tabular
Hardness	5–6
Luster	Vitreous (glassy)
Specific Gravity	3.23
Streak	Brown
Indicators	Habit, streak, color, cleavage

Neptunite.

Neptunite is found in the United States only in California (some of the best specimens come from San Benito County), New Mexico, and North Carolina.

PHYLLOSILICATES
Kaolinite

Chemical Formula	$Al_2Si_2O_5(OH)_4$
Environment	Clay beds formed by decomposition of feldspars
Locality	Kao-Ling, China; worldwide
Etymology	After Kao-Ling, China

Kaolinite. Clinton Mine, Lawrence County, South Dakata.

Physical Properties of Kaolinite

Cleavage	[001] Perfect
Color	White, brownish white, grayish white, yellowish white, grayish green
Diaphaneity	Transparent to translucent
Fracture	Earthy
Habit	Earthy
Hardness	1.5–2
Luster	Earthy (dull)
Specific Gravity	2.6
Streak	White
Indicators	Habit, hardness, color, luster, clay-like properties

Kaolinite is a very common mineral; it is used primarily in the paper industry to form the glossy coating on paper for magazines, etc. It occurs in every state except Delaware, Hawaii, Kansas, and West Virginia.

SERPENTINE GROUP   *See listing under "Gemstones."*

Pyrophyllite

Chemical Formula	$Al_2Si_4O_{10}(OH)_2$
Environment	Hydrothermal veins and in bedded deposits in schistose rocks
Locality	United States, Belgium, China, Switzerland, Mexico, Brazil, Sweden, Russia
Etymology	Greek *pyro*, "fire," and *philos*, "loving"

Physical Properties of Pyrophyllite

Cleavage	[001] Perfect
Color	Brown green, brownish yellow, greenish, gray green, gray white
Diaphaneity	Translucent to opaque
Fracture	Flexible, earthy
Hardness	1.5–2
Luminescence	Fluorescent
Luster	Pearly
Specific Gravity	2.8–2.9, Average = 2.84
Streak	White
Indicators	habit, color, cleavage, hardness, greasy feel

Pyrophyllite can be either monoclinic or triclinic; the monoclinic variety is isomorphous with talc, and is sometimes used for sculpture. Pyrophyllite is found in Arizona, Arkansas, California, Colorado, Georgia, Maine, Maryland, Michigan, Missouri, Montana, Nevada, New Mexico, New York, North Carolina, Pennsylvania, South Carolina, Texas, Utah, Vermont, Virginia, and Wisconsin.

Talc

Chemical Formula	$Mg_3Si_4O_{10}(OH)_2$
Environment	Hydrothermal alteration of non-aluminous mafic rocks and low-temperature metamorphism of silicaceous dolomites
Locality	Common worldwide
Etymology	Arabic *talq*, "pure"

Physical Properties of Talc

Cleavage	[001] Perfect
Color	Pale green, white, gray white, yellowish white, brownish white
Diaphaneity	Translucent
Fracture	Uneven
Habit	Foliated, massive, scaly
Hardness	1
Luminescence	Fluorescent
Luster	Vitreous – pearly
Specific Gravity	2.7–2.8, Average = 2.75
Streak	White
Indicators	Hardness, color, soapy feel, luster

Talc.

Talc is one of the softest minerals; it is commonly sold in loose form as talcum powder, and has many important industrial and commercial uses. It is very common and, in the United States, is found in Alabama, Arizona, Arkansas, California, Colorado, Connecticut, Georgia, Idaho, Maine, Maryland, Massachusetts, Michigan, Missouri, Montana, Nevada, New Hampshire, New Mexico, New York, North Carolina, Oregon, Pennsylvania, Rhode Island, South Carolina, South Dakota, Tennessee, Texas, Utah, Vermont, Virginia, Washington, Wisconsin, and Wyoming.

Muscovite   *Mica Group*

Chemical Formula	$KAl_2(Si_3Al)O_{10}(OH,F)_2$
Environment	Common as a primary constituent of many types of rocks
Locality	Common worldwide
Etymology	After Muscovy glass (from the Russian province of Muscovy)

Physical Properties of Muscovite

Cleavage	[001] Perfect
Color	White, gray, silver white, brownish white, greenish white

Diaphaneity	Transparent to translucent
Fracture	Brittle – sectile
Habit	Foliated, massive – lamellar, micaceous
Hardness	2–2.5
Luster	Vitreous (glassy)
Specific Gravity	2.77–2.88, Average = 2.82
Streak	White
Indicators	Habit, cleavage, elastic sheets, color

Muscovite is the most common mica. It occurs in Alabama, Alaska, Arizona, Arkansas, California, Colorado, Connecticut, Delaware, Georgia, Idaho, Maine, Maryland, Massachusetts, Michigan, Minnesota, Missouri, Montana, Nevada, New Hampshire, New Mexico, New York, North Carolina, Oregon, Pennsylvania, Rhode Island, South Carolina, South Dakota, Tennessee, Texas, Utah, Vermont, Virginia, Washington, West Virginia, Wisconsin, and Wyoming.

Muscovite. This specimen shows a well formed, pseudo-otahedral crystal of medium orange scheelite on a matrix of coarse grained muscovite.

Phlogopite   *Mica Group*

Chemical Formula	$KMg_3AlSi_3O_{10}(F,OH)_2$
Environment	Common in contact and regional metamorphic limestones and dolomites; also in ultramafic igneous rocks
Locality	St. Lawrence County, at Edwards, New York, United States
Etymology	Greek *flogopos*, "resembling fire"

Physical Properties of Phlogopite

Cleavage	[001] Perfect
Color	Brown, gray, green, yellow, reddish brown
Diaphaneity	Transparent to translucent
Fracture	Uneven
Habit	Lamellar, micaceous, scaly
Hardness	2–2.5
Luster	Vitreous – pearly
Specific Gravity	2.7–2.9, Average = 2.8
Streak	White
Indicators	Habit, color, cleavage, elastic sheets

Phlogopite. Vohitrosy, Madagascar.

Phlogopite is less common than muscovite mica, and is relatively little known. It occurs in Alabama, Arizona, Arkansas, California, Colorado, Connecticut, Georgia, Idaho, Kansas, Kentucky, Louisiana, Maryland, Massachusetts, Michigan, Missouri, Montana, Nebraska, Nevada, New Hampshire, New Mexico, New York, North Carolina, Oregon, Pennsylvania, Rhode Island, South Carolina, South Dakota, Texas, Utah, Vermont, Virginia, Washington, Wisconsin, and Wyoming.

Biotite

Mica Group. Biotite is now a group name for phlogopite, siderophyllite, and eastonite.

Chemical Formula	$K(Mg,Fe)_3(AlSi_3O_{10})(OH,F)_2$
Environment	Common in granitic rocks
Locality	Common worldwide
Etymology	French physicist Jean Baptiste Biot (1774–1862)

Biotite.

Physical Properties of Biotite

Cleavage	[001] Perfect
Color	Dark brown, greenish brown, blackish brown, yellow, white
Diaphaneity	Transparent to translucent to opaque
Fracture	Uneven
Habit	Lamellar, micaceous, pseudo hexagonal
Hardness	2.5–3
Luster	Vitreous – pearly
Specific Gravity	2.8–3.4, Average = 3.09
Streak	Gray
Indicators	Habit, color, cleavage, elastic sheets

Biotite, unlike other micas, has little industrial value, and is mined primarily for collectors; it is also a useful index mineral. It occurs in Alabama, Arizona, Arkansas, California, Colorado, Connecticut, Georgia, Idaho, Kansas, Kentucky, Louisiana, Maryland, Massachusetts, Michigan, Missouri, Montana, Nebraska, Nevada, New Hampshire, New Mexico, New York, North Carolina, Oregon, Pennsylvania, Rhode Island, South Carolina, South Dakota, Texas, Utah, Vermont, Virginia, Washington, Wisconsin, and Wyoming.

Lepidolite

Mica Group. Lepidolite is now a series name.

Chemical Formula	$K(Li,Al)_3(Si,Al)_4O_{10}(F,OH)_2$
Environment	Lithium-bearing pegmatites
Locality	Brazil, Russia, United States, Afghanistan, Algeria, Madagascar, Namibia
Etymology	Greek *lepidion*, "scale," and *lithos*, "stone"

Physical Properties of Lepidolite

Cleavage	[001] Perfect
Color	Colorless, gray white, lilac, yellowish, white

Diaphaneity	Translucent
Fracture	Uneven
Habit	Foliated, massive, platy
Hardness	2.5–3
Luster	Vitreous – pearly
Specific Gravity	2.8–2.9, Average = 2.84
Streak	White
Indicators	Habit, color, cleavage, elastic sheets

Lepidolite.

Lepidolite is an unusual rose or lilac-colored mica; it is also a field term loosely applied to any light-colored lithium-bearing mica whose species has not yet been determined. It occurs in Alabama, Arizona, California, Colorado, Connecticut, Maine, Massachusetts, Nevada, New Hampshire, New Mexico, North Carolina, Rhode Island, South Carolina, Texas, Virginia, Washington, Wisconsin, and Wyoming.

Clinochlore   *Chlorite Group*

Chemical Formula	$(Mg,Fe)_5Al(Si_3Al)O_{10}(OH)_8$
Environment	Occurs through hydrothermal, contact, and regional metamorphism of mafic minerals
Locality	Common worldwide
Etymology	Greek *klino,* "oblique," and *chloros,* "green"

Physical Properties of Clinochlore

Cleavage	[001] Perfect
Color	Blackish green, bluish green, white, yellowish green, olive green
Diaphaneity	Transparent to translucent
Fracture	Uneven
Habit	Granular, massive – fibrous, pseudo hexagonal
Hardness	2–2.5
Luster	Vitreous – pearly
Specific Gravity	2.55–2.75, Average = 2.65
Streak	White
Indicators	Habit, hardness, color, cleavage

Clinochlore is found in in Arizona, California, Colorado, Connecticut, Georgia, Idaho, Maine, Maryland, Massachusetts, Michigan, Nevada, New Hampshire, New Jersey, New Mexico, New York, North Carolina, Oregon, Pennsylvania, Rhode Island, South Dakota, Utah, Texas, Vermont, Virginia, Washington, and Wyoming.

Prehnite

Chemical Formula	$Ca_2Al_2Si_3O_{10}(OH)_2$
Environment	A low-grade secondary metamorphic mineral in hydrothermally altered or volcanic rocks
Locality	South Africa, United States, Canada, Germany, Austria, United Kingdom, France, Italy, Norway, Sweden, China
Etymology	Dutch colonel H. von Prehn (1733–1785)

Physical Properties of Prehnite

Cleavage	[001] Distinct
Color	Colorless, gray, yellow, yellow green, white
Diaphaneity	Subtransparent to translucent
Fracture	Brittle
Habit	Globular, reniform, stalactitic
Hardness	6–6.5
Luster	Vitreous – pearly
Specific Gravity	2.8–2.95, Average = 2.87
Streak	Colorless
Indicators	Habit, color, cleavage, hardness

Prehnite.

Prehnite occurs in Alabama, Alaska, Arizona, Arkansas, California, Colorado, Connecticut, Georgia, Idaho, Iowa, Maine, Maryland, Massachusetts, Michigan, Minnesota, Montana, Nevada, New Hampshire, New Jersey, New Mexico, New York, North Carolina, Oklahoma, Oregon, Pennsylvania, Rhode Island, Tennessee, Texas, Utah, Vermont, Virginia, Washington, and Wisconsin.

Apophyllite

Now a group name for fluorapophyllite, hydroxypophyllite, and natropophyllite.

Chemical Formula	$KCa_4(Si_4O_{10})_2F \cdot 8H_2O$
Environment	A secondary mineral in basaltic or granitic cavities
Locality	Pune, India; United States; Brazil; Germany; Denmark; Italy; Sweden; Japan
Etymology	Greek *apophylliso*, "it flakes off"

Physical Properties of Apophyllite

Cleavage	[001] Perfect
Color	White, pink, green, yellow, violet
Diaphaneity	Transparent to translucent
Fracture	Uneven
Habit	Crystalline – coarse, massive, pseudo cubic
Hardness	4–5
Luster	Vitreous – pearly
Specific Gravity	2.3–2.4, Average = 2.34
Streak	White
Indicators	Habit, cleavage, luster

Apophyllite.

Apophyllites are fairly common, and are popular specimens for collections. They are found in Arizona, Arkansas, California, Colorado, Connecticut, Georgia, Idaho, Maine, Massachusetts, Michigan, Montana, Nevada, New Jersey, New Mexico, New York, North Carolina, Oregon, Pennsylvania, Texas, Utah, Virginia, Washington, and Wisconsin.

Chrysocolla

Chemical Formula	$(Cu,Al)_2H_2Si_2O_5(OH)_4$ · $n(H2O)$
Environment	Oxidized zones of copper deposits
Locality	Worldwide
Etymology	Greek *chrysos*, "gold," and *kolla*, "glue" (from the name of the material used to solder gold)

Physical Properties of Chrysocolla

Cleavage	None
Color	Green; bluish green; blue; blackish blue; brown
Diaphaneity	Translucent to opaque
Fracture	Brittle – sectile
Habit	Botryoidal, earthy, stalactitic
Hardness	2.5–3.5
Luster	Vitreous – dull
Specific Gravity	1.9–2.4, Average = 2.15
Streak	Light green
Indicators	Lack of crystals, color, fracture, density, hardness

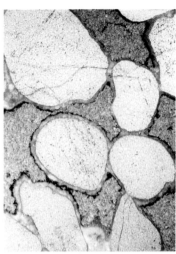

Chrysocolla. This Navajo sandstone is cemented by malachite. Its remaining pores are filled with cuprite and chrysocolla. Copper Mine Trading Post, Coconino County, Arizona.

Chrysocolla has a unique blue-green color from its copper content. It occurs in Alabama, Alaska, Arizona, Arkansas, California, Colorado, Connecticut, Georgia, Idaho, Maine, Massachusetts, Michigan, Minnesota, Missouri, Montana, Nevada, New Jersey, New Mexico, New York, North Carolina, Oklahoma, Oregon, Pennsylvania, Rhode Island, South Dakota, Tennessee, Texas, Utah, Vermont, Virginia, Washington, Wisconsin, and Wyoming.

TECTOSILICATES

Quartz   *See also listing under "Gemstones."*

Chemical Formula	SiO_2
Environment	Common in sedimentary, metamorphic, and igneous rocks
Locality	Very common mineral found worldwide
Etymology	German *quarz*, of uncertain origin

Physical Properties of Quartz

Cleavage	[0110] Indistinct
Color	Brown, colorless, violet, gray, yellow
Diaphaneity	Transparent
Fracture	Conchoidal
Habit	Crystalline – coarse, crystalline – fine, drusy
Hardness	7
Luminescence	Triboluminescent
Luster	Vitreous (glassy)
Specific Gravity	2.6–2.65, Average = 2.62

Streak	White
Indicators	Commonness, transparency, habit, hardness

Quartz is the second most common mineral on Earth, after feldspar. It has many industrial and commercial uses, and many varieties are prized as gemstones. It is found in every U.S. state.

Flint. Flint is a sedimentary cryptocrystalline form of quartz that was one of the primary materials used for toolmaking during the Stone Age. When struck against steel, flint produces sparks useful for starting fires. It was used to ignite the gunpowder in early flintlock rifles. It is also a common building material, especially in parts of England.

Quartz (var. amethyst). Near Amatitlan, Guerrero, Mexico.

Coesite

Chemical Formula	SiO_2
Environment	High-temperature and high-pressure polymorph of quartz; occurs naturally only in meteor craters and ultra-high-pressure kimberlite and eclogite rocks
Locality	Meteor Crater, Arizona, United States, and other meteorite impact craters worldwide
Etymology	American chemist Loring Coes Jr. (1915–1973), who first synthesized it

Physical Properties of Coesite

Cleavage	None
Color	Colorless
Diaphaneity	Transparent
Fracture	Conchoidal
Habit	Inclusions
Hardness	7.5
Luster	Vitreous (glassy)
Specific Gravity	2.93
Streak	White
Indicators	Environment, density

Coesite is a polymorph of quartz. It is metastable at normal surface temeperatures, converting to quartz; it occurs naturally only in meteor craters, in Arizona, Colorado, Indiana, and Oklahoma.

Opal
See listing under "Gemstones."

Orthoclase
See also listing for adularia under "Gemstones."

Chemical Formula	$KAlSi_3O_8$
Environment	Common in granites, syentites, and metamorphic rocks
Locality	Common worldwide
Etymology	Greek *orthos*, "right," and *kalo*, "I cleave" (from its right angle of good cleavage)

Physical Properties of Orthoclase

Cleavage	[001] Perfect, [010] Good
Color	Colorless, greenish, grayish yellow, white; pink
Diaphaneity	Transparent to translucent
Fracture	Uneven
Habit	Blocky, massive – granular, prismatic
Hardness	6
Luster	Vitreous (glassy)
Specific Gravity	2.56
Streak	White
Indicators	Color, cleavage, common occurrence

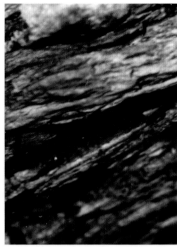

Orthoclase. Crystals of orthoclase deposited in the metashale of the Rome formation, 1.2 miles west of the Kelly mine, circa 1944. Bartow County, Georgia.

Orthoclase is an alkali feldspar and, as with all feldspars, commonly forms twins. It is the state gem of Florida. It is found in in Alabama, Alaska, Arizona, Arkansas, California, Colorado, Connecticut, Delaware, Georgia, Idaho, Iowa, Maine, Maryland, Massachusetts, Michigan, Minnesota, Missouri, Montana, Nevada, New Hampshire, New Jersey, New Mexico, New York, North Carolina, North Dakota, Oklahoma, Pennsylvania, Rhode Island, South Carolina, South Dakota, Tennessee, Texas, Utah, Vermont, Virginia, Washington, Wisconsin, and Wyoming.

Microcline   *See also listing for amazonite under "Gemstones."*

Chemical Formula	$KAlSi_3O_8$
Environment	Granitic pegmatites; hydrothermal, metamorphic, and plutonic felsic rocks
Locality	Common worldwide
Etymology	Greek *mikron*, "little," and *klinein*, "to stoop"

Physical Properties of Microcline

Cleavage	[001] Perfect, [010] Good
Color	Bluish green, green, gray, grayish yellow, yellowish
Diaphaneity	Translucent to transparent
Fracture	Uneven
Habit	Blocky, crystalline – coarse, prismatic
Hardness	6
Luster	Vitreous (glassy)
Specific Gravity	2.56
Streak	White
Indicators	Common occurrence, twinning, color, luster

Microcline is a triclinic form of orthoclase. It is found in Alabama, Arizona, Arkansas, California, Colorado, Connecticut, Delaware, Georgia, Idaho, Maine, Maryland,

Massachusetts, Michigan, Minnesota, Missouri, Montana, Nevada, New Hampshire, New Jersey, New Mexico, New York, North Carolina, Oklahoma, Pennsylvania, Rhode Island, South Carolina, South Dakota, Texas, Utah, Vermont, Virginia, Washington, Wisconsin, and Wyoming.

Plagioclase

Plagioclase Group (group name for sodium and calcium feldspars)

Chemical Formula	$(Na,Ca)(Si,Al)_4O_8$
Environment	Common in igneous and metamorphic rocks
Locality	Common worldwide
Etymology	Greek *plagios*, "oblique," and *klao*, "I cleave" (from its obtuse angles of good cleavage)

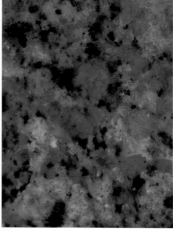

Plagioclase. Rock surface chemically etched and stained to differentiate potassium feldspar (orange-yellow), plagioclase (red), and quartz (uncolored). El Capitan Granite, Yosemite National Park, California.

Physical Properties of Plagioclase

Cleavage	[001] Good, [010] Good
Color	White, gray, bluish white, reddish white, greenish white
Diaphaneity	Transparent to translucent
Fracture	Brittle
Habit	Massive – granular
Hardness	6–6.5
Luster	Vitreous (glassy)
Specific Gravity	2.61–2.76, Average = 2.68
Streak	White
Indicators	Twinning

Albite

Plagioclase Group. See also listing under "Gemstones."

Chemical Formula	$NaAlSi_3O_8$
Environment	Primary constituent of pegmatitic igneous and magmatic rocks
Locality	United States, Brazil, Sweden, France, Switzerland
Etymology	Latin *albus*, "white"

Physical Properties of Albite

Cleavage	[001] Perfect, [010] Good
Color	White, gray, greenish gray, bluish green, gray
Diaphaneity	Transparent to translucent to subtranslucent
Fracture	Uneven
Habit	Blocky, granular, striated
Hardness	7
Luster	Vitreous (glassy)
Specific Gravity	2.61–2.63, Average = 2.62
Streak	White
Indicators	Habit, twinning

Albite is technically a plagioclase feldspar with less than 10% anorthite. All plagioclase feldspars exhibit a form of twinning known as albite law twinning, referring to the stacks if twin layers characterstic of albite. It occurs in Alabama, Arizona, Arkansas, California, Colorado, Connecticut, Delaware, Georgia, Idaho, Louisiana, Maine, Maryland, Massachusetts, Michigan, Minnesota, Missouri, Montana, Nevada, New Hampshire, New Jersey, New Mexico, New York, North Carolina, Oklahoma, Oregon, Pennsylvania, Rhode Island, South Carolina, South Dakota, Texas, Utah, Vermont, Virginia, Washington, West Virginia, Wisconsin, and Wyoming.

Oligoclase

Plagioclase Group. Oligoclase is a variety of albite.

Chemical Formula	$(Na,Ca)(Si,Al)_4O_8$
Environment	Primary constituent of pegmatitic igneous and magmatic rocks
Locality	Sri Lanka, Russia, Norway, Sweden, Canada, United States
Etymology	Greek *oligos* and *kasein*, "little cleavage"

Physical Properties of Oligoclase

Cleavage	[001] Perfect, [010] Good
Color	Brown, colorless, greenish, gray, yellowish
Diaphaneity	Transparent to translucent
Fracture	Uneven
Habit	Euhedral crystals, granular
Hardness	7
Luminescence	Fluorescent
Luster	Vitreous (glassy)
Specific Gravity	2.64–2.66, Average = 2.65
Streak	White
Indicators	Twinning, shimmer, density

Sunstone and moonstone are both gem-quality forms of oligoclase. Oligoclase occurs in Alabama, Arizona, Arkansas, California, Colorado, Connecticut, Delaware, Georgia, Idaho, Louisiana, Maine, Michigan, Montana, Nevada, New Hampshire, New Jersey, New Mexico, New York, North Carolina, Oklahoma, Oregon, Pennsylvania, Rhode Island, South Carolina, South Dakota, Texas, Utah, Vermont, and Virginia.

Andesine

Plagioclase Group. Andesine is a variety of albite.

Chemical Formula	$(Na,Ca)(Si,Al)_4O_8$
Environment	Primary constituent of pegmatitic igneous and magmatic rocks
Locality	Andes Mountains, Colombia; Greenland; North America; Europe
Etymology	After the Andes Mountains

Physical Properties of Andesine

Cleavage	[001] Perfect, [010] Good
Color	Colorless, gray, yellow green, white
Diaphaneity	Transparent to subtransparent to translucent
Fracture	Uneven
Habit	Crystalline – coarse, granular
Hardness	7
Luster	Vitreous (glassy)
Specific Gravity	2.66–2.68, Average = 2.67

Streak	White
Indicators	Occurrence, twinning, density

Andesine is found in Alabama, Arizona, Arkansas, California, Colorado, Connecticut, Georgia, Idaho, Maine, Massachusetts, Nevada, New Hampshire, New Mexico, New York, North Carolina, Rhode Island, South Dakota, Utah, Virginia, Washington, and Wisconsin.

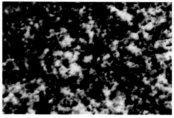

Andesine.

Labradorite

Plagioclase Group. See listing under "Gemstones."

Anorthite

Plagioclase Group

Chemical Formula	$CaAl_2Si_2O_8$
Environment	Within mafic plutonic rocks
Locality	Italy, United States, Japan, New Zealand
Etymology	Greek *an*, "not," and *orthos*, "upright"

Physical Properties of Anorthite

Cleavage	[001] Perfect, [010] Good
Color	Colorless, gray, white, red, reddish gray
Diaphaneity	Transparent to subtransparent to translucent
Fracture	Uneven
Habit	Euhedral crystals, granular, striated
Hardness	6
Luster	Vitreous (glassy)
Specific Gravity	2.72–2.75, Average = 2.73
Streak	White
Indicators	Occurrence, twinning, density

Anorthite is a calcium-rich plagioclase, and is rarer than other plagioclase minerals. It occurs in Alabama, Arizona, Arkansas, California, Colorado, Connecticut, Georgia, Idaho, Kansas, Maine, Massachusetts, Michigan, Montana, Nebraska, Nevada, New Hampshire, New Jersey, New Mexico, New York, North Carolina, Ohio, Oregon, Pennsylvania, Rhode Island, South Carolina, South Dakota, Texas, Utah, Vermont, Virginia, Washington, Wisconsin, and Wyoming.

Nepheline

Chemical Formula	$(Na,K)AlSiO_4$
Environment	Characteristic of silica-poor igneous rocks
Locality	Italy, Russia, Canada, United States, Brazil, Greenland
Etymology	Greek *nephele*, "cloud" (for its tendency to become clouded when placed in acid)

Physical Properties of Nepheline

Cleavage	[1010] Poor
Color	White, gray, brown, brownish gray, reddish white
Diaphaneity	Transparent to translucent to opaque

Fracture	Subconchoidal
Habit	Massive – granular, prismatic
Hardness	6
Luster	Vitreous – greasy
Specific Gravity	2.55–2.65, Average = 2.59
Streak	White
Indicators	Luster, reaction to acid, hardness

Nepheline is found in Arizona, Arkansas, California, Colorado, Maine, Massachusetts, Michigan, New Hampshire, New Jersey, New Mexico, Pennsylvania, South Dakota, Tennessee, Texas, Utah, Vermont, Virginia, Washington, Wisconsin, and Wyoming.

Nepheline.

Leucite

Chemical Formula	$KAlSi_2O_6$
Molecular Weight	218.25 gm
Environment	Within potassium-rich mafic and ultramafic rocks
Locality	Italy, Germany, United States
Etymology	Greek *leukos*, "white"

Physical Properties of Leucite

Cleavage	[110] Indistinct
Color	Colorless, gray, yellow gray, white
Diaphaneity	Translucent to transparent
Fracture	Brittle – conchoidal
Habit	Crystalline – coarse
Hardness	6
Luster	Vitreous (glassy)
Specific Gravity	2.47
Streak	White
Indicators	Habit, density, hardness, luster

Leucite is fairly rare, but popular for collections because it is one of few minerals with an isometric trapezohedral crystal form. It is found in Arizona, Maine, Montana, New Mexico, and Wyoming.

Sodalite

Chemical Formula	$Na_4Al_3(SiO_4)_3Cl$
Environment	Formed in nepheline syenites, phonolites, calcareous metamorphic rocks, and volcanic ejecta
Locality	Greenland, Canada, Italy, Brazil, Russia
Etymology	After its composition

Physical Properties of Sodalite

Cleavage	[110] Poor
Color	Azure blue, white, pink, gray, green
Diaphaneity	Transparent to translucent

Fracture	Brittle – conchoidal
Habit	Disseminated, massive – granular
Hardness	6
Luster	Vitreous – greasy
Specific Gravity	2.29
Streak	White
Indicators	Color (when blue), lack of pyrite association, hardness

Sodalite is a rare rock-forming mineral, but its striking royal blue color makes it popular for carving when it can be found in large enough specimens. It can be found in Arkansas, California, Colorado, Maine, Massachusetts, Montana, New Hampshire, New Jersey, New Mexico, South Dakota, Utah, Vermont, and Wisconsin.

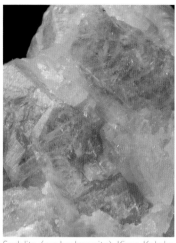

Sodalite (var. hackmanite). Kiran, Kokcha Valley, Badakhshan, Afghanistan.

Lazurite

See also listing for lapis lazuli under "Gemstones."

Chemical Formula	$(Na,Ca)_8(Al,Si)_{12}O_{24}(S,SO)_4$
Environment	Forms as a contact metamorphic mineral in limestone
Locality	Afghanistan, Russia, Italy, Chile, United States
Etymology	Persian *lazward*, "blue"

Physical Properties of Lazurite

Cleavage	[110] Imperfect
Color	Blue, azure blue, violet blue, greenish blue
Diaphaneity	Translucent
Fracture	Conchoidal
Habit	Massive – granular
Hardness	5.5
Luminescence	Fluorescent
Luster	Vitreous – dull
Specific Gravity	2.38–2.42, Average = 2.4
Streak	Light blue
Indicators	Color, pyrite association, density

Lazurite. Sar-e-Sang, Badakhshan, Afghanistan.

Lazurite is the blue component of lapis lazuli. While rare in the United States it can be found in Alabama, Arkansas, California, Colorado, and North Carolina.

Marialite

Chemical Formula	$Na_4(Al_3Si_9O_{24})Cl$
Environment	Forms in regional and contact metamorphic rocks, pegmatites, and volcanic ejecta; forms a series with meionite

| Locality | Italy, Canada, United States, Norway |
| Etymology | Named by German mineralogist Gerhard vom Rath in honor of his wife, Maria Rosa vom Rath (1830–1888) |

Physical Properties of Marialite

Cleavage	[100] Distinct, [110] Distinct
Color	Bluish, brownish, colorless, violet, greenish
Diaphaneity	Transparent to translucent
Fracture	Brittle – conchoidal
Habit	Columnar, prismatic
Hardness	5.5–6
Luminescence	Fluorescent
Luster	Vitreous – pearly
Specific Gravity	2.5–2.62, Average = 2.56
Streak	White
Indicators	Color, habit, cleavage, fluorescence

Marialite is found in Arizona, California, Colorado, Maine, Massachusetts, Nevada, New Jersey, New Mexico, New York, and Pennsylvania.

Meionite

Chemical Formula	$Ca_4(Al_6Si_6O_{24})CO_3$
Environment	Occurs in metamorphic, pegmatitic, and altered mafic igneous rocks, and volcanic ejecta; forms a series with marialite
Locality	Italy, Canada, United States, Mexico, Norway, Germany
Etymology	Greek for "less" (from its less-acute pyramidal form compared with vesuvianite)

Physical Properties of Meionite

Cleavage	[100] Distinct, [110] Distinct
Color	Bluish, brownish, colorless, violet, greenish
Diaphaneity	Transparent to subtranslucent
Fracture	Subconchoidal
Habit	Columnar, fibrous, massive – granular
Hardness	5–6
Luster	Vitreous – resinous
Specific Gravity	2.66–2.73, Average = 2.69
Streak	Colorless
Indicators	Color, habit, cleavage, fluorescence

Meionite occurs in California, Georgia, Idaho, Maine, Massachusetts, Michigan, Nevada, New Hampshire, New Jersey, New Mexico, New York, North Carolina, Rhode Island, Vermont, and Washington.

ZEOLITE TECTOSILICATES

Analcime

| Chemical Formula | $NaAlSi_2O_6 \cdot H_2O$ |
| Environment | Occurs frequently in basalts, phonolites, and tuffs |

Locality	Canada, United States, Iceland, Greenland, Switzerland
Etymology	Greek for "weak" (from the weak electrical charge developed on rubbing)

Physical Properties of Analcime

Cleavage	[001] Indistinct, [010] Indistinct, [100] Indistinct
Color	White, grayish white, greenish white, yellowish white; reddish white
Diaphaneity	Transparent to subtransparent to translucent
Fracture	Subconchoidal
Habit	Euhedral crystals, granular, massive
Hardness	5
Luminescence	Fluorescent
Luster	Vitreous (glassy)
Specific Gravity	2.3
Streak	White
Indicators	Habit, density, hardness, luster

Analcime is one of few minerals that forms an isometric trapezohedral crystal. It occurs in Arizona, Arkansas, California, Colorado, Connecticut, Hawaii, Idaho, Iowa, Maine, Massachusetts, Michigan, Minnesota, Montana, Nevada, New Hampshire, New Jersey, New Mexico, New York, North Carolina, Oklahoma, Oregon, Pennsylvania, Rhode Island, South Dakota, Texas, Utah, Vermont, Virginia, Washington, West Virginia, Wisconsin, and Wyoming.

Laumontite

Chemical Formula	$CaAl_2Si_4O_{12} \cdot 4H_2O$
Environment	Secondary mineral in basalt, andesite, granite, and metamorphic rocks
Locality	France, Iceland, United Kingdom, India
Etymology	French mineraologist F.P.N. Gillet de Laumont (1747–1834)

Physical Properties of Laumontite

Cleavage	[010] Perfect, [110] Perfect
Color	Brownish, gray, yellowish, pearl white, pink
Diaphaneity	Transparent to translucent to opaque
Fracture	Brittle – conchoidal
Habit	Bladed, crystalline – fine, prismatic
Hardness	3.5–4
Luster	Vitreous (glassy)
Specific Gravity	2.25–2.35, Average = 2.29
Streak	White
Indicators	Habit, luster, density

Laumontite. Megascopic features of Ohanapecosh metamorphism. Spherical concentrations of laumontite in pumiceous tuff-breccia on the east side of Backbone Ridge. Note the friability of the rock. Circa 1959. Mount Rainier National Park, Washington.

Laumontite will dehydrate into a white powder, so it should always be kept in an airtight container. It can be found in Alabama, Alaska, Arizona, California, Colorado, Connecticut, Delaware, Georgia, Hawaii, Idaho, Maine, Maryland, Massachusetts, Michigan, Minnesota, Montana, Nevada, New Hampshire, New Jersey, New Mexico, New York, North Carolina, Oregon, Pennsylvania, Rhode Island, Utah, Virginia, Washington, Wisconsin, and Wyoming.

Chabazite

Renamed chabazite-Ca by IMA zeolite committee.

Chemical Formula	$CaAl_2Si_4O_{12} \cdot 6H_2O$
Environment	Within volcanic vesicles, hydrothermal veins, and tuffs
Locality	Italy, Germany, New Zealand, Canada
Etymology	Greek *chabazios*, "tune" or "melody"

Physical Properties of Chabazite-Ca

Cleavage	[1011] Imperfect
Color	Colorless, green, yellow, white, pink
Diaphaneity	Translucent to transparent
Fracture	Brittle – uneven
Habit	Drusy, pseudo cubic
Hardness	4
Luster	Vitreous (glassy)
Specific Gravity	2.05–2.15, Average = 2.09
Streak	White
Indicators	Habit, density, hardness, luster

Chabazite forms in the vesicles of volcanic rocks, which often appear similar to geodes. It can be found in Colorado, New Jersey, North Carolina, Oregon, Rhode Island, and Washington.

Heulandite

Chemical Formula	$(Ca,Na)(Al_2Si_7O_{18}) \cdot 6H_2O$
Environment	Forms in volcanic vesicles.
Locality	Brazil, India, United States, Canada, Iran, Italy
Etymology	English mineral collector John Henry Heuland (1778–1856)

Physical Properties of Heulandite-Ca

Cleavage	[010] Perfect
Color	White, reddish white, grayish white, brownish white, yellow
Diaphaneity	Transparent to subtranslucent
Fracture	Brittle
Habit	Crystalline – coarse, tabular
Hardness	3–3.5
Luster	Vitreous – pearly
Specific Gravity	2.2
Streak	White
Indicators	Habit, density, cleavage, luster

Heulandites are the most common zeolites. They are found in Colorado, Idaho, Michigan, New Jersey, New York, North Carolina, Oregon, and Rhode Island.

Stilbite

Chemical Formula	$NaCa_4(Al_8Si_{28}O_{72}) \cdot nH_2O$ (n=28-32)
Environment	Forms in cavities in basalts
Locality	Iceland, India, United Kingdom, United States, Canada
Etymology	Greek *stilbe*, "luster"

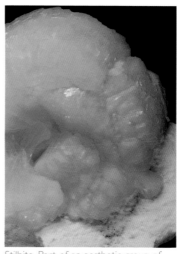

Physical Properties of	Stilbite
Cleavage	[010] Perfect
Color	White, red, yellow, brown, cream
Diaphaneity	Transparent to subtransparent to translucent
Fracture	Brittle – conchoidal
Habit	Fibrous, globular, wheat sheaf
Hardness	3.5–4
Luster	Vitreous – pearly
Specific Gravity	2.1–2.2, Average = 2.15
Streak	White
Indicators	Habit, luster, density

Stilbite. Part of an aesthetic group of stilbite on a matrix, this was collected in Maharashtra State, India. The group sold for $977.50 at auction in early 2008.

Stilbite is a popular mineral for collections because of its "wheat sheaf" crystals. It occurs in Alaska, California, Colorado, Connecticut, Idaho, Maine, Michigan, New Jersey, New York, North Carolina, Oregon, Pennsylvania, and Rhode Island.

Natrolite

Chemical Formula	$Na_2Al_2Si_3O_{10} \cdot 2H_2O$
Environment	Forms in cavities of amygdaloidal basalts and related rocks
Locality	Czech Republic, India, United States
Etymology	Greek *natron*, "soda," and *lithos*, "stone"

Physical Properties of Natrolite	
Cleavage	[110] Perfect, [010] Imperfect
Color	White, colorless, red, yellowish white, reddish white
Diaphaneity	Transparent to translucent
Fracture	Brittle
Habit	Acicular, nodular, prismatic
Hardness	5.5–6
Luster	Vitreous – silky
Specific Gravity	2.25
Streak	White
Indicators	Habit, density

Natrolite forms radiating sprays of acicular crystals which are popular among collectors. It can be found in Arizona, Arkansas, California, Colorado, Connecticut, Delaware, Georgia, Hawaii, Idaho, Maine, Massachusetts, Michigan, Minnesota, Montana, Nevada,

New Jersey, New Mexico, New York, North Carolina, Oregon, Pennsylvania, Rhode Island, South Dakota, Texas, Utah, Virginia, Washington, West Virginia, and Wisconsin.

Mesolite

Chemical Formula	$Na_2Ca_2(Al_6Si_9)O_{30} \cdot 8H_2O$
Environment	Forms in cavities in amygdaloidal basalt and similar rocks
Locality	Italy, Iceland, India, United States, Denmark
Etymology	Greek *mesos*, "middle"

Physical Properties of Mesolite

Cleavage	[101] Perfect, [001] Perfect
Color	White, gray, pale yellow
Diaphaneity	Transparent to translucent
Fracture	Uneven
Habit	Acicular, capillary, spherical
Hardness	5
Luster	Vitreous – silky
Specific Gravity	2.2–2.4, Average = 2.29
Streak	White
Indicators	Habit, density

Mesolite, like natrolite, is popular in collections because of its radiating needle-like crystals. It occurs in Arizona, Arkansas, California, Colorado, Georgia, Idaho, Michigan, Minnesota, New Jersey, New Mexico, New York, North Carolina, Oregon, Pennsylvania, Utah, Virginia, Washington, and West Virginia.

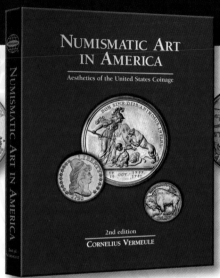

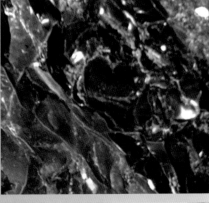

Rocks

CATALOG OF ROCKS

◼ IGNEOUS ROCKS ◼

PLUTONIC
Granite

Texture	Phaneritic, commonly porphyritic
Structure	Typically homogeneous, but may have banded characteristics. Xenoliths are common.
Color	White, gray, pink, red, black
Mineralogy	Quartz, potassium feldspars, plagioclase feldspars, hornblende and micas

Field Features: Granite is one of the most common rocks on Earth, forming a major component of the crust. It is massive, occurring throughout the world in batholiths, sills, dikes, and intrusions. Because of its strength and hardness it often forms mountains, peaks, and crags. Mount Rushmore, Half-Dome in Yosemite National Park, and Stone Mountain, Georgia, are all granite outcroppings.

Notes: Granite has been used as a building material since antiquity, because of its durability, strength, and resistance to weathering. The Egyptian pyramids were built of granite and covered with a sheath of polished limestone. It remains popular today for flooring tiles, building facades, kitchen counters, and cemetery monuments for the same reasons and for its ability to take a high polish.

Granodiorite

Texture	Phaneritic, sometimes porphyritic
Structure	Typically homogeneous, but may have banded characteristics. Xenoliths are common.
Color	White, grey, black
Mineralogy	Quartz, plagioclase feldspars, potassium feldspars, hornblende and micas. Granodiorite is similar to granite but has more plagioclase feldspar than potassium feldspar. Micas and hornblende are often abundant, giving it a darker color than granite.

Granodiorite. This specimen of Sentinel Granodiorite is a Glacier Point facies, with large ragged flakes of biotite, collected from the base of the cliff below Glacier Point in Yosemite National Park, California, in January 1923.

Field Features: Same as granite.

Notes: Granodiorite is at least as common as granite, perhaps more so. The Rosetta Stone was carved in granodiorite.

Pegmatite

Texture	Pegmatitic, uneven, highly variable grain size from coarse to giant
Structure	Complex dikes commonly exhibit zones. Drusy cavities may occur.
Color	Widely variable, but generally white, pink, light red; uneven due to very large crystals
Mineralogy	Alkali feldspars, micas, quartz

Field Features: Pegmatites tend to concentrate in the margins and vicinity of granite intrusions.

Notes: Pegmatite forms during rapid cooling of granitic magma, and so provides a near-perfect environment for the formation of large mineral crystals. Pegmatite often contains gem-quality minerals such as apatite, aquamarine, fluorite, topaz, and tourmaline, and is therefore of great

Pegmatite. This pegmatite was captured in migmatite at Clear Creek Canyon, Front Range, Colorado, in March 1955.

economic importance. Because of this it is one of the most prized mineral environments for collectors. Pegmatite is also a primary source of such industrial ores and rare-earth elements as beryllium, feldspar, mica, lithium, niobium, and tantalum.

Syenite

Texture	Phaneritic, sometimes porphyritic. Similar to granite.
Structure	Same as granite, although commonly with drusy cavities
Color	Pink, white, gray, light green
Mineralogy	Alkali feldspar, plagioclase. Very similar to granite, but with no or very little (less than 5 percent) quartz.

Field Features: Same as for granite.

Notes: Syenite has generally the same economic uses and value as granite, but is uncommon and so is rarely exploited.

Syenite. Syenite in a creek bed cut by seams of aplite, observed circa 1936. Boren Creek, La Plata County, Colorado.

Nepheline syenite

Texture	Same as syenite
Structure	Same as syenite
Color	Gray, pink, green
Mineralogy	Alkali feldspar, plagioclase, nepheline

Field Features: Generally forms in association with other highly alkaline rocks. Occurs frequently in contact with or near limestone.

Notes: Forms primarily from intrusive magma, but sometimes from the partial melting of silica-poor alkali rocks such as syenites, where orthoclase is replaced by feldspathoids. Nepheline syenite is very rare.

Monzonite

Texture	Phaneritic to porphyritic
Structure	Same as granite
Color	Light to medium gray
Mineralogy	Plagioclase feldspar, orthoclase feldspar. Less than 10 percent quartz.

Field Features: Uncommon rock; found usually along the borders of diorite or granodiorite masses.

Diorite

Texture	Phaneritic, rarely porphyritic
Structure	Essentially the same as granite. Xenoliths are common.
Color	Gray to dark gray
Mineralogy	Primarily plagioclase feldspar and hornblende. Minimal quartz content.

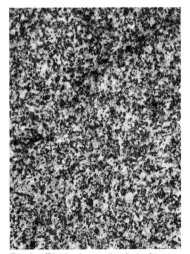

Diorite. Diorite is mostly plagioclase and dark minerals with a little quartz and potassium feldspar. Yosemite National Park, California.

Field Features: Occurs in stocks, sills, and dikes in marginal portions of granite or granodiorite masses.

Notes: Diorite is extremely hard and durable. Because of its dark color it has little economic use today. However, it was prized by the ancient Middle Eastern cultures of Egypt, Mesopotamia, Babylonia, and Assyria for sculpture, despite the difficulty in working the rock. The Code of Hammurabi was inscribed upon a seven-foot pillar of black diorite. The Incan and Mayan civilizations used diorite for constructing fortresses. Diorite was also commonly used for cobblestones in Great Britain.

Gabbro

Texture	Phaneritic
Structure	Massive, often layered, with strata producing alternating light and dark bands
Color	Gray to black
Mineralogy	Plagioclase feldspar; pyroxene; hornblende; olivine

Gabbro. This September 1961 close-up of Circle volcanics "bedded gabbro" was taken in Circle district, Yukon region, Alaska.

Field Features: Massive intrusions, or, more rarely, sheetlike intrusions called *lopoliths*.

Notes: Gabbro weathers more rapidly then granitic rocks, so exposed outcroppings are relatively small. Finer-grained gabbro is called *diabase*. Gabbro is often (and incorrectly) referred to as "black granite," and is popular for countertops and cemetery monuments.

Anorthosite

Texture	Phaneritic
Structure	Same as gabbro
Color	White, gray, black, blue
Mineralogy	Minimum 90 percent plagioclase

Field Features: Usually associated with gabbro, but may form huge masses within metamorphic rocks.

Notes: Labradorite (see listing under "Gemstones") is a form in which the plagioclase crystals can exhibit a specific type of refractive iridescence known as *labradorescence*. Gemstone-quality labradorite is also called spectrolite.

Peridotite

Texture	Phaneritic
Structure	May be layered
Color	Dull green to black
Mineralogy	Olivine, pyroxene

Field Features: Occurs as dikes and sills, often very large. May also appear in layers in gabbro lopoliths.

Notes: Peridotite is the primary rock in the upper part of the Earth's mantle. It is the world's primary source of chromium ore and is also a valuable source of nickel and platinum. Most surface outcroppings of peridotite have altered to serpentine through low-temperature hydration. A mica-rich peridotite called *kimberlite* is one of only two sources for diamonds (the other is lamproite).

VOLCANIC

Rhyolite

Texture	Aphanitic; may be aphanitic-porphyritic
Structure	May exhibit flow banding (layers that form as lava oozes onto the surface and cools as it flows, creating many thin strata)
Color	White, gray, red
Mineralogy	Quartz, potassium feldspars, plagioclase feldspars, and hornblende. Rhyolite is the volcanic equivalent of granite.

Rhyolite. Spherulitic rhyolite found at Paku Point on Coromandel Peninsula on the North Island, New Zealand, in November 1965.

Field Features: Rhyolite occurs as lava flows and small intrusions. Rhyolite magma flows very slowly because of its viscosity, so extrusions are generally very short.

Notes: When rhyolitic magma erupts explosively from a volcano, gases trapped in the magma can expand rapidly, causing the magma to become "foamy" before it cools, creating a glassy rock known as *pumice*. Because of the gas bubbles trapped within it, pumice can actually float on water. Large "rafts" of pumice have been known to float for hundreds of miles—some as large as 19 miles wide!

Trachyte

Texture	Aphanitic to aphanitic-porphyritic
Structure	Flow banding is much less common than in rhyolite. A subparallel fluidal alignment of phenocrysts is characteristic, but is not visible to the naked eye due to the fine grain size.
Color	Light to medium gray, white, pink
Mineralogy	Potassium feldspar, biotite, hornblende. Less SiO_2 than rhyolite. Trachyte is the volcanic equivalent of syenite.

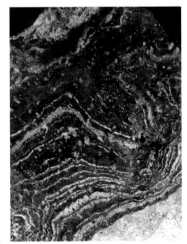

Trachyte. Nye County, Nevada.

Field Features: Occurs in surface lava flows and as dikes and sills.

Notes: Although trachyte rarely provides an environment for mineral crystals, thin seams are often filled with opal, turquoise, or chalcedony.

Dacite

Texture	Ahanitic to aphanitic-porphyritic
Structure	Flow banding is common; phenocrysts are often abundant and show marked flow alignment
Color	White, gray, red, brown, black
Mineralogy	Plagioclase feldspar, quartz, biotite, hornblende, augite. Dacite has a high iron content. Dacite is the volcanic equivalent of quartz diorite.

Field Features: Occurs as lava flows and dikes.

Notes: Dacite is a primary rock at Mount St. Helens, a volcano near Portland, Oregon, which erupted violently in 1980.

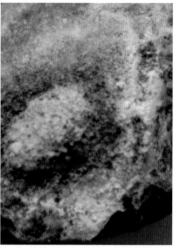

Dacite. This dacite cobble was collected on May 29, 1980, from the Mount St. Helens debris avalanche. Dark-red iron hydroxide was deposited first at high temperature, followed by yellow encrustations, consisting mostly of calcium sulfate in various hydration stages, that were deposited in the cooler zone away from the orifice. Skamania County, Washington.

Andesite

Texture	Apahnitic-porphyritic
Structure	Flow banding uncommon but may develop under certain conditions
Color	Gray, brown, green, purple
Mineralogy	Plagioclase feldspar, pyroxene, hornblende. Andesite is the volcanic equivalent of diorite.

Field Features: Lava flows or shallow dikes. Andesite is the second most common lava after basalt.

Notes: Andesite is generally associated with areas of mountain building and is named for the Andes in South America, where it is very common.

Andesite. New cobblestones of consanguineous Miocene diorite and andesite on Coromandel Peninsula on the North Island, Zealand.

Basalt

Texture	Aphanitic, occasionally porphyritic
Structure	Prominent vesicular structure, usually filled in after cooling with quartz and zeolite minerals. Basalt is the volcanic equivalent of gabbro.
Color	Dark gray to black; fresh flows often reddish; may weather to green
Mineralogy	Plagioclase feldspar, pyroxene, olivine

Basalt. This specimen of quartz basalt is from the cinder cone, circa 1890. Lassen Volcanic National Park, California.

Field Features: Occurs as massive lava flows. Hexagonal columnar jointing is common, as in the Giant's Causeway (Ireland) or Devil's Tower, Wyoming.

Notes: Basalt is the most common and widespread volcanic igneous rock, in many areas forming flows thousands of feet thick. Basalt rises from deep within the Earth's mantle, and so carries with it an abundance of heavier elements, including iron, which accounts for the rusty hue of fresh flows. Iceland and the Hawaiian Islands are basaltic formations.

Obsidian

Texture	Glassy
Structure	Conchoidal fracture due to the amorphous, glassy nature. Flow banding may be evident as bands or streaks of colors.
Color	Black, but smoky along thinner edges. Impurities may give a greenish or brownish hue. Some varieties, known as "rainbow obsidian," may exhibit iridescence. Small white clusters of cristobalite crystals produce "snowflake" obsidian.
Mineralogy	Forms from rapidly cooling silica-rich granitic magma, generally greater than 70 percent SiO_2

Obsidian. This obsidian specimen was found in the Flagstaff area. Coconino County, Arizona.

Field Features: Dikes and lava flows

Notes: Rhyolite that cools very quickly forms a dense, black, glassy rock called "obsidian." Obsidian was used for knives and arrowheads by Stone Age cultures because of its even, regular fracture; the fracture is so smooth that obsidian blades are used in modern cardiac surgery because they create a finer cut and less scarring than even the sharpest metal scalpels.

Tuff

Texture	Fragmental; dense to fine-grained (less than 1/16")
Structure	Tuff is consolidated volcanic ash; it has no defined structure, but can appear in particulate layers like sedimentary rock
Color	White, gray, light brown, yellow, pink, green
Mineralogy	Tuffs are classified according to the volcanic rock composing them; they can therefore be rhyolitic, trachytic, andesitic, or basaltic

This specimen of metamorphosed tuff, showing faults, was collected from the southwest slope of Mount Dana, circa 1923. Yosemite National Park, California.

Field Features: Occurs in well-defined layers associated with successive volcanic eruptions. Grain size generally decreases with distance from the site of the eruption.

Notes: The moai statues of Easter Island were carved from tuff.

SEDIMENTARY ROCKS

Mudstone

Texture	Dense; composed of microscopic particles (less than 0.0025" diameter)
Structure	Massive
Color	Light to dark gray
Mineralogy	Phyllosilicate clay minerals (e.g., kaolinite); silt

Field Features: Often forms layers with shale. Mudstone erodes more rapidly than shale, and on exposed cliff faces the layers are quite apparent, with the laminar bands of shale standing out in relief against the mudstone.

Notes: Mudstone is, as the name implies, hardened mud. If clay predominates it may be called "claystone," and if silt predominates it may be called "siltstone."

Mudstone. In the Red Rocks area near Sterling, the view looking southward reveals some of the red and gray mudstone beds of the Cedar Mountain Formation in Spring 1980. These beds are mantled locally by limestone nodules. Sanpete County, Utah.

Shale

Texture	Dense; composed of microscopic particles (less than 0.0025" diameter).
Structure	Laminar
Color	Light to dark gray
Mineralogy	Same as mudstone; shale is simply a laminar variety of mudstone

Shale. This close-up view shows crumpled beds of Arapien in Spring 1982. Juab County, Utah.

Field Features: Shale forms when the extremely fine and lightweight particles of clay and silt settle out of slow-moving water.

Notes: Shale often contains fossils, and oil shales are a potential source of fossil fuels. Shale is the most common sedimentary rock; shale and mudstones together account for about two-thirds of all sedimentary rocks.

Sandstone

Texture	Even-grained, clastic; grains are sand-sized (less than 0.08" diameter)
Structure	Bedding is very apparent; cross-bedding and ripple marks are common; may contain fossils
Color	Widely varied; generally red, tan, and brown; often gray, white, green, yellow
Mineralogy	Primarily quartz; grains may be cemented by silica, clay, carbonates, or iron oxide

Sandstone. This view shows the sandstone above a tunnel entrance through Wingate Sandstone on the west side of No Thoroughfare Canyon. Colorado National Monument, Colorado.

Field Features: Sandstone is resistant to weathering, and so often stands out in massive ridges from nearby rock that has eroded.

Notes: Sandstone is subclassified according to mineral its content: *Arkose* is sandstone with a high feldspar content (25 to 50 percent). It has a composition similar to granite. *Graywacke* is a sandstone composed of fragments of quartz, feldspar, granite, basalt, or slate. It is gray to black, often with a green tint. *Orthoquartzite* is sandstone in which both the grains and the cement are primarily quartz; this high quartz content (greater than 90 percent) makes orthoquartzite extremely hard and crystalline.

Breccia

Texture	Uneven, coarse-grained, containing angular rock fragments anywhere from 0.08" to several feet in size held together by a variety of cements
Structure	Generally massive; bedding is uncommon but very thick when it does occur
Color	Variable
Mineralogy	Variable; breccias can form from almost any type of rock

Breccia with copper.

Field Features: Breccia often consolidates fragments created in mountain rockfalls, and so often appears as cliffs or outcroppings.

Conglomerate

Texture	Uneven, coarse-grained; containing smooth, well-rounded rock fragments anywhere from 0.08" to several feet in size held together by a variety of cements
Structure	Generally massive; bedding is uncommon but very thick when it does occur.
Color	Variable
Mineralogy	Variable; conglomerates can form from almost any type of rock

Field Features: Conglomerate often consolidates fragments created in mountain rockfalls, and so often appears as cliffs or outcroppings.

Notes: Conglomerates that accumulate in alluvial fans are called "fanglomerates." Fanglomerates form the basis for the North Sea oil fields. The only difference between conglomerate and breccia is that the grains of conglomerate are rounded by abrasion and erosion, whereas the grains of breccia remain sharp and angular.

Limestone

Texture	Dense to fine-grained, though sometimes with visible crystals; often contains fossils
Structure	Bedding from one inch to 100 feet thick; may occur as masses or, due to its high solubility and tendency to reprecipitate, as a variety of isolated structures such as stalagmites and stalactites in caves
Color	White or light gray to dark gray; impurities may create a wide range of subtle colors
Mineralogy	Calcite ($CaCO_3$)

Field Features: Limestone is easily soluble, especially in acid, and therefore weathers easily, forming erosional landscapes known as "karsts," with hills, cliffs, outcroppings, and often an abundance of caves.

Notes: Limestone has a vast range of economically important uses. Limestone block is widely used as a building stone or for sculpture. Crushed limestone is used for concrete, cement, and mortar. It is a source of dietary calcium, and is also used as a mild abrasive in toothpaste. Limestone is used in the manufacture of quicklime and in glassmaking. Agricultural lime is important as a soil additive in farming.

The remains of marine organisms settling to the sea floor are the primary source for the calcite in limestone, and for this reason limestone is often an excellent source of fossils.

Oolitic limestone is compose of spherical grains less than .08" in diameter. The facade of the Empire State Building is clad in oolitic limestone.

Travertine is a banded, crystalline deposit formed in hot springs and caves. It comes in a variety of colors and features natural pits and troughs that make it very visually interesting. For these reasons travertine is used extensively in architecture for wall and floor tiles as well as for outdoor paving stones.

Limestone. Exposure of Twin Creek limestone beds, possibly overturned, in the valley of Chicken Creek, Levan area, in Spring 1982. Juab County, Utah.

Chalk is a soft, white, porous form of limestone. It tends to form in clay fields that erode more readily then the chalk, so chalk often appears as tall, stark, seaside cliffs. Chalk has been replaced by other substances for such traditional uses as blackboard chalk or for marking lines on playing fields, even though the name "chalk" is still used.

Dolomite rock

Texture	Dense, fine- to coarse-grained
Structure	Usually massive; bedding is thick when it occurs
Color	White to light gray
Mineralogy	At least 50 percent dolomite; formed by chemical replacement of the calcium in limestone

Field Features: Same as limestone. Dolomite rock forms under the same conditions as limestone and appears interbedded with it. In the field, it is usually indistinguishable from limestone.

Notes: Dolomite rock has most of the same uses as limestone. Dolomite rock is sometimes called "dolostone" to avoid confusion with the mineral dolomite, but this usage is not widely accepted.

Dolomite.

Chert

Texture	Dense, smooth
Structure	Massive, bedded, nodular
Color	White to gray to black
Mineralogy	Crypotcrystalline quartz (primarily chalcedony)

Field Features: Chert is very hard and durable, and therefore appears as outcroppings in eroded rocks.

Notes: Chert is a more general term for flint, jasper, or other cryptocrystalline quartz rocks. Chert will spark when struck against steel; hence its use in starting fires or in the construction of flintlock rifles. Jasper is a semiprecious chert with a deep red color caused by iron inclusions.

Coal

Texture	Dense, semi-glassy
Structure	Varies by variety (see below)
Color	Brown to black
Mineralogy	Carbon; forms from compression and lithification of peat (plant remains)

Coal.

Field Features: Occurs in layers called seams up to 15 feet thick

Notes: Coal is a combustible fossil fuel, and an important energy source.

Coal forms in stages, and each successive stage, or grade, has specific properties.

Peat, the precursor to coal, is an accumulation of partially decayed plant matter that forms in marshy areas. It is harvested for fuel in Ireland, Scotland, and Scandinavia.

Lignite, also called "brown coal," is slightly more solid than peat. It is the lowest grade of true coal, with a fixed carbon content of less than 25 percent. A compacted form of lignite is called "jet"; when polished, it is used as a gemstone.

Bituminous coal is a dense black or dark-brown coal used for industrial power generation. It has a fixed carbon content between 50 and 65 percent.

Anthracite is a very hard coal, glossy black, with a fixed carbon content as high as 95 percent. It is the most familiar grade of coal, used for residential heating.

EVAPORITES

Gypsum rock

Texture	Fine- to coarse-grained, crystalline, sugary
Structure	Massive; may show thin layers due to seasonal deposition
Color	White to light gray
Mineralogy	Primarily selenite (mineral gypsum); often with anhydrite, halite, calcite, and clay minerals

Field Features: Gypsum rock forms from salt-water evaporation in desert environments. Freshly broken fragments sparkle due to the exposed selenite cleavage planes.

Notes: Gypsum is used primarily for the manufacture of plaster of Paris, for building materials such as wallboard and lathing plaster.

Rock salt

Texture	Fine- to coarse-grained, crystallines sugary
Structure	Well-defined beds; massive
Color	Colorless to white; impurities may produce yellow, pink, or blue tints
Mineralogy	Halite (95 to 99 percent); impurities may include anhydrite, gypsum, and dolomite

Field Features: Subterranean salt domes; salt glaciers or outcroppings occur only in desert climates due to the extreme solubility of halite in water.

Notes: Pressure may cause salt beds to intrude upward into overlying sediments, forming salt domes or salt plugs, which are often associated with petroleum deposits. Rock salt is often spread on roads and walkways to manage ice.

Rock salt. Salt stalactites on overturned slab of rock salt, formed by solution of salt, rainwater, and fog, on the eastern side of Salar de Atacama, circa 1962. Antofagasta Province, Chile.

METAMORPHIC ROCKS

Slate

Texture	Dense; microcrystalline or fine-grained
Structure	Foliated; cleavage into thin, flat, parallel sheets is so characteristic that "slaty" is the descriptive term for this kind of cleavage in all rocks
Color	Gray to black, blue, purple, green, yellow
Mineralogy	Quartz, muscovite, chlorite

Field Features: Occurs as outcroppings, with exposed edges jagged and flaky from weathering.

Notes: Slate is a low-grade metamorphism of shale or mudstone. It is still used for roofing shingles and floor tiles due to its durability and fireproof

Slate. Prichard slate near Wallace, Idaho, circa 1947.

nature; for billiard tables and laboratory benchtops because of its thermal stability; and for whetstones for sharpening knives. In the past, slate was also used for blackboards and as an electrical insulator.

Phyllite

Texture	Dense, medium-grained
Structure	Foliated
Color	Same as for slate
Mineralogy	Quartz, micas, muscovite, chlorite

Field Features: Occurs as outcroppings, less irregular and more rounded than slate due to higher mica content.

Notes: Phyllite is a further metamorphism of slate. It is less brittle than slate, with a wavy rather than flat cleavage surface and a micaceous sheen.

Phyllite. This image from 1954 of sheared sandstone and green phyllite is in the Anakeesta Formation north of Newfound Gap. Great Smoky Mountains National Park, Tennessee and North Carolina.

Schist

Texture	Irregular, medium- to coarse-grained, crystalline
Structure	Foliated; splitting into flakes (this flakiness is called a "schistose" foliation)
Color	Gray, silver, white, yellow, brown, depending on the specific mineral content
Mineralogy	Micas, chlorite, hornblende, quartz

Field Features: Occurs in outcroppings, often showing foliated or folded cross sections.

Notes: Schist is the final stage of the metamorphism of shale through slate and phyllite. Schist is actually a group of related rocks, which are individually named according to the principal minerals that cause the foliation, e.g., chlorite, glaucophane, muscovite, biotite, garnet, staurolite, albite, kyanite, or hornblende schist. Some of the more durable schists are used as building stones, and some (such as graphite schist) are minor sources of minerals.

Schist. Mica schist with granite injections, this specimen (6" x 5") from under side of large inclusions at Boutwell quarry, Barre, shows light granite bands alternating with dark bands of schist parallel to its foliation. Caledonia County, Vermont.

Gneiss

Texture	Irregularly medium- to coarse-grained; crystalline
Structure	Foliated, with evident banding of discontinuous alternating light

(granular) and dark (micaceous) layers. This type of banding is characteristic and is called "gneissose" structure.

Color	Variable
Mineralogy	Feldspars, quartz, muscovite, biotite, hornblende. Micas account for less than 50 percent of total content.

Field Features: Gneisses are as strong as granite and therefore as resistant to weather and erosion; they commonly form mountains and other prominent features as does granite, but can be distinguished by their characteristic banding.

Notes: There is no clear line separating gneiss from schist, and it is often difficult to tell the two apart. Like schist, gneiss is named for its parent rock or characteristic minerals (granite gneiss, garnet gneiss, etc.). Many gneisses with lower mica contents are used similarly to granite, for building purposes.

Greenschist

Texture	Dense, crystalline
Structure	Massive; compact; may be foliated due to chlorite or actinolite content
Color	Pale to dark green
Mineralogy	Principally chlorite, epidote, actinolite, and albite. Greenschist forms from metamorphism of basalt, gabbro, or other silica-rich rocks.

Field Features: Occurs in mountains and outcroppings.

Notes: Greenschist is used as a crushed stone for roadway beds. It is also sometimes called "greenstone" or "chlorite schist."

Amphibolite

Texture	Medium- to coarse-grained
Structure	Generally schistose; may be massive
Color	Dark green to black
Mineralogy	Amphibole minerals (primarily hornblende), plagioclase feldspars

Field Features: Occurs in outcroppings; distinguished from schist and gniess by the dark color.

Notes: Amphibolite is commonly used for building construction and paving because of its durability, color, and ability to take a high polish.

Amphibolite. This large amphibolite sphere has been fashioned by a master sphere maker from Melbourne, Australia. Amphibolite is a term that is restricted to metamorphic rocks. The boulder that was used to make this large sphere was from the Australian island of Tasmania. Large spheres such as this require special equipment. This finely polished exotic sphere measures a significant 8-1/2" in diameter. Dundas, Tasmania, Australia.

Hornfels

Texture	Dense, fine-grained
Structure	Compact and massive; may exhibit distinct banding due to bedding
Color	Black, dark gray, dark green, bluish
Mineralogy	Hornfels form through contact metamorphism from slates, shales, and clays, or from basalts, diabases, etc. Mineralogy therefore varies greatly depending on the parent rock.

Field Features: Generally forms in contact with or proximity to plutonic igneous rocks. Very similar in appearance to basalt, hornfelses fracture into cubical or sharply angular fragments.

Hornfels. This specimen of hornfels developed in previously folded phyllite, from half a mile west of Stagger Inn camp, at an altitude of 4,400 feet. Pend Oreille County, Washington.

Notes: Hornfels may contain inclusions of well-formed garnet, andalusite, epidote, cordierite, pyrite, vesuvianite, scheelite, or sphalerite crystals.

Marble

Texture	Granuloblastic, fine- to medium-grained, even textured
Structure	Massive
Color	Typically white or light gray, but accessory minerals can produce red, green, black, yellow, or brown veins, streaks, and patches
Mineralogy	Marble forms from metamorphism of limestone or dolostone

Field Features: Commonly interbedded with schists, gneisses, or hornfels. Also found in the vicinity of limestone, from which it metamorphoses.

Marble. This marble and schist on the Charley River was photographed in August 1961. Alaska.

Notes: Marble has many uses—in construction, paper-making, toothpaste, paint, plastics, and cement—but is best known for its use in sculpture. The pure white crystal marbles of Carrara, Italy, and of China have been prized for sculpture for thousands of years, so much so that any light-colored stone that takes a high polish is now often referred to as "marble."

Serpentinite

Texture	Fine-grained, compact
Structure	Massive; serpentinite forms from the metamorphosis of magnesium-rich igneous rock, primarily peridotite
Color	Green
Mineralogy	Principally chrysotile, antigorite, and lizardite

Field Features: Occurs as layers in areas of mountain building or at subduction zones of undersea tectonic plates.

Notes: Serpentinite is associated with platinum, iron, nickel, and chromium deposits. More colorful and striated specimens of serpentinite are widely used for floor and wall tiles.

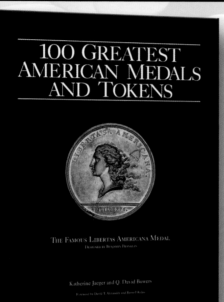

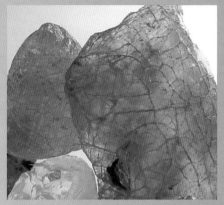

GEMSTONES

CATALOG OF GEMSTONES

Diamond

Chemical Formula	C
Environment	Very deep, very high-pressure volcanic intrusives in Kimberlite rocks
Locality	Kimberly, South Africa; Angola; Ivory Coast; India; Brazil; Ural Mountains, Russia; Murfreesboro, Arkansas
Etymology	Greek *adamas*, "invincible" or "hardest"

Diamond. This well-formed, twinned, octahedral crystal is close to 100 carats. Diamond crystals more than 10 carats are considered extremely rare. South Africa. This diamond sold for $14,950 at auction in early 2008.

Physical Properties of Diamond

Cleavage	[111] Perfect, [111] Perfect, [111] Perfect
Color	Colorless, white, gray, black, blue
Diaphaneity	Transparent to subtransparent to translucent
Fracture	Conchoidal
Habit	Euhedral crystals, granular
Hardness	10
Luminescence	Fluorescent (about 1/3 of all diamonds fluoresce—primarily blue, although green, yellow, and red fluorescence has been observed in rare specimens)
Luster	Adamantine
Specific Gravity	3.5–3.53, Average = 3.51
Streak	Colorless
Indicators	Hardness

Diamond is the hardest natural substance known. Synthetic diamond naonrods and ultrahard fullerite are harder, but have been manufactured only in laboratories and only in extremely minute quantities. It is their hardness, along with their brilliance of reflection, that make diamonds one of the most prized—and most expensive—gemstones.

Gem-quality diamonds are judged according the "four C's": carat (weight), clarity, color, and cut.

Pure diamonds are colorless, but impurities can create a variety of hues. Yellow, the most common color, is created by nitrogen in the carbon lattice structure; other colors (blue, green, pink, violet, or black) are quite rare, and diamonds with intense colors are extremely valuable. In October 2007, a 6.04-carat flawless blue diamond sold for $7.98 million, a record price per carat. The blue color is the result of trace boron impurities, and is only found at the Premier Mine in South Africa, where a number of famous and record-setting diamonds have been found. A rare red diamond, weighing 2.26 carats and possibly mined in Australia, sold for $2.7 million in November 2007. At $1,180,340 per carat, that is a record price for a red diamond at auction.

Throughout most of history, colored diamonds have been more sought after than the clear variety. The advent of the brilliant cut in the 17th century increased the popularity of white or colorless diamonds; in 1919 the modern brilliant cut was designed mathematically to produce the maximum possible brilliance and fire—the "sparkle" caused by light passing through the diamond and reflecting off its facets.

The largest gem-quality diamond yet found is the Cullinan Diamond, which weighed 3,106.75 carats before it was cut and 530.20 carats afterwards. Today, the Cullinan Diamond ("Star of Africa") is the centerpiece of King Edward VII's scepter. The largest flawless, colorless diamond is the Centenary Diamond; it weighed 599 carats rough, and has been cut into a modified heart-shaped brilliant gemstone weighing 273.685 carats. Its value is estimated at greater than $100 million. Like the blue diamond mentioned above, both the Cullinan and the Centenary came from the Premier Mine.

Only about 20 percent of all diamonds have the color and clarity necessary to make gemstone quality. The remaining 80 percent are reserved for industrial uses such as cutting and grinding.

Corundum   *See also listing under "Minerals."*

Corundum may be naturally clear. Due to its extreme hardness, it is used industrially as an abrasive (called "emery"). Impurities create colors in the corundum, and if transparent these specimens are used as gemstones.

Ruby. Ruby is the name given to red specimens of corundum. The color is caused by chromium impurities. The deeper the color, the more valuable the stone.

All natural rubies have imperfections, including the inclusion of rutile. The needle-like crystals of rutile reflect light, creating an effect known as "silk." In some cases this silk effect can cause "asterism," an effect in which a six-pointed star can be seen within the stone as light reflects off the crystal inclusions. Asterism is one of the rare cases where impurities can actually increase the value of a gemstone.

Corundum. This sapphire variety was collected at Passara, Uva Province, Sri Lanka.

Rubies exhibit pleochroism—a shifting of color when viewed at different angles—and many specimens also show a fluorescence that causes a brightening of their red color under strong light. These qualities not only increases the value of rubies, but also helps to distinguish them from other red gemstones.

An 8.62 carat cushion-cut, unnamed Burma ruby sold for $3.64 million in February 2006, setting the record price of $425,000 per carat for rubies. The new owner named the stone the "Graff Ruby," after himself.

Ninety percent of the world's rubies are found in Burma (Myanmar). The political situation in Burma and the working conditions in the mines there have caused the ruby trade to become very controversial in recent years.

Sapphire. Corundum gems of colors other than pure red are called "sapphire." Sapphires are typically blue, although they can also be violet, green, yellow, or pink. The blue color is caused by iron and titanium impurities; violet by vanadium; yellow and green varieties by iron; and pink by chromium, as in rubies. There is no specific distinction between pink sapphires and rubies, and pink sapphires are often marketed as low-cost rubies—though more expensive than sapphires, simply because of the name.

Ruby Corundum. Bajouri, Hassanabad, Northern Area, Pakistan.

Like rubies, sapphires may exhibit both silk and asterism due to rutile impurities; sapphires are also pleochroic (exhibiting one color when viewed from one angle and a different color when viewed from a different angle).

Sapphires are often treated with heat or chemical diffusion to artificially enhance their color and therefore their value.

Sapphire. Collected in Montana, this specimen is the sapphire variety of corundum.

Hematite   *See also listing under "Minerals."*

Hematite can be polished to a metallic luster and used for low-cost jewelry, specifically rings. It is relatively soft and brittle, and therefore has little value as a gemstone.

Hematite. This flattened hematite crystal has a highly reflective luster. Brumado, Bahia, Brazil. This crystal sold for $1,955 in early 2008.

Spinel

Chemical Formula	$MgAl_2O_4$
Environment	An accessory in basalts, peridotites, and kimberlites
Locality	Gem gravels of Sri Lanka and other notable locations
Etymology	Uncertain; possibly from Latin *spina*, "thorn"

Physical Properties of Spinel

Cleavage	None
Color	Colorless, red, blue, green, brown
Diaphaneity	Transparent to translucent to opaque
Fracture	Uneven
Habit	Euhedral crystals, massive – granular
Hardness	8
Luminescence	Sometimes fluorescent
Luster	Vitreous (glassy)
Specific Gravity	3.57–3.72, Average = 3.64
Streak	Grayish white
Indicators	Twinning, color

Spinel.

Spinel is the name of a class of minerals which includes franklinite, chromite, magnetite, and the gem spinel.

The gem spinel can be red, blue, violet, dark green, or black.

Red spinel is very similar to and is sometimes substituted for ruby—although red spinel is the most valuable variety, its value is still less than 1/10 that of ruby. Spinel can be distinguished from ruby by its lack of pleochroism.

Blue spinel is very similar to sapphire and can be as valuable, although deeply colored and transparent specimens of blue spinel are very rare and generally extremely small. More typically, blue spinel is light in color and cloudy, and worth much less than sapphires. Because sapphires do not always exhibit pleochroism, this is not a reliable characteristic for distinguishing them from spinel.

Chrysoberyl

Chemical Formula	$BeAl_2O_4$
Environment	Occurs in granitic pegmatite dikes
Locality	Ural Mountains, Russia; Sri Lanka; Burma; Brazil
Etymology	Greek chrysos, "golden," and the mineral beryl

Physical Properties of Chrysoberyl

Cleavage	[110] Distinct, [010] Imperfect, [001] Poor
Color	Yellow, brown, brownish green, green; gray, blue green
Diaphaneity	Transparent to translucent
Fracture	Brittle

Habit	Prismatic, tabular, twinning common
Hardness	8.5
Luster	Vitreous (glassy)
Specific Gravity	3.5–3.84, Average = 3.67
Streak	White
Indicators	Twinning, hardness, color

Common chrysoberyl is yellow, yellow-green, or brown. Despite being the third-hardest gem (only diamond and corundum are harder), chrysoberyl itself is not as highly regarded as its sub-varieties, due primarily to its rather weak color.

Alexandrite. Alexandrite is a rare form of chrysoberyl that exhibits a striking pleochroism—it is a bright green in sunlight but turns red under incandescent light. The largest alexandrite found, in Sri Lanka, is 1,876 carats. The largest cut alexandrite is 66 carats and is housed at the Smithsonian Institution in Washington, DC.

Cymophane. Cymophane is a yellow or greenish-yellow variety of chrysoberyl noted for its chatoyancy, an internal reflectivity caused by fibrous inclusions of rutile that create an effect that gives cymophane its more common name: cat's eye. Cymophane is especially noted for the "milk-and-honey" coloration of its chatoyancy. While not as valuable as alexandrite, it is still highly prized by collectors, and the more pronounced the cat's eye effect, the greater the value of the specimen.

Rhodochrosite

Chemical Formula	MnCO3
Environment	Commonly occurs as a gangue mineral in low- to moderate-temperature hydrothermal veins and metamorphic and sedimentary deposits
Locality	Romania, Germany, Argentina, Mexico, Namibia, South Africa, North America, many other localities worldwide
Etymology	Greek rhodon, "rose," and chroma, "color"

Chrysoberyl. Espirito Santo, Minas Gerais, Brazil.

Alexandrite. Occasionally found associated with emerald crystals at this locality are the often rumored, seldom seen variety of chrysoberyl named for Alexander II, tsar of all the Russias. This cyclicly twinned crystal exhibits the fine green to purple color change for which this gem mineral is noted. It is perched upon a mica schist matrix very consistent with other material from this locality. The alexandrite crystal measures 1-1/4" across. Emerald Mines, Malashevskoye Deposit, Malyshevo, Ekaterinburg, Sverdlovskaya Oblast, Urals Region, Russia.

Physical Properties of Rhodochrosite

Cleavage	[1011] Perfect, [1011] Perfect, [1011] Perfect
Color	Pinkish red, red, rose red, yellowish gray, brown
Diaphaneity	Translucent to subtranslucent
Fracture	Brittle – conchoidal
Habit	Botryoidal, columnar, massive – granular
Hardness	3
Luster	Vitreous (glassy)
Specific Gravity	3.69
Streak	White
Indicators	Color, habit, hardness

Rhodochrosite.

Rhodochrosite is fairly common and has little value as a gem. Slabs often show veining or banding, and are used for sculpture or boxes, but the mineral is fragile and therefore not often used for jewelry.

Azurite

Chemical Formula	$Cu_3(CO_3)_2(OH)_2$
Environment	Secondary mineral in the oxidized zone of copper deposits
Locality	Utah, Arizona, New Mexico, Mexico, Namibia, Congo, Australia
Etymology	Persian *lazward*, "blue"

Physical Properties of Azurite

Cleavage	[011] Perfect, [100] Fair
Color	Azure blue, blue, light blue, dark blue
Diaphaneity	Transparent to subtranslucent
Fracture	Brittle – conchoidal
Habit	Prismatic, stalactitic, tabular
Hardness	3.5–4
Luster	Vitreous (glassy)
Specific Gravity	3.77–3.89, Average = 3.83
Streak	Light blue
Indicators	Color, hardness, habit, association

Azurite. This large rosette of pale blue azurite is associated with minor malachite. Chessy, near Lyon, France. This piece brought $805 at auction in early 2008.

Azurite is a less-common relative of malachite, and the two often occur together. Azurite oxidizes into malachite, its deep blue color changing to green in the process. Although azurite is used as a gemstone, typically for beads, this oxidation and its softness limit its desirability for use in jewelry.

Powdered azurite has also been used for centuries as an artists' pigment. Its color change from oxidation has been of great concern to conservators.

Malachite

Chemical Formula	$Cu_2CO_3(OH)_2$
Environment	Most common secondary mineral in the oxidized zones of copper ore deposits
Locality	Ural Mountains, Russia; Mexico; Congo; Namibia; Australia; Southwestern United States.
Etymology	From the Greek *malache*, "mallow"

Malachite. This choice 4 cm velvet malachite crystal sits on a matrix of light green malachite and a grayish white matrix. Milpillas Copper Mine, Milpillas, Sonora, Mexico. In early 2008, this crystal brought $460 at auction.

Physical Properties of Malachite

Cleavage	[201] Perfect, [010] Fair
Color	Green, Dark green, Blackish green
Diaphaneity	Translucent to subtranslucent to opaque
Fracture	Uneven
Habit	Botryoidal, massive – fibrous, stalactitic
Hardness	3.5–4
Luster	Vitreous – silky
Specific Gravity	3.6–4, Average = 3.8
Streak	Light green
Indicators	Color banding, hardness, association

Malachite has little value and is not often used as a gemstone, but it is prized for use in sculpture for the beauty of its whorls and striations of color, which range from pale whitish-green to dark blackish-green, and its ability to take a high polish.

Turquoise

Chemical Formula	$CuAl_6(PO_4)_4(OH)_8 \cdot 4H_2O$
Environment	Secondary mineral found in potassic alteration zone of copper deposits
Locality	Southwestern United States, Australia, Middle East
Etymology	Named for Turkey

Physical Properties of Turquoise

Cleavage	[001] Perfect, [010] Good
Color	Blue, blue green, green
Diaphaneity	Subtranslucent to opaque
Fracture	Conchoidal

Habit	Concretionary, encrustations, massive
Hardness	5–6
Luster	Waxy
Specific Gravity	2.6–2.8, Average = 2.7
Streak	Pale bluish white
Indicators	Habit, hardness, luster, color

Turquoise has been used as a gem for thousands of years by such diverse and widespread cultures as ancient Egypt, China, and Native Americans. Its value is based primarily on color, increasing as the color becomes more purely blue; green color or mottling substantially reduce the value.

Because of its phosphate content, turquoise is fragile and its color and finish can be adversely affected by solvents, cosmetics, and skin oils, so care should be taken when wearing turquoise jewelry.

Turquoise. Bishop Mine, Campbell County, Virginia.

Because it is relatively soft for a gemstone and rarely forms crystals, turquoise can be easily carved into surprisingly delicate scultpures.

Olivine (Peridot)

Chemical Formula	$(Mg,Fe)_2SiO_4$
Environment	Mafic and ultramafic igneous rocks and marble
Locality	Common worldwide
Etymology	Named for the green color

Physical Properties of Olivine

Cleavage	[001] Good, [010] Distinct
Color	Yellowish green, olive green
Diaphaneity	Transparent to translucent
Fracture	Brittle – conchoidal
Habit	Massive – Granular
Hardness	6.5–7
Luster	Vitreous (glassy)
Specific Gravity	3.27–3.37, Average = 3.32
Streak	White
Indicators	Color, hardness, environment, lack of cleavage

Olivine (Peridot).

Olivine is the gem-quality variety of forsterite, which ranges from colorless to green, depending on iron content. The gem we call olivine today has gone by many names throughout history. The ancient Greeks called it chrysotile (meaning "gold stone"). The Romans called it topazos, after an island (now called Zebirget) in the Red Sea where it was found; the name topaz was initially applied to any yellowish stone, but is now applied only to one specific gem. The transparent gemstone variety of olivine is often called *peridot*, the French word for olivine.

GARNET GROUP

Garnet actually comprises a group of related but distinct minerals. The name "garnet" comes from the Latin name for pomegranate, *malum granatum,* because of the mineral's resemblance to pomegranate seeds.

Low-quality garnet is used as an industrial abrasive; the "sand" in sandpaper is often garnet.

Pyrope

Garnet Group

Chemical Formula	$Mg_3Al_2(SiO_4)_3$
Environment	Occurs in ultrabasic igneous rocks
Location	Bohemia, South Africa, Zimbabwe, Tanzania, United States, Mexico, Australia
Etymology	From the Greek *pyropos,* "fiery-eyed"

Physical Properties of Pyrope

Cleavage	None
Color	Bright red, dark red.
Diaphaneity	Transparent to subtranslucent
Fracture	Conchoidal
Habit	Crystalline – fine, granular, lamellar
Hardness	7.5
Luster	Vitreous (glassy)
Specific Gravity	3.65–3.84, Average = 3.74
Streak	White
Indicators	Habit, color, hardness

Pyrope is usually a bright red, although it can be darker—sometimes so dark that it appears almost black. Pyrope is fairly common, and therefore is less valuable than other garnets.

Almandine

Garnet Group

Chemical Formula	$Fe_3^{2+}Al_2(SiO_4)_3$
Environment	Occurs in metamorphic and pegmatitic rocks
Locality	Alabanda, Asia Minor; worldwide
Etymology	Named for its locality

Physical Properties of Almandine

Cleavage	None
Color	Red, deep red, reddish-purple
Diaphaneity	Transparent to Subtransparent to translucent
Fracture	Brittle – conchoidal
Habit	Granular, massive – lamellar
Hardness	7–8
Luster	Vitreous – resinous
Specific Gravity	4.09–4.31, Average = 4.19
Streak	White
Indicators	Habit, color, hardness

Almandine is the most common variety of garnet. Even exceptionally bright and clear specimens have little value.

Spessartine *Garnet Group*

Chemical Formula	$Mn_3Al_2(SiO_4)_3$
Environment	Occurs in magmatic, metamorphic, and pegmatitic rocks
Locality	Spessart Mountains, Germany; Sri Lanka; Burma; Madagascar; Brazil; United States
Etymology	Named for its locality

Physical Properties of Spessartine

Cleavage	None
Color	Red, reddish-orange, pink, yellow, violet-red
Diaphaneity	Transparent to translucent
Fracture	Subconchoidal
Habit	Crystalline – fine, lamellar, massive
Hardness	6.5–7.5
Luster	Vitreous – Resinous
Specific Gravity	4.18
Streak	White
Indicators	Habit, color, hardness

Spessartine. Quartz provides an accent for this spessartine garnet. Tongbei, Fujian Province, China.

Gem-quality spessartine is uncommon. Its value is therefore generally higher than that of pyrope and almandine. A beautiful orange-yellow variety is found in Madagascar; a violet-red species is commonly found in the United States.

Andradite *Garnet Group*

Chemical Formula	$Ca_3 Fe_3^{2+}Al_2(SiO_4)_3$
Environment	Forms from contact metamorphism of impure limestones and calcic igneous rocks.
Locality	Arizona and California, United States; Ural Mountains, Russia; Italy.
Etymology	Named for Brazilian mineralogist J.B. de Andrada de Silva (1763–1838)

Physical Properties of Andradite

Cleavage	None
Color	Black, yellowish brown, red, greenish yellow, gray

Andradite.

Diaphaneity	Transparent to translucent
Fracture	Conchoidal
Habit	Crystalline – coarse, euhedral crystals, massive
Hardness	6.5–7
Luster	Vitreous (glassy)
Specific Gravity	3.7–4.1, Average = 3.9
Streak	White
Indicators	Habit, color, hardness

Andradite comprises three varieties. Melanite is a glossy black due to high titanium content; it is not used as a gem. Topazolite is a honey yellow color, and is sometimes, though rarely, used as a gem. Demantoid is a bright, vivid green due to chromium substitution. It is the rarest and most valuable garnet—indeed, one of the rarest and most valuable of all gems, often selling for thousands of dollars per carat.

Grossular — *Garnet Group*

Chemical Formula	$Ca_3Al_2(SiO_4)_3$
Environment	Occurs in contact and regional metamorphic calcareous rocks
Locality	North America, Madagascar, Kenya, Tanzania, Sri Lanka
Etymology	From the Latin *grossularia*, "gooseberry"

Physical Properties of Grossular

Cleavage	None
Color	Brown, colorless, green, gray, yellow
Diaphaneity	Transparent to subtranslucent
Fracture	Subconchoidal
Habit	Crystalline – fine, euhedral crystals, massive – granular
Hardness	6.5–7.5
Luster	Vitreous – resinous
Specific Gravity	3.42–3.72, Average = 3.57
Streak	Brownish white
Indicators	Habit, color, hardness

Grossular. This specimen, circa 1944, shows a zoned garnet with grossularite-rich cores and andradite margins. Jumbo Mine, Prince of Wales Island, Alaska.

Grossular occurs in the widest range of colors of any garnet. It is a common gem, and has little value except for the brilliant green variety known as tsavorite, which is found in Kenya and Tanzania.

Uvarovite — *Garnet Group*

Chemical Formula	$Ca_3Cr_2(SiO_4)_3$
Environment	Formed by metamorphism of chromium-containing silicaceous limestones
Locality	Ural Mountains, Russia; Finland; Norway; South Africa

Etymology	Named for Count Sergey Semeonovich Uvarov (1765–1855), Russian statesman, president of the Academy of St. Petersburg

Physical Properties of Uvarovite

Cleavage	None
Color	Green
Diaphaneity	Transparent to translucent
Fracture	Brittle
Habit	Crystalline – fine, lamellar
Hardness	6.5–7
Luster	Vitreous (glassy)
Specific Gravity	3.4–3.8, Average = 3.59
Streak	White
Indicators	Habit, color, hardness

Uvarovite is the only consistently green species of garnet, its color the result of its chromium content. It is rare—almost never found large enough for gems—and highly prized for its bright color and exceptional brilliance.

Zircon

Chemical Formula	$ZrSiO_4$
Environment	Occurs as an accessory mineral in igneous and metamorphic rocks
Locality	United States, Canada, Brazil, Australia, Scandinavia
Etymology	Named for its composition

Zircon. The large, light brown, emerald-cut zircon is from Ceylon; the rest were collected in Siam. Part of a collection (nine pieces) that brought $1,495 at auction in February 2008.

Physical Properties of Zircon

Cleavage	[110] Indistinct
Color	Brown, red, colorless, gray, black, green
Diaphaneity	Transparent to translucent to opaque
Fracture	Uneven
Habit	Crystalline –fine, prismatic, tabular
Hardness	7.5
Luminescence	Fluorescent and radioactive, short UV = yellow, long UV = dull red.
Luster	Adamantine
Specific Gravity	4.6–4.7, Average = 4.65
Streak	White
Indicators	Habit, hardness, luster

While zircon is often substituted for diamond because of its clarity and high index of refraction (1.95; diamond approximately 2.4), it should not be confused with the synthetic diamond substitute cubic zirconia, which is zirconium dioxide (ZrO_2).

The color of zircon can be readily changed by heating, but the color often reverts to the original through exposure to sunlight. Because of this and zircon's brittleness, it is not suitable for daily wear, and therefore has little value as a gemstone.

Topaz

Topaz.

Chemical Formula	$Al_2SiO_4(F,OH)_2$
Environment	Occurs in pegmatites and high-temperature quartz veins and in cavities in granites and rhyolites
Locality	Mexico, United States, Brazil, Europe, Sri Lanka, Japan, Afghanistan
Etymology	Named for Topazios Island (see Olivine)

Physical Properties of Topaz

Cleavage	[001] Perfect
Color	Colorless, pale blue, yellow, yellowish brown, red
Diaphaneity	Transparent
Fracture	Brittle – uneven
Habit	Crystalline – coarse, massive – granular, prismatic
Hardness	8
Luminescence	Fluorescent, short UV = golden yellow, long UV = cream
Luster	Vitreous (glassy)
Specific Gravity	3.5–3.6, Average = 3.55
Streak	White
Indicators	Habit, color, hardness

Pure topaz is colorless, but impurities give it a range of colors. Typically, topaz is yellow—raging from pale straw yellow to the color of sherry. Sherry-colored specimens will turn pink when heated; when irradiated, topaz turns blue. Although both colors do occur naturally, deliberate alteration is considered acceptable in the gem trade.

Topaz is considered one of the more valuable secondary gems. The value of topaz increases as the color becomes deeper and more intense.

Zoisite

Chemical Formula	$Ca_2Al_3(SiO_4)_3(OH)$
Environment	Occurs in metamorphic and pegmatite rocks
Locality	Austria, Switzerland, Norway, Tanzania, Kenya, India, Pakistan, United States
Etymology	Named for Slovene natural scientist Baron Sigmund Zois von Edelstein (1747–1819)

Physical Properties of Zoisite

Cleavage	[001] Perfect
Color	Blue, green, gray, pink, yellow, brown

Diaphaneity	Transparent to subtranslucent
Fracture	Even
Habit	Columnar, prismatic, striated
Hardness	6.5
Luster	Vitreous – pearly
Specific Gravity	3.3
Streak	White
Indicators	Cleavage, color, pleochroism

Zoisite. Found in Tanzania, this specimen is blue zoisite, or tanzanite. Merelani Hills, Umba Valley Arusha, Tanzania.

Blue zoisite, called *tanzanite* after its main locality (Tanzania, but also found in Pakistan), when transparent is a rare and valuable gem. It is pleochroic, shifting color to violet or even green.

Green zoisite (from Tanzania) and pink zoisite (called thulite, after its locality in Thule, Norway) are opaque and massive, and often carved into sculpture. Green zoisite often forms with non-gem-quality ruby inclusions; the contrast between the green and red give the stone a striking and unique appearance, making it especially prized for carving.

Beryl

Chemical Formula	$Be_3Al_2Si_6O_{18}$
Environment	Commonly found in granitic pegmatites
Locality	Worldwide
Etymology	From the Greek *beryllos*, "blue-green color of sea water"

Physical Properties of Beryl

Cleavage	[0001] Imperfect
Color	Colorless, green, blue, yellow, pink
Diaphaneity	Transparent to subtranslucent
Fracture	Brittle – conchoidal
Habit	Columnar, crystalline – coarse, prismatic
Hardness	7.5–8
Luster	Vitreous – Resinous
Specific Gravity	2.63–2.9, Average = 2.76
Streak	White
Indicators	Habit, cleavage, hardness, color

Beryl. Colorado.

Beryl, which in its pure state is colorless, is little known by itself; it is instead widely regarded for its colored varieties.

The largest known crystal of any mineral is a beryl from Madagascar that measures almost 60 feet long and almost 12 feet across.

Aquamarine. Aquamarine is a blue beryl found in Russia, Sri Lanka, Africa, Brazil, and the United States. It is pleochroic, showing a green tinge in one direction. The larger deep-blue specimens are especially valuable, often worth more than comparable blue topaz. Aquamarine is often heated to deepen its color.

Emerald. Emerald is perhaps the best known beryl, famous for its distinctive bright green color. The best specimens come from Colombia, though emeralds are found throughout Africa, India, Pakistan, and Afghanistan. Emeralds almost always contain inclusions; however, unlike with other gems, these inclusions are not considered flaws because they are so widespread. In fact, the inclusions are often used to distinguish natural emerald from synthetics. Rarely, carbon inclusions will produce a form of asterism in an emerald. Such specimens, called trapiche emeralds, are found only in Colombia.

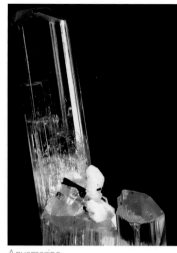
Aquamarine.

Famous emeralds include the Gachala emerald, the largest uncut emerald in the world. Now housed at the Smithsonian Institution, this 858-carat stone was discovered in Colombia 1967.

Heliodor. Heliodor, also called golden beryl, is a comparatively little-known yellow beryl.

Emerald. This beautiful group of fine, dark green emerald prisms sit on a matrix of shiny pyrite crystals. A single emerald stands 1.5 cm tall in the center. Chivor, Columbia. This specimen brought $310.50 at auction in early 2008.

Heliodor. This brought $1,725 at auction in February 2008. Volodarsk, Volynski, Ukraine.

Morganite. Morganite is a pink variety of beryl, the color caused by manganese impurities. It is named for the banker and financier J.P. Morgan, who at one time had one of the most important mineral collections in the world.

Cordierite

Chemical Formula	$Mg_2Al_4Si_5O_{18}$
Environment	Occurs in metamorphic, sedimentary, and mafic igneous rocks
Locality	Germany, Sri Lanka, India, Burma, Madagascar, Connecticut, Canada
Etymology	Named for French geologist P.L.A. Cordier (1777–1861)

Physical Properties of Cordierite

Cleavage	[010] Poor
Color	Colorless, pale blue, violet, yellow
Diaphaneity	Transparent to translucent
Fracture	Conchoidal
Habit	Massive – granular, prismatic
Hardness	7
Luster	Vitreous (glassy)
Specific Gravity	2.55–2.75, Average = 2.65
Streak	White
Indicators	Hardness, cleavage, color, pleochroism

Cordierite exhibits strong dichroism in sunlight. The transparent variety is sometimes called iolite, dichroite, or water sapphire when used as a gemstone.

Tourmaline Group

Tourmaline is a complex group of related but widely varying silicate minerals. Schorl (see listing under "Minerals") accounts for 95 percent of all tourmaline but has no value as a gem.

All tourmaline crystals are trigonal and piezoelectric, meaning that they produce a small electric charge when compressed or vibrated. Many tourmalines are pyroelectric as well, generating an electric charge when heated.

Morganite. Spectacular pink morganite growing on a matrix of platy clevelandite. The crystal is 11 cm in length and has a few green elbaite crystals attached. Lavra de Serra do Urucom, Galileia, Minas Gerais, Brazil. This specimen sold for $12,650 at auction in early 2008.

Tourmaline. Jonas Mine, Itatiaia District, Minas Gerais, Brazil. This specimen brought $3,680 at auction in February 2008.

Elbaite

Tourmaline Group

Chemical Formula	Na(Li,Al)3Al6(BO3)3Si6O18 (OH)4
Environment	Forms in lithium-rich granitic pegmatites and high-temperature hydrothermal veins
Locality	Elba, Italy; Brazil; United States; Russia; Sri Lanka; Pakistan
Etymology	Named for its locality

Physical Properties of Elbaite

Cleavage	[1011] Indistinct
Color	Blue, violet, colorless, green, pink
Diaphaneity	Transparent to translucent to opaque
Fracture	Subconchoidal
Habit	Prismatic, striated
Hardness	7.5
Luminescence	Piezoelectric
Luster	Vitreous (glassy)
Specific Gravity	2.9–3.2, Average = 3.05
Streak	White
Indicators	Habit, triangular cross section, color

Elbaite.

Elbaite is the most colorful tourmaline, and the only one routinely used as a gemstone. It is highly pleochroic, appearing much darker when viewed down the long axis of the crystal.

Specific colors of elbaite have their own names. Rubellite is a red or pink variety. Indicolite is deep blue variety, often with some violet or even greenish tint. Verdelite is the green variety. Only the most colorful stones of all varieties are valuable.

Elbaite often exhibits distinct color zoning, the most familiar example of this being "watermelon" tourmaline, which is green at one end and pink at the other (if transversely zoned) or green on the outside and pink on the inside (if concentrically zoned). Watermelon tourmaline is very popular among collectors, and for this reason often carries a higher price than single-colored specimens.

Jadeite

Chemical Formula	Na(Al,Fe)Si$_2$O$_6$
Environment	Occurs in sodium-rich metamorphic serpentinous rocks
Locality	California, Guatemala, Japan, Tibet, Burma, Russia, Alaska, British Columbia
Etymology	From the Spanish, *piedra de ijada,* "stone of the side," because it was believed to cure kidney ailments when applied to the side of the body

Physical Properties of Jadeite

Cleavage	[110] Good
Color	Light to deep jade green, white, gray, grayish green, pale purple, yellow, black
Diaphaneity	Translucent to subtranslucent
Fracture	Tough
Habit	Fibrous, granular, massive – fibrous
Hardness	6.5
Luster	Vitreous (glassy)
Specific Gravity	3.25–3.35, Average = 3.3
Streak	White
Indicators	Tenacity, fibrousness, color

Jadeite is one of two minerals commonly known as jade (the other is nephrite). Jadeite can occur in a range of colors, but the pale emerald green color known as "imperial jade" is the best known and the most valuable—in fact, imperial green jade sometimes sells for more per weight then diamond. However, in China the white variety has been the most highly prized. A blue-green variety from Guatemala, which was carved by the ancient Olmecs, is increasing in popularity.

Because of its massive habit, extremely fine crystals, and tenacity, jade can be carved in exceptionally fine detail and with great delicacy. Jadeite's toughness makes it suitable not only for fine sculpture, but for wares such as teacups, vases, and even decorative knife and sword blades.

Rhodonite

Chemical Formula	$(Mn^{++},Fe^{++},Mg,Ca)SiO_3$
Environment	Within metamorphic rocks and hydrothermal veins
Locality	Ural Mountains, Russia; Sweden; Australia; United States
Etymology	Greek *rhodos*, "rose colored"

Rhodonite. Franklin, New Jersey.

Physical Properties of Rhodonite

Cleavage	[110] Perfect, [110] Perfect
Color	Pink, rose red, brownish red, black, yellow
Diaphaneity	Semiopaque to translucent
Fracture	Uneven
Habit	Massive – granular, massive, tabular
Hardness	6
Luster	Vitreous (glassy)
Specific Gravity	3.5–3.7, Average = 3.6
Streak	White
Indicators	Color, inclusions

Rhodonite is little used as a gemstone, due to its generally patchy color (pink with black veins or blotches), but this same property makes it popular for beads and cabochons, as well as for carving as an ornamental stone. Very small transparent crystals are occasionally found and faceted as gems, however, although they are not in great demand.

Nephrite

See also listings for tremolite and actinolite under "Minerals."

Nephrite is the gemstone variety of two distinct minerals, tremolite and actinolite; it is also one of two minerals commonly called "jade" (the other is jadeite). Nephrite has a "felted" texture, which distinguishes it from jadeite, but is otherwise similar in appearance and properties to jadeite, and has the same uses.

Nephrite is found in New Zealand, where it plays an important role in the native culture of the Maori, who carve it into weapons and ornaments and often exchange it to signify treaties.

SERPENTINE GROUP

Serpentine is a group of more than 20 related minerals, although only three are of any importance. All of the serpentine minerals have generally the same chemistry, but different structures. These minerals rarely occur alone, and because their appearance and other properties are so similar, distinctions are not often made; instead, mixtures of serpentine group minerals are simply referred to as a single specimen of serpentine.

The group name comes from the Latin *serpens*, "snake," because of the scaly, reticulated appearance.

Antigorite

Serpentine Group

Chemical Formula	$(Mg,Fe)_3Si_2O_5(OH)_4$
Environment	Common in regional and contact metamorphosed serpentinites
Locality	Valle di Antigorio, Italy; New Zealand; United States
Etymology	After Valle di Antigorio, Italy

Physical Properties of Antigorite

Cleavage	[001] Good
Color	Green, gray, bluish gray, brown, black
Diaphaneity	Translucent to subopaque
Fracture	Brittle
Habit	Massive, platy, scaly
Hardness	3.5–4
Luster	Vitreous – greasy
Specific Gravity	2.5–2.6, Average = 2.54
Streak	Greenish white
Indicators	Hardness, color, silky feel, luster

Antigorite is lamellar and often translucent. Translucent specimens are called "precious serpentine" and are popular for ornamental carving. Antigorite is the serpentine most often used for jewelry.

Lizardite — *Serpentine Group*

Chemical Formula	$Mg_3Si_2O_5(OH)_4$
Environment	Forms most of the serpentine in the serpentine marbles
Locality	Lizard Point, Cornwall, England
Etymology	After Lizard Point, Cornwall

Physical Properties of Lizardite

Cleavage	[001] Perfect
Color	Green, green blue, yellow, white
Diaphaneity	Translucent
Fracture	Uneven
Habit	Hexagonal crystals
Hardness	2.5
Luster	Dull to greasy
Specific Gravity	2.55–2.6, Average = 2.57
Streak	White
Indicators	Hardness, color, silky feel, luster

Lizardite comprises most of the serpentine found in serpentine marble. It is very fine grained and scaly, although this has nothing to do with its name.

Chrysotile — *Serpentine Group*

Chemical Formula	$Mg_3Si_2O_5(OH)_4$
Environment	Forms in many metamorphic and igneous rocks
Locality	Quebec, Canada; United States
Etymology	Greek *chrysos,* "gold," and *tilos,* "fiber"

Physical Properties of Chrysotile

Cleavage	None
Color	Green
Diaphaneity	Translucent
Fracture	Splintery
Habit	Acicular
Hardness	2.5
Luster	Silky
Specific Gravity	2.53
Streak	White
Indicators	Hardness, color, silky feel, luster

Chrysotile.

Chrysotile is a very fibrous mineral that is the only source of asbestos currently in use, as it seems to be eliminated from the body more easily than other forms of asbestos. Although some controversy still surrounds chrysotile, it is used in the manufacture of chrysotile cement, a tough, lightweight cement product which is used around the world for roof and wall shingles, pipes, sewers, and water tanks.

Quartz

Chemical Formula	SiO_2
Environment	Common in sedimentary, metamorphic, and igneous rocks
Locality	Very common; found worldwide
Etymology	German *quarz*, of uncertain origin

Physical Properties of Quartz

Cleavage	[01 10] Indistinct
Color	Colorless (see also specific varieties)
Diaphaneity	Transparent
Fracture	Conchoidal
Habit	Crystalline – coarse, crystalline – fine, druse
Hardness	7
Luminescence	Triboluminescent
Luster	Vitreous (glassy)
Specific Gravity	2.6–2.65, Average = 2.62
Streak	White
Indicators	Commonness, transparency, habit, hardness

Quartz. Near Amatitlan, Guerrero, Mexico.

Quartz is the second-most-common mineral in the Earth's crust, after feldspar. Pure quartz is transparent and colorless, but impurities give it an astonishing range of diapheneity and color. Quartz often forms geodes (hollow pockets of beautiful drusy crystals formed inside cavities of rock); geodes are split and sold as ornaments, usually unpolished to highlight the raw crystals themselves.

All quartzes are piezoelectric, that is, producing an electric charge under mechanical stress, and

Amethyst.

vibrating when electrical current is applied to them. Because of this, quartz is commonly used as a crystal oscillator in electronics and watches.

Amethyst. Amethyst is the transparent or translucent purple variety of quartz, the color being due to iron and aluminum impurities. Amethyst is highly prized for its color, and after pure quartz is perhaps the best-known variety, and the most popular. It is faceted into gemstones, carved into beads or figures, and sold in its raw state as an ornament. Amethyst often forms especially large and impressive geodes.

Chatoyant quartz. Chatoyancy is a reflective sheen, caused by light glancing off fibrous inclusions within a stone. The greenish varieties of chatoyant quartz are called "cat's eye." Blue varieties are called "hawk's eye." Golden yellow or brown varieties are called "tiger's eye." Chatoyant quartz is generally polished as cabochons, beads, or slabs, to highlight the chatoyancy.

Citrine. Citrine is a transparent yellow or orange quartz. Though rare, its value is low. It is most often faceted as a gemstone. It is sometimes sold fraudulently as topaz.

Rock crystal. Colorless quartz when faceted as a gemstone or carved is called "rock crystal."

Rose quartz. Rose quartz is a delicate-pink to red variety often carved into cabochons or figurines; it is always translucent, never transparent, because of the mineral inclusions that produce its color, so it is rarely faceted as a gemstone. Rutile inclusions may produce a faint asterism.

Smoky quartz. Smoky Quartz is a brown to black, usually translucent, quartz. The color is caused by natural or intentional irradiation of aluminum impurities. It is one of the few brown or black minerals popular as a gemstone. An opaque black variety is called "morion."

Rose quartz. These quartz crystals, ranging in color from pale pink to rose, are growing a large, pale smoky quartz crystal. The pink color is due to titanium or iron. Sapucaia do Norte, Minas Gerais, Brazil. This piece sold for $34,500 at a February 2008 auction.

Smoky quartz. A large, spectacular, completely transparent, gem-quailty smoky quartz with great luster, this specimen is a "floater," with no points of attachment. It brought $7,475 at auction in early 2008.

Chalcedony. Chalcedony is the name given to any cryptocrystalline quartzes that form from concretions of silica-rich deposits.

Agate. Agate is multi-colored, banded chalcedony. The banding occurs when silicaceous solutions deposit layers of crystals onto the walls of cavities in volcanic rock. Variations in the chemistry of successive solutions cause the range of colors seen in the striped bands. Moss agate is a dendritic form featuring beautiful patterns suggesting moss of other vegetable growth.

Aventurine. Aventurine is a vaguely translucent chalcedony, with platy mineral inclusions causing a characteristic glistening or shimmering appearance known as aventurescence. Aventurine is most commonly green, but can be yellow, orange, brown, or blue. Because of its inclusions, aventurine rarely takes a good polish, and so is used primarily for beads and pendants. Exceptional specimens are carved into cabochons.

Carnelian. Carnelian is a red or reddish-brown chalcedony. It was used in ancient Rome for making signets to seal letters and documents.

Chalcedony. This exotically sinuous bit of Nature's whimsy was discovered in the course of operations at one of the numerous road metal quarries that are scattered about the Deccan Plateau, a vast lava flow covering thousands of square miles in central India. Bubbles in the lava are occasionally found to harbor strange wormlike growths formed of chalcedony, a form of silica closely related to agate. In this case, erratically radiating crystals of an unidentified black mineral were coated by translucent chalcedony. As a final touch, Mother Nature gave the structure an overcoat of sparkling, druzy quartz sprinkled with a few pearlescent blades of stilbite. It measures 6" x 4-1/2" x 2-3/4" deep. Deccan Plateau, India.

Agate. Amygdaloid Island Flow with characteristic agate amygdules (sawed surface) from the northeast end of Amygdaloid Island, circa 1971. Isle Royale National Park, Michigan.

Chrysoprase. Chrysoprase is the name given to green chalcedony. It is often used for carving.

Jasper. Jasper is an opaque red or brown chalcedony exhibiting banded or swirling patterns of inclusions. It takes a high polish, and is used as a gemstone or carved into vases, boxes, and figures.

Plasma. Plasma is a bright green chalcedony that is often spotted with jasper.

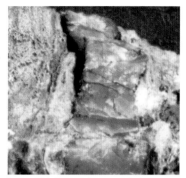

Jasper. This image shows typical "banded" jasper in limestone. Manakacha Formation, Parashant Canyon, Grand Canyon National Park, Arizona.

Opal

Chemical Formula	$SiO_2 \cdot nH_2O$
Environment	Forms by the alteration of siliceous igneous extrusive rocks
Locality	Worldwide
Etymology	Old Indian *upala*, "precious stone"

Physical Properties of Opal

Cleavage	None
Color	White, yellow, red, brown, blue, green
Diaphaneity	Transparent to translucent to opaque
Fracture	Conchoidal
Habit	Amorphous, massive, reniform
Hardness	5.5–6
Luminescence	Fluorescent, short UV = greenish yellow, long UV = white
Luster	Vitreous – dull
Specific Gravity	1.9–2.3, Average = 2.09
Streak	White
Indicators	Play of color, fluorescence, lack of cleavage or crystal face

Black Opal. Small step faults in black opaline chert occurring in diatomaceous rock, circa 1931. Malaga Cove, Palos Verdes Hills, Los Angeles County, California.

Opal is a hydrated form of quartz, but is technically an amorphous mineraloid, since it does not form crystals. Precious, gem-quality opal displays a shifting interplay of internal colors. Opal is generally polished in cabochons to show off this dazzling iridescence. Because opal is hydrous—normally from 2 percent to 3 percent water, though sometimes containing as much as 20 percent—it has a tendency to dry out and crack or shatter.

Opal is categorized according to its background color. White opal is the most widely known, and is the most easily recognized gemstone because of its unmistakable iridescent appearance when polished. Black opal, which has a blue, gray, or black background, is the most valuable variety. Fire opal, or common opal, is generally cloudy and lacks the iridescence of the precious or "noble" opals.

Ninety percent of the world's opals are found in Australia. Fire opals are found in Mexico and Latin America. Opal can often replace organic minerals to form fossils, which, when polished, can be quite striking.

Adularia
See also listing for orthoclase under "Minerals."

Adularia, or moonstone, is a gemstone variety of orthoclase. It is almost transparent and almost colorless, showing a pale gray with a faint silvery or bluish shimmer that occurs deep within the stone. This kind of internal pearly reflection is called "adularescence." Adularia is polished as cabochons or beads to highlight the adularescence. Its value is quite low, although specimens with the blue shimmer are more desirable.

Amazonite
See also listing for microcline under "Minerals."

Amazonite is a semiopaque green to blue-green microcline with a mottled or striated appearance. It polishes well and is often used as a gemstone, although it has a low hardness and is easily fractured.

Albite

The gemstone variety of albite is also called "moonstone" and shares the properties of adularia moonstone, although it is distinct from adularia.

Labradorite
See also listing for anorthosite under "Rocks."

Labradorite. This labradorite specimen exhibits samples of Bytownite.

Chemical Formula	$(Ca,Na)(Si,Al)_4O_8$
Environment	Within metamorphic and mafic igneous rocks
Locality	Labrador, Canada; Scandinavia
Etymology	After Labrador, Canada

Physical Properties of Labradorite

Cleavage	[001] Perfect, [010] Good, [110] Distinct
Color	Colorless, gray, gray white, white, light green
Diaphaneity	Translucent to transparent
Fracture	Uneven
Habit	Crystalline – coarse, granular, striated
Hardness	7
Luminescence	Non-fluorescent
Luster	Vitreous (glassy)
Specific Gravity	2.68–2.71, Average = 2.69

Streak	White
Indicators	Labradorescence, twinning

Although the background of labradorite is a dull, smoky gray, when light strikes the surface in a particular direction it produces a spectacular form of iridescence called "labradorescence," a shifting interplay of violet, blue, green, yellow, and gold caused by light refracting back and forth among lamellar layers in the stone. The labrodorescence is most noticeable on polished surfaces, so as a gemstone labradorite is most often made into cabochons or slabs.

Lapis Lazuli

Lapis lazuli is actually a rock, composed primarily of the mineral lazurite. Calcite, pyrite, and sodalite are also usually present.

Lapis is an intense, opaque blue with flecks of white and gold. It is massive in habit, and has been used for jewelry, carvings, vases, boxes, mosaics, and even in architecture for cladding walls and columns in churches, chapels, and shrines. Until a synthetic (and cheaper) substitute became available in the early 19th century, lapis lazuli was also ground for use in the pigment ultramarine for tempera and oil paint.

Lazurite. Sar-e-Sang, Badakhshan, Afghanistan.

ORGANIC GEMS

Amber

Chemical Formula	[C,H,O]
Environment	Fossilized tree resin
Locality	Baltic Coast, Russia, Poland, Romania, Dominican Republic, United States
Etymology	German *bernstein*, "burn stone" (for its tendency to burn in high heat)

Physical Properties of Amber

Cleavage	None
Color	Yellow, brown, colorless, brownish red
Diaphaneity	Transparent
Fracture	Conchoidal
Habit	Nodular, pulverulent
Hardness	2–2.5
Luminescence	Fluorescent

Amber.

Luster	Resinous
Specific Gravity	1.05–1.15, Average = 1.1
Streak	White
Indicators	Color, density, tenacity, trapped insects

Amber is a fossilized resin or tree sap. It often contains perfectly preserved insects, spiders, and even frogs or other small animals that became trapped in the sap when it was still liquid. Such specimens are highly prized for jewelry. Amber is also widely used for beads, ornaments, tobacco pipes, cigarette holders, and drinking vessels. When heated, amber becomes pliable, and pieces can be joined together to form larger pieces or pressed into sheets.

In 1701 King Friedrich Wilhelm I of Prussia commissioned a collection of chamber wall panels made of more than 6-1/2 tons of amber. In 1716 he presented the panels to Emperor Peter the Great of Russia. The so-called Amber Room was looted from the Catherine Palace by the Nazis during World War II, and was subsequently lost. Between 1979 and 2003 it was reconstructed, following photographs, in the Catherine Palace.

Jet

Opaque and either black or dark brown, jet is actually a mineraloid formed by the high-pressure decomposition of wood. Jet that forms in salt water is much harder than jet that forms in fresh water. Jet has been used for jewelry for at least 10,000 years, although it enjoyed its greatest popularity during the reign of Queen Victoria, who wore it as part of her mourning dress because of its dark, somber appearance. Today its use is almost unheard of.

Jet.

Pearl

Pearls are technically cysts, formed by a mollusk as it secretes layers of calcium carbonate and hornlike conchiolin—the materials it uses to create its shell—around a grain of sand or other irritant that gets inside its shell. Pearls are often cultured by deliberately securing an irritant inside a mollusk's shell.

Because they are organic, very few pearls are of gem quality. The most valuable pearls are almost perfectly spherical and with a smooth, uniform surface and color and a pale luster or iridescence. While the most desirable color is white with a hint of gray or yellow, pearls can be pink or black. In April 2007, the legendary Baroda pearl necklace sold for $7 million at auction. The world's largest pearl, the "Pearl of Lao Tzu," is valued at almost $60 million. Also called the "Pearl of Allah" because of its resemblance to a turbaned head, the pearl measures 9.45" long, weighs 14.1 pounds, and is 31,893.5 carats.

Coral

The gemstone coral is actually the calcareous skeletons of coral colonies, marine anthozoans that produce vast structures of calcite bound together with secreted proteins. Coral can be red, pink white, blue, or black. It is sometimes carved into figurines or beads for jewelry.

Ivory

Ivory is obtained from the tusks and teeth of elephants, walri, hippopotami, or other mammals. It has been carved and used as ornaments and jewelry for tens of thousands of years. Since 1989 there has been a worldwide ban on ivory trade due to overharvesting that caused dangerous declines in animal populations, in some cases leading to near-extinction. Poaching remains widespread, however, and the United Nations partially lifted the ban in 2002 for economic reasons.

Plastic substitutes for ivory exist. The tagua nut, a renewable vegetable source, is also a substitute, although its size limits its use.

Coral. This figure of a woman with attendants is exhibited at the Stanford Museum, Stanford University, California.

The Expert's Guide
to
COLLECTING & INVESTING IN RARE COINS

Coin collecting—the "Hobby of Kings"—pays rich dividends in fun and enjoyment. But it can also pay the old-fashioned way: with a huge return on your investment. Now you can learn how to be a smart collector and investor, straight from the expert: award-winning author and numismatist Q. David Bowers.

With hands-on advice, real-life examples, and entertaining storytelling, the "dean of American numismatics" shares 50 years of experience buying and selling rare coins, tokens, medals, and paper money.

Want to know how to evaluate a coin's potential? Use the four-step process in chapter 2. What's the best way to predict the rare-coin market? It doesn't take a crystal ball; find out in chapter 13. To avoid getting burned in online auctions, read chapter 15. And if you want to be a smart seller, you can learn the ropes in chapter 34. All of these expert secrets, and more, are waiting inside. . . .

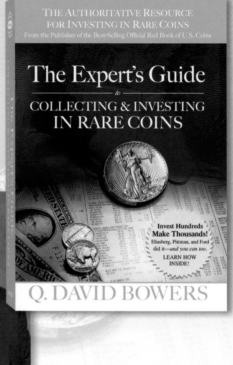

Whitman
Publishing, LLC
PUBLISHING SINCE 1934
www.whitman**books**.com

"[Bowers brings] proper balance to the interplay of collecting and investing in our hobby community."

—Clifford Mishler, numismatic author and researcher

"Are there really 'secrets' to successful coin buying? You bet! And Dave Bowers reveals them here. His style is entertaining, informative, and motivating. . . ."

—Kenneth Bressett, editor of the *Guide Book of United States Coins*

Order online at www.whitmanbooks.com
Call 1-800-546-2995 • Email info@whitman**books**.com

APPENDIX A: METEORITES

Meteorites are stony or metallic pieces of the solar system that have fallen to Earth. Most are broken-off pieces of asteroids, but scientists have traced the origin of some to the Moon and even to the planet Mars. Meteorites are the oldest objects found on Earth, up to 4.55 billion years old. They are also some of the rarest—much rarer than gold and diamonds (about 500 fall each year, and fewer than 2 percent of those are ever recovered). These extraterrestrial minerals are fascinating, beautiful, and highly collectible.

Notable meteorite sites in North America include:

the Barringer Crater in Arizona, also known as "Meteor Crater"
the Manson crater in Iowa
the Chesapeake Bay impact crater
Sudbury Basin in Ontario, Canada
Manicouagan Reservoir in Quebec, Canada
Clearwater Lakes (a double-crater impact in Quebec, Canada)

The following specimens were all sold in the February 15, 2008, Tucson Sale (featuring selections from the Robert and Edna Whitmore Collection), conducted by Stack's of New York.

Allende. In the early morning of February 8, 1969, a very rare class of meteorite called carbonaceous chondrite fell in northern Mexico. To date, scientists have identified only 17 meteorites of this type. Allende specimens are special because they contain unique, somewhat finger-like projections of a whitish material. Called calcium aluminum inclusions, these are mixtures of high-temperature oxides and silicates of calcium, aluminum, and titanium. Scientists believe this might be some of the first matter to have crystallized out of the solar nebula, and thus older than the Earth itself. The composition of Allende is very close to that of the Sun (minus the hydrogen and helium). This quarter-pound example with a very dark, thick fusion crust sold for just under $1,000.

Allende.

Canyon Diablo.

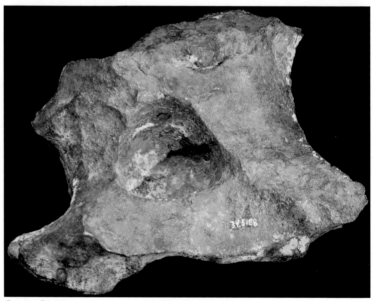

Canyon Diablo.

Canyon Diablo. The Canyon Diablo meteorite comes from the most famous and best-preserved impact crater on Earth—the Barringer Crater, near Flagstaff, Arizona. Once very easily collected, this metallic meteorite is becoming increasingly more difficult to obtain, as the adjacent lands are now off limits to collectors. The magnificent specimen at top weighs slightly more than five pounds and is extremely well preserved; it sold for $1,610 in the Tucson Sale. A heavier specimen (bottom), weighing almost eight pounds, sold for $4,600.

Cape York. The Cape York meteorite was "discovered" in 1894 by Arctic explorer Robert Peary, who brought the specimen to New York three years later, after several expeditions to the site. For centuries, Eskimos had used fragments of this meteorite as a source of iron for knives and other weapons. The American Museum of Natural History has exhibited an enormous mass of Cape York as the featured specimen in their spectacular meteorite exhibit. The piece pictured was discovered in 1963 in a separate mass (named *Agpalilic*). It is esti-

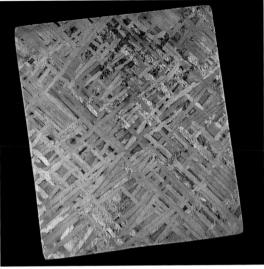

Cape York.

mated to have fallen to Earth 10,000 years ago. This beautiful specimen, which weighs about a third of a pound, was professionally cut, polished, and etched to bring out a Widmanstätten pattern, a structure of long nickel-iron crystals found only in meteorites. This specimen sold for $977.50.

Gibeon. In the 1830s, masses of native iron up to two feet square were found on the east side of the Great Fish River in Namibia. This was the first reported evidence of the Gibeon Meteorite. In subsequent years, European cattle farmers in the area recovered many large meteorites, including a 511-pound mass found in 1857. The Gibeon Meteorite is very stable and is not subject to the usual corrosions of most other iron meteorites. It is so distinctive that Rolex featured it as a watch face in one of its special models. The specimen pictured at left, which weighs about two-thirds of a pound, sold for $460.

The larger specimen at right, weighing more than 18 pounds, sold for nearly $4,000.

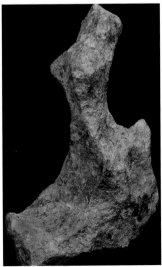

Gibeon.

Gibeon.

Northwest Africa 032. This is a real piece of the Moon that has fallen to Earth—a lunar specimen quite different from all others, as it is a pure sample of volcanic lunar basalt, and not a mixture of basalt and anorthosite. It came from the mare regions of the Moon (known as the "dark regions"). According to the *Meteoritical Bulletin,* the primary assemblage is essentially unaltered by terrestrial weathering. This rare specimen, weighing only 1.57 grams, sold for $2,530.

Northwest Africa 032.

Odessa. The Odessa iron meteorite pictured is a highly curved specimen from the largest meteorite-bearing crater in Texas. Dr. Lincoln Lapaz (an early officer of the Meteoritical Society) found it in the 1950s. The crater has recently been protected and a museum now resides there. Decades ago, a mastodon was found in the crater by a local university excavating for scientific study. Apparently the animal fell in and was unable to climb out because of the steep sides. This two-pound meteorite sold for $2,645.

Odessa.

Seymchan.

Seymchan. The Seymchan meteorite was discovered in 1967. Two large iron pieces were found in a streambed flowing into the Hekandue River in Russia. Analysis revealed they were of a rare type of iron. In 2004, another expedition traveled to the extremely remote location and found several more masses. The Widmanstätten pattern of the Seymchan meteorite is one of the most striking in the world. This etched and polished specimen, weighing about 20 ounces, exhibits a "lightning bolt" of iron streaming through the olivine phase. It sold for $2,990.

Sikhote Alin. The Sikhote Alin meteorite hit Earth in a massive impact event on February 12, 1947. It landed near the village of Paseka, approximately 275 miles northeast of Vladivostok, Russia. Residents saw a fireball "brighter than the sun" that came out of the north and descended at an angle of about 41 degrees. The bright flash and the deafening sound of the fall were observed for hundreds of miles around the point of impact. A smoke trail estimated at 20 miles in length remained in the sky for several hours. Some of the meteorite's fragments made craters up to 85 feet across and 20 feet deep. Others were found driven into trees. A Soviet postage stamp was issued to commemorate this amazing extraterrestrial event. The specimen pictured, with its glassy black fusion crust and many deep indentations, weighs just over two pounds. It sold for $3,680.

Sikhote Alin.

APPENDIX B: GALLERY OF MINERALS AND GEMSTONES

This gallery provides full illustrations of some of the mineral formations included in *A Guide Book of Minerals, Rocks, and Gemstones*.

Amethyst, see page 211.

Apolphyllite, see page 155.

Aquamarine, see page 204.

Aragonite, see page 83.

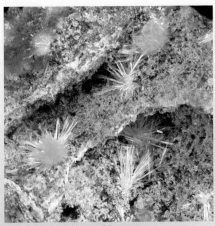

Aurichalcite, see page 86.

Azurite, see page 195.

Beryl, see page 203.

Brochanitite, see page 96.

Calcite, see page 81.

Cerussite, see page 85.

Chalcedony, see page 212.

Chalcopyrite, see page 48.

Childrenite, see page 118.

Chrysoberyl, see page 193.

Copper, see page 35.

Coral, see page 217.

Cuprite, see page 62.

Ferberite, see page 122.

Flourite, see page 80.

Gold, see page 34.

Inesite, see page 148.

Legrandite, see page 119.

Mimetite, see page 116.

Olivenite, see page 112.

Pyromorphite, see page 115.

Rose quartz, see page 211.

Selenite, see page 94.

Siderite, see page 82.

Strengite, see page 107.

Strontianite, see page 84.

Sulfur, see page 40.

Vanadinite, see page 116.

Wavellite, see page 120.

Wulfenite, see page 124.

229

GLOSSARY

accessory mineral. A mineral that occurs in small quantities within a rock.

acicular. Needlelike. Used to describe the crystal habit of single long, thin, slender crystals.

adamantine. Having a very high luster, like diamond.

adularescence. A ghostly bluish-whitish reflection color emanating from one plane when cut and polished. It is caused by structural anomalies or buildup of water in the mineral.

amorphous. Lacking a crystalline structure.

amphibole group (amphibole). A group of related dark rock-forming silicate minerals that contain iron, magnesium, silicon, oxygen, and hydroxyl (OH).

amygdule. A rounded mineral mass formed in a solidified gas bubble in volcanic igneous rock.

anhydrous. Without water.

aphanitic. Composed of crystals too small to be distinguished with the unaided eye.

aqueous. Formed from precipitating hard water. *Stalagmites* and *stalactites* are common examples.

arborescent. Dendritic.

argillaceous. Composed mostly of clay.

asterism. Effect seen in some polished minerals causing a usually six-pointed star-like formation of concentrated light within the mineral. Asterism is caused by dense inclusions of slender parallel fibers that reflect light.

axis of symmetry. An imaginary line drawn through the center of a crystal that replicates the exact shape if the crystal is turned to 360°. Minerals can have symmetry on their x axis (horizontal symmetry), on their y axis (vertical symmetry), or on both or other axes.

banding. The presence of usually different colored zoning lines in some minerals.

batholith. A massive pluton with a surface area greater than 100 square kilometers, typically having a depth of about 30 kilometers. Batholiths are generally found in elongated mountain ranges after the country rock above them has eroded.

bedding. The division of sediment or sedimentary rock into parallel layers (beds) that can be distinguished from each other by such features as chemical composition and grain size.

bladed. Crystal habit described by flat, elongated, "knife-like" crystals.

botryoidal. Resembling a cluster of grapes. Also known as *globular*. Smaller than *reniform*.

breccia. A clastic rock composed of sharp, angular particles and fragments greater than 2 mm in diameter.

brilliant. Adamantine.

brittle. Tending to fracture when subjected to stress, with little tendency to deform or strain before fracture.

cabochon. An unfaceted stone that is highly polished and has smooth, rounded edges.

calcareous. Containing the compound calcium carbonate.

calcic. Containing calcium.

carat. Weight measurement used in reference to gemstones in regard to their evaluation. A carat is .2 grams (or 200 milligrams).

carbonaceous. Containing carbon.

cementation. The process by which sediment grains are bound together by precipitated minerals.

chatoyancy. Phenomenon where the fibrous structure of a mineral or fibrous inclusions cause a silky internal reflection of a concentrated, narrow band of light across the center of the mineral. Usually visible only in polished cabochons.

clast. A fragment of rock or mineral broken off from a larger piece.

clastic. Pertaining to a sedimentary rock composed primarily of fragments of pre-existing rocks or fossils.

cleavage. The tendency of some minerals to break along distinct, smooth planes in their crystal structures where the bonds are weakest.

columnar. Having parallel, slender, compact, adjoining crystals.

compaction. The process by which the thickness of sediment is reduced due to pressure from overlying layers of sediment.

conchoidal. (fracture type) Having a broken surface with a smoothly curved, glasslike or shell-like character.

concretion. A mass of sedimentary rock in which a mineral cement fills the porosity between grains.

contact metamorphism. Metamorphism caused by intrusion of magma and taking place at or near the area of contact.

contact twinning. Form of twinning where two crystals join together.

cross-bedding. An arrangement of inclined or scalloped strata in sedimentary rock formed by the action of wind or waves on the sediment before compaction.

crust. The outermost layer of the Earth, consisting of relatively low-density rocks.

cryptocrystalline. Composed of tiny, microscopic crystals. Also called *microcrystalline.*

crystal. A solid mineral mass with a regular geometric form bounded by smooth, flat plane faces.

crystal face. A flat side of a crystal.

crystal habit. The actual form that a mineral habitually takes as it crystallizes.

crystal system. A group of 32 symmetry classes that crystals may form. The primary method of classification of crystals.

crystalline. Having a crystal structure; composed of visible crystals.

dendritic. Tree-like or branching in form.

diaphaneity. Transparency.

dichroism. An effect in which a mineral exhibits one color when viewed from one angle and a different color when viewed from a different angle. Literally means "two colors." See also *pleochroism.*

dike. A wall-like intrusive pluton, substantially wider than it is thick. Dikes are often steeply inclined.

doubly terminated. Exhibiting a tapered crystal figure on both bases.

drusy. Composed of prismatic crystals protruding from a cavity or wall.

ductile. Capable of being stretched into a thin wire. A form of *tenacity.*

evaporite. An inorganic chemical sediment that precipitates from evaporating salty water.

extrusive. (of rock) Formed from lava solidifying on the Earth's surface.

feldspathoid. A group of minerals that are very similar to the feldspars but containing less silica.

felsic. Consisting of more than 65 percent silica in the form of quartz and feldspar.

ferromagnetic. Greatly attracted to magnetic fields.

ferric. Containing iron (Fe+3).

ferrous. Containing iron (Fe+2).

fibrous. Constructed of fine, usually parallel threads.

fissile. Easily split along parallel layers.

flakey. Containing flat, sometimes bendable flakes.

flaw. An inclusion or crack in a gemstone that usually lowers its value.

flow banding. A layered grouping of different rocks formed from flowing lava.

fluorescence. Luminescence caused by exposure to ultraviolet light or X-rays.

foliated. Composed of thin, parallel layers.

fossil. The remains of an ancient plant or animal.

friable. Easily crumbling.

gabbro. A group of dark, dense, phaneritic, intrusive rocks that are the plutonic equivalent to basalt.

gangue. Commercially worthless matter surrounding valuable minerals in ore deposits.

gem. A cut, shaped, and usually polished mineral or pearl used as an ornament.

gemstone. Any mineral or naturally occurring substance in an raw, uncut state that is capable of being used as a gem.

geode. A hollow rock filled or partially filled with drusy crystals.

globular. See *botryoidal.*

graded bedding. Bedding where the size of the grains increases from top to bottom.

It is caused by a current gradually slowing down, so that larger and therefore heavier particles settle out first.

granuloblastic. (of metamorphic rock) Even-textured with large mineral grains.

greasy. (of luster) Appearing to be coated with grease.

groundmass. Matrix.

habit. The general shape of a crystal.

hackly. Fracture exhibiting sharp, jagged surfaces, resembling broken metal.

hardness. The degree of resistance of a given mineral to scratching. Measured by rubbing the mineral with other substances of known hardness.

hemimorphic. Descriptive of doubly terminated crystal with two differently shaped ends.

hopper crystals. Edges grow faster than interior.

hornfelsic. (of metamorphic rock) Dense, even-textured, and fine-grained, without any evident crystalline structure.

host mineral. Mineral that is the primary constituent of a rock.

hydrous. Containing water.

hydrothermal. Relating to hot water, espeically the formation of minerals from rising hot solutions

igneous. Of volcanic origin.

igneous rock. Rock formed by the solidification of magma.

impurity. Any item present in a mineral which is not part of its integral structure or composition.

inclusion. Material trapped inside a mineral as it is forming.

index mineral. A mineral that, because of its high melting point, can be used to determine the degree of metamorphism in rock.

intrusive. (of rock) Formed from magma before reaching the Earth's surface.

iridescence. An optical effect in which a surface changes hue when viewed at different angles.

isomorphic. Composed of different elements but having the same crystal form.

japanese twin. A form of contact twinning in quartz, where two single crystals are joined at their bases at an angle of 84°.

jewel. A gem, whether cut or uncut, capable of being used as an ornament.

karst. A topography that forms when groundwater dissolves pockets of limestone, dolomite, or gypsum in bedrock. Characterized by caves, sinkholes, and underground drainage.

labradorescence. An iridescence characterized by dark, metallic shimmers of color, commonly blue, green, and gold. Caused by light refracting back and forth among lamellar layers in the mineral. Synonymous with *schiller*.

lamellar. Composed of thin overlapping layers, plates, or scales. Synonymous with *scaly*.

lava. Magma that comes to the Earth's surface through a volcano or fissure.

lenticular. Lens-shaped.

lithification. The conversion of loose sediment into solid sedimentary rock through compaction and cementation.

locality. The area where a specific mineral is found or occurs.

luminescence. The property of emitting non-incandescent light under certain conditions. See *fluorescence, triboluminescence,* and *thermoluminescence.*

luster. The manner in which the surface of a mineral reflects light.

macrocrystalline. Having crystals large enough to be seen with the unaided eye.

mafic. Describing dark-colored rocks or minerals composed primarily of magnesium and iron.

magma. Molten rock that forms naturally within the Earth.

malleable. Able to be pounded into thin sheets without breaking.

mantle. The middle layer of the Earth, just below the crust.

massive. Having no particular shape, either because it is non-crystalline or because it is composed of poorly defined small crystals.

matrix. The material that surrounds larger crystals or particles in sedimentary or porhyritic rock.

metamorphic rock. Rock that has been transformed under heat and pressure.

meteor. An extraterrestrial rock that gets caught in the earth's gravitational pull.

meteorite. The fragment of a meteor that did not fully burn up in the atmosphere and landed on the Earth.

micaceous. Composed of compact, flat, parallel, flexible, and peelable sheets.

microcrystalline. See *cryptocrystalline.*

migmatite. A rock that incorporates both metamorphic and igneous materials.

mineral. Any naturally occurring, solid, homogeneous inorganic substance with a definite chemical composition.

mineral group. A scientifically recognized selection of minerals similar in structure.

mineraloid. A naturally occurring—usually inorganic—solid consisting of either a single element or a compound, having a definite chemical composition but lacking a systemic (crystalline) internal arrangement of atoms.

Mohs hardness scale. A relative measurement system devised by Fredrick Mohs to determine the hardness of a mineral.

mother rock. The rock in which a mineral is found.

nodular. Shaped like or composed of small, rounded lumps.

non-crystalline. Not containing or forming crystals; amorphous.

occurrence. The area where a particular mineral is found.

oolitic. Composed of very small, spherical particles 0.25 to 2.00 millimeters in diameter.

opalescence. A form of iridescence characterized by a shifting interplay of internal colors when viewed from different angles.

opaque. Not able to transmit light.

ore. A mineral deposit that can be mined for a profit.

organic. Composed of carbon compounds from living organisms.

outcrop. Bedrock revealed at the surface of the Earth.

oxidation. The process of combining with oxygen ions.

oxidation zone. An area of a deposit where the rock is exposed to air and therefore is affected by wind, rain, and air, which may affect the minerals embedded in the rock and alter them to secondary minerals.

parent material. The source rock from which a soil is chiefly derived.

parting. The tendency of certain minerals to split along stressed areas or along twinned crystals.

pearly. Exhibiting a luster similar to the inside of a mollusk shell.

pegmatite. A coarse-grained igneous rock with very large crystals, formed from magma that contained a high proportion of water.

penetration. The formation of a crystal through a rock or another crystal.

penetration twinning. A form of twinning wherein two or more crystals are intergrown.

phaneritic. Composed of large, regular grains.

phantom growth. A phenomenon wherein a crystal grows, and then new crystal grows over the old in the same direction.

phenocryst. A large crystal surrounded by much smaller crystals in porphyritic igneous rock.

phosphorescence. A form of luminescence in which a substance continues to emit light even after the source of ultraviolet light that stimulated the luminescence is removed.

piezoelectric. A substance that generates an electrical charge under mechanical stress, or that vibrates when an electric current is passed through it.

pisolitic. Composed of small, spherical particles, larger in size and more distorted than oolitic minerals.

placer. An alluvial, marine, or glacial mineral deposit.

plagioclase twinning. The twinning of two or more crystals in a repeated pattern. Also called *repeated twinning.*

plane of symmetry. Imaginary lines traced on polyhedrons depicting a point or line on the polyhedron that exhibits symmetry.

platy. Small, flat, and flaky.

pleochroism. An effect in which a mineral exhibits one color when viewed from one angle and a different color when viewed from a different angle. Whereas *dichroism* refers specifically to two colors, pleochroism can produce more than two colors.

plug. The solidified rock covering the opening of a dormant volcano.

pluton. A deep, intrusive igneous rock.

poikiloblast. A porphyroblast that contains inclusions of the original parent rock.

polyhedron. A three-dimensional figure composed of regular geometric shapes.

polymorph. A mineral identical in chemical composition to another mineral, but differ in crystal structure.

porphyritic. Containing large, noticeable crystals, usually feldspars.

porphyroblast. A large, well-shaped mineral crystal that has grown within fine-grained matrix rock.

precipitation. The process in which dissolved minerals become freed from water, forming a deposit.

prism. A crystal that is elongated in one direction.

pyroclastic. (of rock fragments) Formed in a volcanic eruption.

pyroelectric. (of a substance) Able to generate an electrical charge during a temperature change.

radiating. Composed of tiny, slender crystals radiating from a central point.

refraction. The bending of light when moving between materials, such as from air to a crystal, and splitting of the white light into the colors of the spectrum.

reniform. Forming smooth, rounded, kidney-like shapes. Larger than *botryoidal*.

replacement. A process by which some or all of the atoms of a mineral are exchanged for atoms of a similar element.

reticulated. Composed of long crystals in a net-like form, with the crystals crossing each other.

rock. A naturally formed aggregate of an indefinite mixture of naturally occurring substances, mainly minerals. The composition of a type of rock may vary and is never exact.

rock cycle. The series of events through which a rock changes over time among igneous, sedimentary, and metamorphic forms.

rutilated. Containing impurities of the needle-like mineral rutile.

saline. Containing salt.

schiller. Iridescence; color reflections or "flashes" in a mineral.

secondary mineral. A mineral altered to a new form after undergoing a chemical change.

secondary enrichment. Natural removal of valueless material in solution, concurrent with the solution and redeposition of valuable minerals.

sectile. Able to be cut by a knife or other sharp object. A form of tenacity.

sedimentary rock. Rock formed from the consolidation of solid fragments of other rocks or organic remains, or by precipitation of minerals from solution.

series. A group consisting of minerals that have nearly identical crystal structures but differ only in their elemental composition.

silky. Exhibiting a luster that displays optical properties similar to silk cloth, caused by a very fine fibrous structure.

sill. An intrusive sheet of lava that has injected between sedimentary strata.

silt. Accumulation of very small grains of rock, finer than sand.

soil. Rock that has been ground finer than sand and mixed with organic materials and other substances.

soluble. Able to be dissolved.

specific gravity. The ratio of the weight of a particular volume of a given substance to the weight of an equal volume of pure water. Density.

specimen. A mineral or rock of interest to collectors or scientists.

sphenoidal. (of a prism) Featuring wedge-shaped corners.

spherulitic. Consisting of rounded, ball-like structures composed of radiating crystals.

spinel twin. Form of contact twinning, in which two octahedral crystals twin at the base.

stalactite. An icicle-like mineral formation that hangs from the ceiling of a cave.

stalagmite. A cone-shaped mineral deposit that forms on the floor of a cave.

staurolite twin. Form of penetration twinning where two monoclinic crystals form interpenetrating twins at 90°, in the shape of a cross.

stellate. See *radiating.*

stone. Any piece of rock.

stratification. Layering.

streak. The color of a mineral in its powdered form. Streak is usually determined by rubbing the mineral against an unglazed porcelain slab and observing the mark it makes.

streak plate. An unglazed piece of porcelain, such as a tile, used to test a mineral's streak.

striated. Exhibiting tiny parallel lines or grooves.

structure. The form of a mineral; the features of rock masses.

subconchoidal fracture. Fracture between conchoidal and even; smooth with irregularly rounded corners.

submetallic luster. Luster of opaque to nearly opaque minerals with good reflective properties.

tabular. (of a crystal habit) Flat, tough, usually four-sided.

talus. A pile of rock fragments lying at the bottom of the cliff or steep slope from which they have broken off.

tarnish. The tendency of a surface to discolor when placed in certain environments.

tenacity. The ability of a substance to resist separation.

termination. The end of a crystal face, usually referring to its base.

tetrahedron. A four-sided polyhedron with all sides triangular and equidimensional.

texture. The feel and appearance of a mineral.

thermoluminescence. A form of luminescence in which a mineral emits light when heated.

translucent. Able to transmit light partially but not clearly.

transparent. (of a substance) Able to transmit light clearly, without obscuring an image seen through the substance.

triboluminescence. A form of luminescence in which a mineral emits orange or yellow "flashes" or sparks when scratched or struck.

trilling. An intergrowth of three orthorhombic crystals that twin at the center and form a hexagonal crystal.

twin. Two or more crystals that intergrow in a specific method.

twinning. The tendency of some crystals to intergrow in a distinct manner.

uneven fracture. Fracture that leaves a rough or irregular surface.

waxy. Exhibiting a luster with the appearance of being coated by a layer of wax.

xenolith. A pre-existing rock embedded in a newer igneous rock.

zoning. The distinction of particular rock material from surrounding rock material.

INDEX

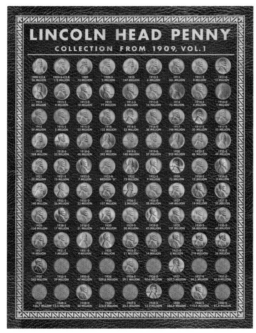